AF816902

CHRONOLOGICAL INDEX

IN RE THE GOODALL TRUST/ SAMUEL H. SLOAN VS. SAM WARE

PTR-99-273030

COURT OF APPEAL NO. A137739 DIV 4

DOCUMENT	DATE FILED	PAGE
REGISTER OF ACTIONS		1
PETITION RE DETERMINATION THAT PARTICULAR ACTION BY BENEFICIARY DOES NOT CONTSTITUTE A CONTEST	12/21/99	9
PROOF OF SERVICE	12/21/99	68
CONSENT TO ACT AS SUCCESSOR-TRUSTEE	01/11/00	72
POINTS AND AUTHORITIES IN OPPOSITION TO PETITION RE DETERMINATION OF THE PARTICULAR ACTION BY BENEFICIARY DOES NOT CONSTITUTE A CONTEST	02/02/00	73
DECLARATION OF SUSAN D. SCRIBNER FOR BANK OF AMERICA, AS TRUSTEE, IN OPPOSITION TO PETITION RE DETERMINATION OF THE PARTICULAR ACTION BY BENEFICIARY DOES NOT CONSTITUTE A CONTEST	02/03/00	78
ORDER RE PETITION RE DETERMINATION THAT PARTICULAR ACTION BY BENEFICIARY DOES NOT CONSTITUTE A CONTEST	02/09/00	89
PETITION FOR REMOVAL OF TRUSTEE	02/14/00	91
PROOF OF SERVICE	02/14/00	96
CONSENT TO ACT AS SUCCESSOR TRUSTEE	02/16/00	100
DECLARATION OF JAMES R. HASTINGS IN OPPOSITION TO PETITION TO REMOVE TRUSTEE	03/21/00	101

DOCUMENT	DATE FILED	PAGE
MEMORANDUM OF POINTS AND AUTHORITIES IN OPPOSITION TO PETITION TO REMOVE TRUSTEE	03/21/00	171
DECLARATION OF SUSAN SCRIBNER IN OPPOSITION TO PETITION FOR REMOVAL OF TRUSTEE	03/21/00	175
PROOF OF SERVICE	03/21/00	178
POINTS AND AUTHORITIES IN SUPPORT OF PETITION TO REMOVE TRUSTEE	03/21/00	179
PETITION FOR ORDER CONFIRMING REAL PROPERTY AS AN ASSET OF THE TRUST	04/21/11	186
NOTICE OF HEARING	04/21/11	278
PROOF OF SERVICE	04/25/11	282
OPPOSITION TO PETITION AS UTTER NONSENCE AND TOTALLY WITHOUT JURISDICTION PETITION FILED BANK OF AMERICA FOR ORDER CONFIRMING THE RESIDENCE OF THE LATE K. MICHAEL GOODALL AS AN ASSET OF THE TRUST TO BE CREATED BY THIS PETITION	05/20/11	286
MINI-MINUTES FOR 05/25/11		296
ORDER CONFIRMING REAL PROPERTY AS AN ASSET OF THE TRUST	06/03/11	297
PETITION FOR DETERMINATION OF THE BENEFICIARIES TO WHOM TRUST PROPERTY SHALL PASS UPON TERMINATION OF TRUST	06/08/11	300
NOTICE OF HEARING	06/08/11	355
PROOF OF SERVICE	06/10/11	358

DOCUMENT	DATE FILED	PAGE
OBJECTION TO PETITION FOR DETERMINATION OF BENEFICIARIES AND REQUEST FOR CONTINUANCE OF HEARING	07/05/11	361
MINI-MINUTES FOR 07/11/11		370
PROOF OF SERVICE	07/25/11	371
FURTHER PROBATE OPPOSITION/OBJECTION TO PETITION FOR DETERMINATION OF THE BENEFICIARIES TO WHOM TRUST PROPERTY SHALL PASS UPON TERMINATION OF TRUST FILED BY OBJECTOR SAMUEL H. SLOAN	07/29/11	373
SUPPLEMENTAL OBJECTIONS TO PETITION FOR DETERMINATION OF BENEFICIARIES AND REQUEST FOR CONTINUANCE OF HEARING	08/12/11	418
PETITIONER BANK OF AMERICA N.A.'S REPLY IN SUPPORT OF PETITION FOR DETERMINATION OF THE BENEFICIARIES TO WHOM TRUST PROPERTY SHALL PASS UPON TERMINATION OF TRUST	08/19/11	471
DECLARATION OF JAMES R. HASTINGS FAMILY AND ESTATE PLANNING ATTORNEY FOR THE GOODALLS	08/19/11	490
MINI-MINUTES FOR 08/23/11		504
SUBSTITUTION OF ATTORNEY	11/10/11	505
SEPARATE STATEMENT IN SUPPORT OF MOTION TO COMPEL PROCUCTION OF DOCUMENTS AND FURTHER DEPOSITION	12/14/11	508

DOCUMENT	DATE FILED	PAGE
NOTICE OF MOTION AND MOTION TO COMPEL PRODUCTION OF DOCUMENTS AND FURTHER DEPOSITION AND DECLARATION OF SAM WARE IN SUPPORT THEREOF AND MEMORANDUM OF POINTS AND AUTHORITIES	12/14/11	517
DEPONENT JAMES R. HASTINGS OPPOSITION TO RESPONDENT SAM SLOAN'S MOTION TO COMPEL PRODUCTION OF DOCUMENTS AND FURTHER DEPOSITION	12/29/11	566
PROOF OF SERVICE	12/29/11	574
DECLARATION OF DON A. LESSER OPPOSING RESPONDENT SAM SLOAN'S MOTION TO COMPEL PRODUCTION OF DOCUMENTS AND FURTHER DEPOSITION	12/29/11	576
GUIDE DOGS FOR THE BLIND, INC.'S JOINDER IN DEPONENT JAMES R. HASTINGS OPPOSITION TO RESPOND SAM SLOAN'S MOTION TO COMPEL DOCUMENTS AND FURTHER DEPOSITION	01/04/12	601
REPLY TO OPPOSITION TO MOTION TO COMPEL	01/05/12	604
MINI-MINUTES FOR 01/12/12		609
ORDER DENYING MOTION TO COMPEL PRODUCTION OF DOCUMENTS AND FURTHER DEPOSITION	01/20/12	610
DECLARATION OF JAMES R. HASTINGS PURSUANT TO COURT ORDER ON RESPONDENT'S MOTION TO COMPEL PRODUCTION OF DOCUMENTS AND FURTHER DEPOSITION	02/02/12	612
FURTHER SUPPLEMENTAL OBJECTIONS TO PETITION FOR DETERMINATION OF BENEFICIARIES	02/06/12	615
DECLARATION OF SAM SLOAN	02/06/12	623

DOCUMENT	DATE FILED	PAGE
OBJECTIONS TO EVIDENCE	02/06/12	646
DECLARATION OF NANCY RODGERS	02/06/12	652
PETITION OF SAM SLOAN FOR FORENSIC DOCUMENT EXAMINATION OF DOCUMENTS PURPORTED TO BE TRUST DOCUMENTS OF THE GOODALL FAMILY TRUST	03/01/12	665
PROOF OF SERVICE	03/01/12	770
DECLARATION OF ALICIA ADORNATO IN SUPPORT OF GUIDE DOGS FOR THE BLIND, INC.'S OPPOSITION TO SAM SLOAN'S FURTHER SUPPLEMENTAL OBJECTIONS TO PETITION FOR DETERMINATION OF BENEFICIARIES	03/01/12	774
GUIDE DOGS FOR THE BLIND, INC.'S OPPOSITION TO SAM SLOAN'S FURTHER SUPPLEMENTAL OBJECTIONS TO PETITION FOR DETERMINATION OF BENEFICIARIES	03/01/12	805
PETITIONER BANK OF AMERICA, N.A.'S FURTHER REPLY IN SUPPORT OF PETITION FOR DETERMINATION OF THE BENEFICIARIES TO WHOM TRUST PROPERTY SHALL PASS UPON TERMINATION OF TRUST	03/02/12	811
MINI-MINUTES FOR 03/07/12		817
ORDER (1) CONTINUING HEARING OF PETITION FOR DETERMINATION OF THE BENEFICIARIES TO WHOM TRUST PROPERTY SHALL PASS UPON TERMINATION OF TRUST; AND (2) REQUIRING PAYMENT OF RENT	03/20/12	818
NOTICE OF ENTRY OF ORDER (1) CONTINUING HEARING OF PETITION FOR DETERMINATION OF THE BENEFICIARIES TO WHOM TRUST PROPERTY SHALL PASS UPON TERMINATION OF TRUST; AND (2) REQUIRING PAYMENT OF RENT	03/26/12	821

DOCUMENT	DATE FILED	PAGE
AMENDED PETITION OF SAM SLOAN FOR FORENSIC DOCUMENT EXAMINATION OF DOCUMENTS PURPORTED TO BE TRUST DOCUMENTS OF THE GOODALL FAMILY TRUST	04/10/12	827
PETITIONER BANK OF AMERICA, N.A.'S ADDITIONAL REPLY IN SUPPORT OF PETITION FOR DETERMINATION OF THE BENEFICIARIES TO WHOM TRUST PROPERTY SHALL PASS UPON TERMINATION OF TRUST	04/24/12	850
GUIDE DOGS FOR THE BLIND, INC.'S OPPOSITION TO SAM SLOAN'S FURTHER SUPPLEMENTAL OBJECTIONS TO PETITION FOR DETERMINATION OF BENEFICIARIES	04/24/12	924
MINI-MINUTES FOR 05/07/12		930
SLOAN'S REPLY TO BANK OF AMERICA AND GUIDE DOG'S OPPOSITION FILED LAST WEEK	05/10/12	931
ORDER RESULTING FROM HEARING ON MAY 7, 2012: (1) DENYING THE AMENDED PETITION OF SAM SLOAN FOR FORENSIC DOCUMENT EXAMINATION OF DOCUMENTS PURPORTED TO BE TRUST DOCUMENTS OF THE GOODALL FAMILY TRUST; AND (2) GRANTING BANK OF AMERICA, N.A.'S PETITION FOR DETERMINATION OF THE BENEFICIARIRES TO WHOM TRUST PROPERTY SHALL PASS UPON TERMINATION OF TRUST	05/16/12	937
NOTICE OF ENTRY OF ORDER RESULTING FROM HEARING ON MAY 7, 2012	05/18/12	943
DECLARATION OF DAVID S. MOORE	05/25/12	955
NOTICE OF MOTION AND MOTION TO COMPEL PRODUCTION OF DOCUMENTS AND FURTHER DEPOSITION AND DECLARATION OF SLOAN IN SUPPORT THEREOF	05/25/12	970

DOCUMENT	DATE FILED	PAGE
AMENDED NOTICE OF MOTION AND MOTION TO RECONSIDER	06/19/12	1039
GUIDE DOGS FOR THE BLIND, INC.'S JOINDER IN TRUSTEE BANK OF AMERICA N.A.'S NOTICE OF MOTION AND MOTION FOR SANCTIONS PURSUANT TO CODE OF CIVIL PROCEDURE SECTIONS 128.7 AND 1008(D); MEMORANDUM OF POINTS AND AUTHORITIES IN SUPPORT THEREOF	06/29/12	1042
PROOF OF SERVICE	07/02/12	1046
DECLARATION OF GARY D. ROTHSTEIN IN SUPPORT OF BANK OF AMERICA, N.A.'S OPPOSITION TO SAM SLOAN'S AMENDED NOTICE OF MOTION AND MOTION FOR RECONSIDERATION	07/02/12	1050
BANK OF AMERICA, N.A.'S OPPOSITION TO SAM SLOAN'S AMENDED NOTICE OF MOTION AND MOTION TO RECONSIDER [ERRONEOUSLY CAPTIONED EARLIER AS MOTION TO COMPEL PRODUCTION OF DOCUMENTS]	07/02/12	1052
JOINDER IN BANK OF AMERICA. N.A.'S RESPONSE TO SAM SLOAN'S MOTION TO RECONSIDER	07/06/12	1060
REPLY MEMORANDUM REGARDING MOTION TO RECONSIDER	07/12/12	1069
DECLARATION OF SAM WARE IN SUPPORT OF REPLY MEMORANDUM REGARDING MOTION TO RECONSIDER	07/12/12	1074
MINI-MINUTES FOR 07/19/12		1078

DOCUMENT	DATE FILED	PAGE
DECLARATION OF GARY D. ROTHSTEIN IN SUPPORT OF BANK OF AMERICA, N.A.'S MOTION FOR SANCTIONS AGAINST SAM SLOAN AND HIS COUNSEL PURSUANT TO CODE OF CIVIL PROCEDURE SECTIONS 128.7 AND 1008(D)	07/20/12	1079
TRUSTEE BANK OF AMERICA, N.A.'S NOTICE OF MOTION AND MOTION FOR SANCTIONS PURSUANT TO CODE OF CIVIL PROCEDURE SECTIONS 128.7 AND 1008(D); MEMORANDUM OF POINTS AND AUTHORITIES IN SUPPORT THEREOF;	07/20/12	1082
PROOF OF SERVICE	07/23/12	1089
OPPOSITION TO MOTION FOR SANCTIONS AND DECLARATION IN SUPPORT THEREOF	08/10/12	1091
STIPULATION TO CONTINUE HEARING OF MOTION FOR SANCTIONS	08/10/12	1110
OPPOSITION TO BANK OF AMERICA'S MOTION FOR SANCTIONS AND CROSS MOTION FOR SANCTIONS AGAINST ATTORNEYS GARY ROTHSTEIN, ALICIA A. ADORNATO, JAMES R. HASTINGS AND DON A. LESSER	08/24/12	1113
DECLARATION IN SUPPORT OF ATTORNEY'S MOTION TO BE RELIEVED AS COUNSEL	09/07/12	1291
NOTICE OF MOTION AND MOTION TO BE RELIEVED AS COUNSEL	09/07/12	1294
DECLARATION OF SAM WARE REGARDING SANCTIONS MOTION	09/07/12	1297
TRUSTEE BANK OF AMERICA, N.A.'S REPLY IN SUPPORT OF MOTION FOR SANCTIONS PURSUANT TO CODE OF CIVIL PROCEDURE SECTIONS 128.7 AND 1008(D)	09/13/12	1300
MINI-MINUTES FOR 09/20/12		1307

DOCUMENT	DATE FILED	PAGE
ORDER DENYING SAM SLOAN'S AMENDED NOTICE OF MOTION AND MOTION TO RECONSIDER [ERRONEOUSLY CAPTIONED EARLIER AS MOTION TO COMPEL PRODUCTION OF DOCUMENTS]	09/27/12	1308
NOTICE OF ENTRY OF ORDER DENYING SAM SLOAN'S AMENDED NOTICE OF MOTION AND MOTION TO RECONSIDER [ERRONEOUSLY CAPTIONED EARLIER AS MOTION TO COMPEL PRODUCTION OF DOCUMENTS]	10/01/12	1313
MINI-MINUTES FOR 10/29/12		1323
SUPPLEMENTAL OPPOSITION TO MOTION FOR SANCTIONS AND DECLARATION IN SUPPORT THEREOF	11/01/12	1324
SUPPLEMENTAL DECLARATION OF GARY D. ROTHSTEIN IN SUPPORT OF BANK OF AMERICA, N.A.'S MOTION FOR SANCTIONS AGAINST SAM SLOAN AND HIS COUNSEL PURSUANT TO CODE OF CIVIL PROCEDURE SECTIONS 128.7 AND 1008(D)	11/07/12	1335
TRUSTEE BANK OF AMERICA N.A.'S SUPPLEMENTAL REPLY IN SUPPORT OF MOTION FOR SANCTIONS PURSUANT TO CODE OF CIVIL PROCEDURE SECTIONS 128.7 AND 1008(D)	11/07/12	1342
FURTHER OPPOSITION TO BANK OF AMERICA'S MOTION FOR SANCTIONS AND CROSS-MOTION FOR SANCTIONS AGAINST ATTORNEYS GARY ROTHSTEIN, ALICIA A. ADORNATO, JAMES R. HASTINGS AND DON A. LESSER	11/14/12	1348
MINI-MINUTES FOR 11/15/12		1481
ORDER GRANTING ATTORNEYS MOTION TO BE RELIEVED AS COUNSEL	11/15/12	1482
NOTICE OF APPEAL	11/21/12	1484
NOTICE OF APPEAL	11/21/12	1492

DOCUMENT	DATE FILED	PAGE
ORDER DENYING MOTION FOR SANCTIONS	11/26/12	1499
CLERK'S NOTICE OF FILING OF NOTICE OF APPEAL	11/29/12	1500
CLERK'S NOTICE OF FILING OF NOTICE OF APPEAL	11/29/12	1502
NOTICE RE: DEFAULT	12/07/12	1504
NOTICE RE: DEFAULT	12/07/12	1506
APPELLANT'S NOTICE DESIGNATING RECORD ON APPEAL	12/26/12	1508
DESIGNATION OF RECORD OF SECOND APPEAL A137190 TO BE THE SAME AS THE RECORD OF FIRST APPEAL A137189	01/11/13	1599
ORDER DISMISSING APPEAL	01/16/13	1603
ORDER DISMISSING APPEAL	01/16/13	1604
NOTICE OF APPEAL	01/28/13	1605
CLERK'S NOTICE OF FILING OF NOTICE OF APPEAL	01/28/13	1611
NOTICE OF APPEAL	01/28/13	1613
CLERK'S NOTICE OF FILING OF NOTICE OF APPEAL	01/28/13	1620
DESIGNATION OF THE RECORD OF APPEAL OF NOVEMBER 26, 2012 ORDER	02/07/13	1622
APPELLANT'S NOTICE DESIGNATING RECORD ON APPEAL	02/07/13	1623
CLERK'S ESTIMATE OF COST OF APPEAL RECORD-RESPONDENT	02/14/13	1715

DE-120

ATTORNEY OR PARTY WITHOUT ATTORNEY *(Name, State Bar number, and address)*:	FOR COURT USE ONLY
MANATT, PHELPS & PHILLIPS, LLP GARY D. ROTHSTEIN (CA # 143157); SUZANNE C. FARLEY (CA # 256693) One Embarcadero Center, 30th Floor San Francisco, CA 94111 TELEPHONE NO.: (415) 291-7400 FAX NO. *(Optional)*: (415) 291-7474 E-MAIL ADDRESS *(Optional)*: GRothstein@manatt.com; SFarley@manatt.com ATTORNEY FOR *(Name)*: Bank of America, N.A.	FILED San Francisco County Superior Court JUN - 8 2011 CLERK OF THE COURT BY: [signature] Deputy Clerk
SUPERIOR COURT OF CALIFORNIA, COUNTY OF SAN FRANCISCO STREET ADDRESS: 400 MacAllister Street MAILING ADDRESS: 400 MacAllister Street CITY AND ZIP CODE: San Francisco, CA 94102 BRANCH NAME: Civic Center	
☐ ESTATE OF *(Name)*: ☒ IN THE MATTER OF *(Name)*: Trust for Michael created under the Goodall Trust dated September 12, 1990 ☐ DECEDENT ☒ TRUST ☐ OTHER	
NOTICE OF HEARING—DECEDENT'S ESTATE OR TRUST	CASE NUMBER: PTR-99-273030

This notice is required by law.
This notice does not require you to appear in court, but you may attend the hearing if you wish.

1. NOTICE is given that *(name)*: Bank of America, N.A.
   (representative capacity, if any): Trustee

   has filed *(specify)*:*
   PETITION FOR DETERMINATION OF THE BENEFICIARIES TO WHOM TRUST PROPERTY SHALL PASS UPON TERMINATION OF TRUST

2. You may refer to the filed documents for more information. *(Some documents filed with the court are confidential.)*

3. A HEARING on the matter will be held as follows:

a. Date: JUL 11 2011	Time: PROBATE DEPARTMENT ...00 A.M., RM. 204	Room:

   b. Address of court ☒ shown above ☐ is *(specify)*:

Assistive listening systems, computer-assisted real-time captioning, or sign language interpreter services are available upon request if at least 5 days notice is provided. Contact the clerk's office for *Request or Accommodations by Persons With Disabilities and Order* (form MC-410). (Civil Code section 54.8.)

* Do not use this form to give notice of a petition to administer estate (see Prob. Code, § 8100 and form DE-121) or notice of a hearing in a guardianship or conservatorship (see Prob. Code, §§ 1511 and 1822 and form GC-020).

☐ ESTATE OF *(Name):* ☒ IN THE MATTER OF *(Name):* Trust for Michael created under the Goodall Trust dated September 12, 1990 ☐ DECEDENT ☒ TRUST ☐ OTHER	CASE NUMBER PTR-99-273030

CLERK'S CERTIFICATE OF POSTING

1. I certify that I am not a party to this cause.
2. A copy of the foregoing *Notice of Hearing—Decedent's Estate or Trust*
   a. was posted at *(address):*

   b. was posted on *(date):*

Date: Clerk by ______________________________, Deputy

PROOF OF SERVICE BY MAIL *

1. I am over the age of 18 and not a party to this cause. I am a resident of or employed in the county where the mailing occurred.
2. My residence or business address is *(specify):*
   One Embarcadero Center, 30th Floor
   San Francisco, CA 94111
3. I served the foregoing *Notice of Hearing—Decedent's Estate or Trust* on each person named below by enclosing a copy in an envelope addressed as shown below AND
   a. ☐ **depositing** the sealed envelope on the date and at the place shown in item 4 with the United States Postal Service with the postage fully prepaid.
   b. ☒ **placing** the envelope for collection and mailing on the date and at the place shown in item 4 following our ordinary business practices. I am readily familiar with this business's practice for collecting and processing correspondence for mailing. On the same day that correspondence is placed for collection and mailing, it is deposited in the ordinary course of business with the United States Postal Service in a sealed envelope with postage fully prepaid.

4. a. Date mailed: b. Place mailed *(city, state):* San Francisco CA

5. ☒ served with the *Notice of Hearing—Decedent's Estate or Trust* a copy of the petition or other document referred to in the Notice.

I declare under penalty of perjury under the laws of the State of California that the foregoing is true and correct.

Date:

______________________________ ______________________________
(TYPE OR PRINT NAME OF PERSON COMPLETING THIS FORM) (SIGNATURE OF PERSON COMPLETING THIS FORM)

NAME AND ADDRESS OF EACH PERSON TO WHOM NOTICE WAS MAILED

	Name of person served	Address *(number, street, city, state, and zip code)*
1.	See Attachment.	
2.		
3.		
4.		

☒ Continued on an attachment. *(You may use* Attachment to Notice of Hearing Proof of Service by Mail, *form DE-120(MA)/GC-020(MA), for this purpose.)*

* Do not use this form for proof of personal service. You may use form DE-120(P) to prove personal service of this Notice.

Trust for Michael created under the Goodall Trust dated September 12, 1990
San Francisco Superior Court Case No. PTR-99-273030

Attachment to Notice of Hearing

Name	Address	Relationship
Julia Bentley Lemons (Adult)	Apt. 308 12800 Marion Lane W Minnetonka, MN 55305-1368	Surviving Sibling of Rachel Goodall; Heir of Rachel Goodall
Robert Bentley (Adult)	Bradford Village #504 906 N Boulevard Street Edmond, OK 73030	Surviving Sibling of Rachel Goodall; Heir of Rachel Goodall
Helen Beth Bentley Perry (Adult)	7926 Praver Drive W Jacksonville, FL 32217	Surviving Sibling of Rachel Goodall; Heir of Rachel Goodall
Glenda Fern Bentley Zinar (Adult)	4536 Chatman Street The Colony, TX 75056	Heir of Rachel Goodall
Beverly Gale Bentley Young (Adult)	2316 Trenton McKinney, TX 75070	Heir of Rachel Goodall
Vickie Bentley Hankins (Adult)	14580 NE 6th Choctaw, OK 73020	Heir of Rachel Goodall
Jeffrey Bentley (Adult)	4701 N Douglas Boulevard Spencer, OK 73084	Heir of Rachel Goodall
Chad Everett Bentley (Adult)	1609 Teepee Trail Kingsland, TX 78639	Heir of Rachel Goodall
Jeanette Goodall Phillips (Adult)	152 S 11th Street Salina, Kansas 67401	Heir of Kenneth Goodall
Kristin Kane (Adult)	University of California, Berkeley College of Engineering College Relations 208 McLaughlin Hall #1722 Berkeley, CA 94720-1722	Potential Heir
Guide Dogs for the Blind	Mr. Thomas Horton, Planned Giving Director Guide Dogs for the Blind, Inc. 350 Los Ranchitos Road San Rafael, CA 94903	Potential Beneficiary

DE-120

ATTORNEY OR PARTY WITHOUT ATTORNEY (Name, State Bar number, and address):
MANATT, PHELPS & PHILLIPS, LLP
GARY D. ROTHSTEIN (CA # 143157); SUZANNE C. FARLEY (CA # 256693)
One Embarcadero Center, 30th Floor
San Francisco, CA 94111

TELEPHONE NO.: (415) 291-7400 FAX NO. (Optional): (415) 291-7474
E-MAIL ADDRESS (Optional): GRothstein@manatt.com; SFarley@manatt.com
ATTORNEY FOR (Name): Bank of America, N.A.

FOR COURT USE ONLY

ENDORSED
FILED
San Francisco County Superior Court
JUN - 8 2011
CLERK OF THE COURT
BY: ALISON YEE AGBAY
Deputy Clerk

FILED
San Francisco County Superior Court
JUN 10 2011
CLERK OF THE COURT
By: Deputy Clerk

SUPERIOR COURT OF CALIFORNIA, COUNTY OF SAN FRANCISCO
STREET ADDRESS: 400 MacAllister Street
MAILING ADDRESS: 400 MacAllister Street
CITY AND ZIP CODE: San Francisco, CA 94102
BRANCH NAME: Civic Center

☐ ESTATE OF (Name): ☒ IN THE MATTER OF (Name):
Trust for Michael created under the Goodall Trust dated September 12, 1990

☐ DECEDENT ☒ TRUST ☐ OTHER

AFFD. OF MAILING

CASE NUMBER:
PTR-99-273030

NOTICE OF HEARING—DECEDENT'S ESTATE OR TRUST

This notice is required by law.
This notice does not require you to appear in court, but you may attend the hearing if you wish.

1. NOTICE is given that *(name):* Bank of America, N.A.
(representative capacity, if any): Trustee

has filed *(specify):**
PETITION FOR DETERMINATION OF THE BENEFICIARIES TO WHOM TRUST PROPERTY SHALL PASS UPON TERMINATION OF TRUST

2. You may refer to the filed documents for more information. *(Some documents filed with the court are confidential.)*

3. A HEARING on the matter will be held as follows:

a. Date: JUL 11 2011	Time: PROBATE DEPARTMENT 9:00 A.M., RM 204	Dept.:	Room:

b. Address of court ☒ shown above ☐ is *(specify):*

Assistive listening systems, computer-assisted real-time captioning, or sign language interpreter services are available upon request if at least 5 days notice is provided. Contact the clerk's office for *Request or Accommodations by Persons With Disabilities and Order* (form MC-410). (Civil Code section 54.8.)

* Do **not** use this form to give notice of a petition to administer estate (see Prob. Code, § 8100 and form DE-121) or notice of a hearing in a guardianship or conservatorship (see Prob. Code, §§ 1511 and 1822 and form GC-020).

Form Adopted for Mandatory Use
Judicial Council of California
DE-120 [Rev. July 1, 2005]

NOTICE OF HEARING—DECEDENT'S ESTATE OR TRUST
(Probate—Decedents' Estates)

Probate Code §§ 851, 1211, 1215, 1216, 1230, 17100
www.courtinfo.ca.gov

☐ ESTATE OF *(Name)*: ☒ IN THE MATTER OF *(Name)*: Trust for Michael created under the Goodall Trust dated September 12, 1990 ☐ DECEDENT ☒ TRUST ☐ OTHER	CASE NUMBER: PTR-99-273030

CLERK'S CERTIFICATE OF POSTING

1. I certify that I am not a party to this cause.
2. A copy of the foregoing *Notice of Hearing—Decedent's Estate or Trust*
   a. was posted at *(address)*:

   b. was posted on *(date)*:

Date: Clerk by ______________________, Deputy

PROOF OF SERVICE BY MAIL *

1. I am over the age of 18 and not a party to this cause. I am a resident of or employed in the county where the mailing occurred.
2. My residence or business address is *(specify)*:
   One Embarcadero Center, 30th Floor
   San Francisco, CA 94111
3. I served the foregoing *Notice of Hearing—Decedent's Estate or Trust* on each person named below by enclosing a copy in an envelope addressed as shown below AND
   a. ☐ **depositing** the sealed envelope on the date and at the place shown in item 4 with the United States Postal Service with the postage fully prepaid.
   b. ☒ **placing** the envelope for collection and mailing on the date and at the place shown in item 4 following our ordinary business practices. I am readily familiar with this business's practice for collecting and processing correspondence for mailing. On the same day that correspondence is placed for collection and mailing, it is deposited in the ordinary course of business with the United States Postal Service in a sealed envelope with postage fully prepaid.

4.a.Date mailed: 6-9-2011 b.Place mailed *(city, state)*: San Francisco CA

5. ☒ served with the *Notice of Hearing—Decedent's Estate or Trust* a copy of the petition or other document referred to in the Notice.

I declare under penalty of perjury under the laws of the State of California ~~that the~~ foregoing is true and correct.

Date: 6-9-2011

Armand B. Anguiano
(TYPE OR PRINT NAME OF PERSON COMPLETING THIS FORM)

[signature]
(SIGNATURE OF PERSON COMPLETING THIS FORM)

NAME AND ADDRESS OF EACH PERSON TO WHOM NOTICE WAS MAILED

	Name of person served	Address *(number, street, city, state, and zip code)*
1.	See Attachment.	
2.		
3.		
4.		

☒ Continued on an attachment. *(You may use* Attachment to Notice of Hearing Proof of Service by Mail, *form DE-120(MA)/GC-020(MA), for this purpose.)*

* Do not use this form for proof of personal service. You may use form DE-120(P) to prove personal service of this Notice.

Trust for Michael created under the Goodall Trust dated September 12, 1990
San Francisco Superior Court Case No. PTR-99-273030

Attachment to Notice of Hearing

Name	Address	Relationship
Julia Bentley Lemons (Adult)	Apt. 308 12800 Marion Lane W Minnetonka, MN 55305-1368	Surviving Sibling of Rachel Goodall; Heir of Rachel Goodall
Robert Bentley (Adult)	Bradford Village #504 906 N Boulevard Street Edmond, OK 73030	Surviving Sibling of Rachel Goodall; Heir of Rachel Goodall
Helen Beth Bentley Perry (Adult)	7926 Praver Drive W Jacksonville, FL 32217	Surviving Sibling of Rachel Goodall; Heir of Rachel Goodall
Glenda Fern Bentley Zinar (Adult)	4536 Chatman Street The Colony, TX 75056	Heir of Rachel Goodall
Beverly Gale Bentley Young (Adult)	2316 Trenton McKinney, TX 75070	Heir of Rachel Goodall
Vickie Bentley Hankins (Adult)	14580 NE 6th Choctaw, OK 73020	Heir of Rachel Goodall
Jeffrey Bentley (Adult)	4701 N Douglas Boulevard Spencer, OK 73084	Heir of Rachel Goodall
Chad Everett Bentley (Adult)	1609 Teepee Trail Kingsland, TX 78639	Heir of Rachel Goodall
Jeanette Goodall Phillips (Adult)	152 S 11th Street Salina, Kansas 67401	Heir of Kenneth Goodall
Kristin Kane (Adult)	University of California, Berkeley College of Engineering College Relations 208 McLaughlin Hall #1722 Berkeley, CA 94720-1722	Potential Heir
Guide Dogs for the Blind	Mr. Thomas Horton, Planned Giving Director Guide Dogs for the Blind, Inc. 350 Los Ranchitos Road San Rafael, CA 94903	Potential Beneficiary

Samuel Sloan
461 Peachstone Ter.
San Rafael, CA 94903
415-894-7201

Pro per administrator
of the Estate of Michael Goodall

Telephone 415-464-4872

FILED
San Francisco County Superior Court
JUL - 5 2011
CLERK OF THE COURT
By: Deputy Clerk

SUPERIOR COURT OF THE STATE OF CALIFORNIA

COUNTY OF SAN FRANCISCO

In the Matter of the Trust for Michael created under the Goodall Trust dated September 12, 1990	Case No. PTR-99-273030 OBJECTION TO PETITION FOR DETERMINATION OF BENEFICIARIES And REQUEST FOR CONTINUANCE OF HEARING Hearing Date: July 11, 2011 Time: 9 AM Department: 204

BY FAX

Samuel Sloan declares:

(1) I am the duly appointed administrator of the the Estate of K. Michael Goodall, action number PR 1100596 pending in the County of Marin and attached hereto are the Order for Probate and Letters of Administration issued in that action;

(2) I have previously appeared in this San Francisco Superior Court action as an interested party as reflected in the

opposition papers filed May 20, 2011;

(3) I recently received notification from one of the other interested parties that the Bank of America had filed the instant Petition for Determination of Beneficiaries which is scheduled for hearing July 11, 2011;

(4) As is plainly reflected on the proof of service of the Notice of Hearing on that petition, I was not included on the service list and I did not receive proper notice of this hearing and petition (see attached);

(5) It is my intention to present an opposition to the instant Petition and to otherwise further participate in this action as the duly appointed Administrator of the Estate of K. Michael Goodall pending in Marin County;

(6) I have this day contacted an attorney to represent me as administrator in this action in San Francisco Superior Court, Sam Ware (105005), 700 Larkspur Landing Cir., #199, Larkspur, CA 94939 (415) 464-4872, but it is impossible for us to meaningfully address the instant Petition presently scheduled for July 11, 2011, because I was not properly noticed as an interested party in this action;

(7) Accordingly, I hereby request that the hearing of this instant Petition scheduled for July 11, 2011 be continued for no less than 30 days so that I may can further consult with and retain my attorney to represent and protect the interests of the

//

//

Estate of [illegible] Michael [illegible] in this matter.

I declare under penalty of perjury under the laws of the state of California that the foregoing is true and correct and that this declaration was executed on July [illegible], 2011.

ATTORNEY OR PARTY WITHOUT ATTORNEY (Name, state bar number, and address)	TELEPHONE AND FAX NOS	FOR COURT USE ONLY
Samuel H. Sloan 461 Peachstone Terrace San Rafael CA 94903 samhsloan@gmail.com ATTORNEY FOR (Name)	415-894-7201	FILED MAR 2 1 2011 KIM TURNER, Court Executive Officer MARIN COUNTY SUPERIOR COURT By: S. Bond, Deputy
SUPERIOR COURT OF CALIFORNIA, COUNTY OF Marin STREET ADDRESS: 3501 Civic Center Drive MAILING ADDRESS: CITY AND ZIP CODE: San Rafael CA 94903 BRANCH NAME:		
ESTATE OF (Name): K. Michael Goodall, DECEDENT		
ORDER FOR PROBATE ORDER APPOINTING ☐ Executor ☑ Administrator with Will Annexed ☐ Administrator ☐ Special Administrator ☐ Order Authorizing Independent Administration of Estate ☐ with full authority ☐ with limited authority		CASE NUMBER: PR 1100596

WARNING: THIS APPOINTMENT IS NOT EFFECTIVE UNTIL LETTERS HAVE ISSUED.

1. Date of hearing: MAR 2 1 2011 Time: 8:30 am Dept./Room: H Judge: VERNA ADAMS

THE COURT FINDS

2. a. All notices required by law have been given.
   b. Decedent died on *(date)*: October 5, 2010
      (1) ☑ a resident of the California county named above
      (2) ☐ a nonresident of California and left an estate in the county named above
   c. Decedent died
      (1) ☐ intestate
      (2) ☑ testate
   and decedent's will dated: January 15, 2004 and each codicil dated:
   was admitted to probate by Minute Order on *(date)*: MAR 2 1 2011

THE COURT ORDERS

3. *(Name)*: Samuel H. Sloan
   is appointed personal representative:
   a. ☐ executor of the decedent's will
   b. ☑ administrator with will annexed
   c. ☐ administrator
   d. ☐ special administrator
      (1) ☐ with general powers
      (2) ☐ with special powers as specified in Attachment 3d(2)
      (3) ☐ without notice of hearing
      (4) ☐ letters will expire on *(date)*:

   and letters shall issue on qualification.
4. a. ☑ **Full authority** is granted to administer the estate under the Independent Administration of Estates Act.
   b. ☐ **Limited authority** is granted to administer the estate under the Independent Administration of Estates Act (there is no authority, without court supervision, to (1) sell or exchange real property or (2) grant an option to purchase real property or (3) borrow money with the loan secured by an encumbrance upon real property).
5. a. ☑ Bond is not required.
   b. ☐ Bond is fixed at: $ to be furnished by an authorized surety company or as otherwise provided by law.
   c. ☐ Deposits of: $ are ordered to be placed in a blocked account at *(specify institution and location)*:
   and receipts shall be filed. No withdrawals shall be made without a court order. ☐ Additional orders in Attachment 5c.
   d. ☐ The personal representative is not authorized to take possession of money or any other property without a specific court order.
6. ☐ *(Name)*: is appointed probate referee.

Date: MAR 2 1 2011

VERNA ADAMS
JUDGE OF THE SUPERIOR COURT

7. Number of pages attached: ____ ☐ SIGNATURE FOLLOWS LAST ATTACHMENT

0365

DE-150

ATTORNEY OR PARTY WITHOUT ATTORNEY (Name, state bar number, and address): Samuel H. Sloan, 461 Peachstone Terrace, San Rafael CA 94903, samhsloan@gmail.com

TELEPHONE AND FAX NOS: 415-894-7201

FOR COURT USE ONLY

FILED
MAR 2 1 2011
KIM TURNER, Court Executive Officer
MARIN COUNTY SUPERIOR COURT
By: S. Bond, Deputy

ATTORNEY FOR (Name):

SUPERIOR COURT OF CALIFORNIA, COUNTY OF Marin
STREET ADDRESS: 3501 Civic Center Drive
MAILING ADDRESS:
CITY AND ZIP CODE: San Rafael CA 94903
BRANCH NAME:

ESTATE OF (Name): K. Michael Goodall, DECEDENT

LETTERS

☐ TESTAMENTARY ☐ OF ADMINISTRATION
☑ OF ADMINISTRATION WITH WILL ANNEXED ☐ SPECIAL ADMINISTRATION

CASE NUMBER: PR 1100596

LETTERS

1. ☑ The last will of the decedent named above having been proved, the court appoints (name): Samuel H. Sloan
   a. ☐ executor.
   b. ☑ administrator with will annexed.
2. ☐ The court appoints (name):
   a. ☐ administrator of the decedent's estate.
   b. ☐ special administrator of decedent's estate
      (1) ☐ with the special powers specified in the *Order for Probate*.
      (2) ☐ with the powers of a general administrator
      (3) ☐ letters will expire on (date):
3. ☑ The personal representative is authorized to administer the estate under the Independent Administration of Estates Act ☑ **with full authority** ☐ **with limited authority** (no authority, without court supervision, to (1) sell or exchange real property or (2) grant an option to purchase real property or (3) borrow money with the loan secured by an encumbrance upon real property).
4. ☐ The personal representative is not authorized to take possession of money or any other property without a specific court order.

WITNESS, clerk of the court, with seal of the court affixed.

(SEAL) SEAL

Date: MAR 2 1 2011

Clerk, by KIM TURNER

S. BOND
(DEPUTY)

AFFIRMATION

1. ☐ PUBLIC ADMINISTRATOR: No affirmation required (Prob. Code, § 7621(c)).
2. ☑ INDIVIDUAL: I solemnly affirm that I will perform the duties of personal representative according to law.
3. ☐ INSTITUTIONAL FIDUCIARY (name):

   I solemnly affirm that the institution will perform the duties of personal representative according to law. I make this affirmation for myself as an individual and on behalf of the institution as an officer.
   (Name and title):
4. Executed on (date): MARCH 3, 2011 at (place): SAN RAFAEL, California.

Samuel H. Sloan
(SIGNATURE)

CERTIFICATION

I certify that this document is a correct copy of the original on file in my office and the letters issued the personal representative appointed above have not been revoked, annulled, or set aside, and are still in full force and effect.

(SEAL)

Date:

Clerk, by

(DEPUTY)

DE-120

ATTORNEY OR PARTY WITHOUT ATTORNEY (Name, State Bar number, and address):
MANATT, PHELPS & PHILLIPS, LLP
GARY D. ROTHSTEIN (CA # 143157), SUZANNE C. FARLEY (CA # 256693)
One Embarcadero Center, 30th Floor
San Francisco, CA 94111
TELEPHONE NO.: (415) 291-7400 FAX NO. (Optional): (415) 291-7474
E-MAIL ADDRESS (Optional): GRothstein@manatt.com, SFarley@manatt.com
ATTORNEY FOR (Name): Bank of America, N.A.

FOR COURT USE ONLY

FILED
San Francisco County Superior Court
JUN 10 2011
CLERK OF THE COURT
By: [signature]

ENDORSED
FILED
San Francisco County Superior Court
JUN - 8 2011
CLERK OF THE COURT
BY: ALISON YEE AGBAY, Deputy Clerk

AFFD OF MAILING

SUPERIOR COURT OF CALIFORNIA, COUNTY OF SAN FRANCISCO
STREET ADDRESS: 400 MacAllister Street
MAILING ADDRESS: 400 MacAllister Street
CITY AND ZIP CODE: San Francisco, CA 94102
BRANCH NAME: Civic Center

☐ ESTATE OF (Name): ☒ IN THE MATTER OF (Name):
Trust for Michael created under the Goodall Trust dated September 27, 1990

☐ DECEDENT ☒ TRUST ☐ OTHER

NOTICE OF HEARING—DECEDENT'S ESTATE OR TRUST

CASE NUMBER: PTR-99-273030

This notice is required by law.
This notice does not require you to appear in court, but you may attend the hearing if you wish.

1. NOTICE is given that *(name)*: Bank of America, N.A.
(representative capacity, if any): Trustee

has filed *(specify)*:*
PETITION FOR DETERMINATION OF THE BENEFICIARIES TO WHOM TRUST PROPERTY SHALL PASS UPON TERMINATION OF TRUST

2. You may refer to the filed documents for more information. *(Some documents filed with the court are confidential.)*

3. A HEARING on the matter will be held as follows:

a. Date: JUL 11 2011	Time: 9:00 A.M., PROBATE DEPARTMENT RM 204	Room:

b. Address of court ☒ shown above ☐ is *(specify)*:

Assistive listening systems, computer-assisted real-time captioning, or sign language interpreter services are available upon request if at least 5 days notice is provided. Contact the clerk's office for *Request or Accommodations by Persons With Disabilities and Order* (form MC-410). (Civil Code section 54.8.)

* Do not use this form to give notice of a petition to administer estate (see Prob. Code, § 8100 and form DE-121) or notice of a hearing in a guardianship or conservatorship (see Prob. Code, §§ 1511 and 1822 and form GC-020).

☐ ESTATE OF *(Name)* ☒ IN THE MATTER OF *(Name)*: Trust for Michael created under the Goodall Trust dated September 12, 1990 ☐ DECEDENT ☒ TRUST ☐ OTHER	CASE NUMBER: PTR-99-273030

CLERK'S CERTIFICATE OF POSTING

1. I certify that I am not a party to this cause.
2. A copy of the foregoing *Notice of Hearing—Decedent's Estate or Trust*
   a. was posted at *(address)*:

   b. was posted on *(date)*:

Date: Clerk by ______________________, Deputy

PROOF OF SERVICE BY MAIL *

1. I am over the age of 18 and not a party to this cause. I am a resident of or employed in the county where the mailing occurred.
2. My residence or business address is *(specify)*:
   One Embarcadero Center, 30th Floor
   San Francisco, CA 94111
3. I served the foregoing *Notice of Hearing—Decedent's Estate or Trust* on each person named below by enclosing a copy in an envelope addressed as shown below AND
   a. ☐ **depositing the sealed envelope on the date and at the place shown in item 4 with the United States Postal Service with the postage fully prepaid.**
   b. ☒ **placing the envelope for collection and mailing on the date and at the place shown in item 4 following our ordinary business practices. I am readily familiar with this business's practice for collecting and processing correspondence for mailing. On the same day that correspondence is placed for collection and mailing, it is deposited in the ordinary course of business with the United States Postal Service in a sealed envelope with postage fully prepaid.**

4 a. Date mailed: 6-9-2011 b. Place mailed *(city, state)*: San Francisco CA

5. ☒ served with the *Notice of Hearing—Decedent's Estate or Trust* a copy of the petition or other document referred to in the Notice.

I declare under penalty of perjury under the laws of the State of California ~~that the foregoing~~ is true and correct.

Date: 6-9-2011

[illegible] B Angriano
(TYPE OR PRINT NAME OF PERSON COMPLETING THIS FORM)

Armand [signature]
(SIGNATURE OF PERSON COMPLETING THIS FORM)

NAME AND ADDRESS OF EACH PERSON TO WHOM NOTICE WAS MAILED

	Name of person served	Address (number, street, city, state, and zip code)
1	See Attachment.	
2		
3		
4		

☒ Continued on an attachment. *(You may use Attachment to Notice of Hearing Proof of Service by Mail, form DE-120(MA)/GC-020(MA), for this purpose.)*

* Do not use this form for proof of personal service. You may use form DE-120(P) to prove personal service of this Notice.

Trust for Michael created under the Goodall Trust dated September 12, 1990
San Francisco Superior Court Case No. PTR-99-273030

Attachment to Notice of Hearing

Name	Address	Relationship
Julia Bentley Lemons (Adult)	Apt. 308 12800 Marion Lane W Minnetonka, MN 55305-1368	Surviving Sibling of Rachel Goodall; Heir of Rachel Goodall
Robert Bentley (Adult)	Bradford Village #504 906 N Boulevard Street Edmond, OK 73030	Surviving Sibling of Rachel Goodall; Heir of Rachel Goodall
Helen Beth Bentley Perry (Adult)	7926 Praver Drive W Jacksonville, FL 32217	Surviving Sibling of Rachel Goodall; Heir of Rachel Goodall
Glenda Fern Bentley Zinar (Adult)	4536 Chatman Street The Colony, TX 75056	Heir of Rachel Goodall
Beverly Gale Bentley Young (Adult)	2316 Trenton McKinney, TX 75070	Heir of Rachel Goodall
Vickie Bentley Hankins (Adult)	14580 NE 6th Choctaw, OK 73020	Heir of Rachel Goodall
Jeffrey Bentley (Adult)	4701 N Douglas Boulevard Spencer, OK 73084	Heir of Rachel Goodall
Chad Everett Bentley (Adult)	1609 Teepee Trail Kingsland, TX 78639	Heir of Rachel Goodall
Jeanette Goodall Phillips (Adult)	152 S 11th Street Salina, Kansas 67401	Heir of Kenneth Goodall
Kristin Kane (Adult)	University of California, Berkeley College of Engineering College Relations 208 McLaughlin Hall #1722 Berkeley, CA 94720-1722	Potential Heir
Guide Dogs for the Blind	Mr. Thomas Horton, Planned Giving Director Guide Dogs for the Blind, Inc. 350 Los Ranchitos Road San Rafael, CA 94903	Potential Beneficiary

PROOF OF SERVICE

I certify and declare as follows:

I am over the age of 18 years, not a party to this action. My business address is 700 Larkspur Landing Circle #199, Larkspur, CA 94939. I am readily familiar with the business practices of my firm for the collection, processing and service of items with the United States Postal Service, express service providers (same day messenger and overnight) and facsimile transmission.

On the date set forth below, I served the foregoing documents described as Objection to Petition for Determination of Beneficiaries and Request for Continuance on the parties in this action as follows:

____: BY FIRST CLASS MAIL — By placing [ ] the original [X] a true and correct copy thereof in each sealed envelope addressed as indicated below. Said sealed envelopes, with postage fully prepaid, were deposited with the United States Postal Service in San Francisco, California this same day in the ordinary course of business.

____: BY FEDERAL EXPRESS — By placing [ ] the original [ ] a true and correct copy thereof in each sealed envelope addressed as indicated below. Said envelopes were deposited for collection and processing by Federal Express, Priority Overnight Service, in San Francisco, California.

__X__: BY PERSONAL SERVICE: By placing [ ] the original [x] a true and correct copy thereof in each sealed envelope addressed as indicated below and causing said envelopes to be delivered by hand, by our firm's messenger, to the offices of the addressees indicated below.

____: BY FACSIMILE TRANSMISSION — The foregoing document was transmitted between 9:00 a.m. and 5:00 p.m. to the fax number indicated below each address.

____: BY EMAIL TRANSMISSION — The foregoing document was transmitted between 9:00 a.m. and 5:00 p.m. to the e-mail address indicated below.

Manatt, Phelps & Phillips
Gary Rothstein
Suzanne Farley
One Embarcadero Center 30th floor
Sam Francisco, CA 94111

I declare under penalty of perjury under the laws of the State of California that the foregoing statements are true and correct.

Executed July 5, 2011

MINI-MINUTES FOR JUL-11-2011 9:00 AM FOR

Appearances: Sam Sloan Aministrator of the Estate of K. Micheal Goodall in Marin County.

This was a continued matter. Mr. Sloan argued that the Trust should be in Marin County and stated that he was not given notice of the petition. The Court advised Mr. Sloan to contact Counsel for the moving Party to ask for notice of the continued hearing and the petition, and to check the tentative ruling line for future hearings. The matter remains continued to August 23, 2011 at 9:00 a.m., in Dept. 204.

Judge Pro Temp: Sue M. Kaplan. Reporter: Diana Chen, CSR#11312. Clerk: Rosie Noguera. Bailiff: Deputy A. Payne.

0371

DE-120

ATTORNEY OR PARTY WITHOUT ATTORNEY *(Name, State Bar number, and address)*
MANATT, PHELPS & PHILLIPS, LLP
GARY D. ROTHSTEIN (CA # 143157); SUZANNE C. FARLEY (CA # 256693)
One Embarcadero Center, 30th Floor
San Francisco, CA 94111

TELEPHONE NO.: (415) 291-7400 FAX NO. *(Optional)*: (415) 291-7474
E-MAIL ADDRESS *(Optional)*: GRothstein@manatt.com; SFarley@manatt.com
ATTORNEY FOR *(Name)*: Bank of America, N.A.

FOR COURT USE ONLY
FILED
SAN FRANCISCO COUNTY SUPERIOR COURT
JUL 25 2011
CLERK OF THE COURT
BY: [signature]
DEPUTY CLERK

AFFD. OF MAILING

SUPERIOR COURT OF CALIFORNIA, COUNTY OF SAN FRANCISCO
STREET ADDRESS: 400 MacAllister Street
MAILING ADDRESS: 400 MacAllister Street
CITY AND ZIP CODE: San Francisco, CA 94102
BRANCH NAME: Civic Center

☐ ESTATE OF *(Name)*: ☒ IN THE MATTER OF *(Name)*:
Trust for Michael created under the Goodall Trust dated September 12, 1990

☐ DECEDENT ☒ TRUST ☐ OTHER

NOTICE OF HEARING—DECEDENT'S ESTATE OR TRUST

CASE NUMBER: PTR-99-273030

This notice is required by law.
This notice does not require you to appear in court, but you may attend the hearing if you wish.

1. NOTICE is given that *(name)*: Bank of America, N.A.
(representative capacity, if any): Trustee
has filed *(specify)*:*
PETITION FOR DETERMINATION OF THE BENEFICIARIES TO WHOM TRUST PROPERTY SHALL PASS UPON TERMINATION OF TRUST

2. You may refer to the filed documents for more information. *(Some documents filed with the court are confidential.)*

3. A HEARING on the matter will be held as follows:

a. Date: August 23, 2011 Time: 9:00 am Dept.: 204 Room:

b. Address of court ☒ shown above ☐ is *(specify)*:

Assistive listening systems, computer-assisted real-time captioning, or sign language interpreter services are available upon request if at least 5 days notice is provided. Contact the clerk's office for *Request or Accommodations by Persons With Disabilities and Order* (form MC-410). (Civil Code section 54.8.)

* Do **not** use this form to give notice of a petition to administer estate (see Prob. Code, § 8100 and form DE-121) or notice of a hearing in a guardianship or conservatorship (see Prob. Code, §§ 1511 and 1822 and form GC-020).

☐ ESTATE OF *(Name)*: ☒ IN THE MATTER OF *(Name)*: Trust for Michael created under the Goodall Trust dated September 12, 1990 ☐ DECEDENT ☒ TRUST ☐ OTHER	CASE NUMBER: PTR-99-273030

CLERK'S CERTIFICATE OF POSTING

1. I certify that I am not a party to this cause.
2. A copy of the foregoing *Notice of Hearing—Decedent's Estate or Trust*
   a. was posted at *(address)*:

   b. was posted on *(date)*:

Date: Clerk by ____________________, Deputy

PROOF OF SERVICE BY MAIL *

1. I am over the age of 18 and not a party to this cause. I am a resident of or employed in the county where the mailing occurred.
2. My residence or business address is *(specify)*:
   One Embarcadero Center, 30th Floor
   San Francisco, CA 94111
3. I served the foregoing *Notice of Hearing—Decedent's Estate or Trust* on each person named below by enclosing a copy in an envelope addressed as shown below AND
   a. ☐ **depositing** the sealed envelope on the date and at the place shown in item 4 with the United States Postal Service with the postage fully prepaid.
   b. ☒ **placing** the envelope for collection and mailing on the date and at the place shown in item 4 following our ordinary business practices. I am readily familiar with this business's practice for collecting and processing correspondence for mailing. On the same day that correspondence is placed for collection and mailing, it is deposited in the ordinary course of business with the United States Postal Service in a sealed envelope with postage fully prepaid.

4.a.Date mailed: 7/13/2011 b.Place mailed *(city, state)*: San Francisco CA

5. ☒ served with the *Notice of Hearing—Decedent's Estate or Trust* a copy of the petition or other document referred to in the Notice.

I declare under penalty of perjury under the laws of the State of California that the foregoing is true and correct.

Date: 7/13/2011

Judy Phoenix
(TYPE OR PRINT NAME OF PERSON COMPLETING THIS FORM)

Judy Phoenix
(SIGNATURE OF PERSON COMPLETING THIS FORM)

NAME AND ADDRESS OF EACH PERSON TO WHOM NOTICE WAS MAILED

	Name of person served	Address *(number, street, city, state, and zip code)*
1.	Samuel H. Sloan	461 Peachstone Terrace San Rafael, CA 94903
2.		
3.		
4.		

☐ Continued on an attachment. *(You may use* Attachment to Notice of Hearing Proof of Service by Mail, *form DE-120(MA)/GC-020(MA), for this purpose.)*

* Do not use this form for proof of personal service. You may use form DE-120(P) to prove personal service of this Notice.

Samuel H. Sloan
Administrator with Will Attached of
Estate of K. Michael Goodall
461 Peachstone Terrace
San Rafael CA 94903
415-419-5980
917-659-3397
samhsloan@gmail.com

FILED
SUPERIOR COURT
COUNTY OF SAN FRANCISCO
2011 JUL 29 AM 11:39
CLERK OF THE COURT
BY: [signature]
DEPUTY CLERK

SUPERIOR COURT OF THE STATE OF CALIFORNIA

FOR THE COUNTY OF SAN FRANCISCO

IN RE: THE GOODALL TRUST,	Case No.: PTR-99-273030 FURTHER PROBATE OPPOSITION/OBJECTION TO PETITION FOR DETERMINATION OF THE BENEFICIARIES TO WHOM TRUST PROPERTY SHALL PASS UPON TERMINATION OF TRUST FILED BY OBJECTOR SAMUEL H. SLOAN.

The undersigned, the court appointed Administrator of the Estate of K. Michael Goodall with will attached, further objects to the Motion of Bank of America to steal the property of the Estate of K. Michael Goodall. Bank of America has conducted this case on an entire fraudulent basis.

1. I intend to seek criminal indictments of Bank of America and their attorneys for their using false documents to bamboozle the courts into believing that this case is entirely different from what it is. In addition, on the afternoon of July 28, 2011 (yesterday) I came home and found a real estate agent rummaging

around in the back yard my house at 461 Peachstone Terrace, San Rafael, California 94903. There were two real estate agents trespassing on Estate Property. They said they had been sent by Guide Dogs for the Blind who, they said, owned the property.

2. One of the real estate agents gave her name as Carol Chapman of CRC Partners, San Anselmo CA 94979. The other, a man, who had opened the gate and whom I found in the back yard and who seemed to be trying to open the windows to get into the house, did not give his name. I told them both in no uncertain terms that Guide Dogs for the Blind does not own the property and has nothing to do with this property. I told them to get out and to tell Guide Dogs that they had better not send anybody again.

3. Bank of America and their attorneys are committing a fraud upon this court by submitting the wrong documents to the courts. They claim that the Goodall Family Trust of 1990 is a "Trust for Michael". They have apparently bamboozled a judge of a court into believing that. The document they submitted to the court is NOT the real 1990 trust. I have the real 1990 trust and here it is. It is marked Exhibit A. I found it in the court file of this case, PTR-99-273030 where it is also marked Exhibit A.

4. The key provision of this trust is on page 13, section 6.3, which states:

6.3. Disposition of Credit Shelter Trust Upon Death of Surviving Spouse.

Upon the death of the surviving spouse, the property in the Credit Shelter Trust shall be disposed of as follows:

(a) To KENNETH MICHAEL GOODALL, by right of representation, those issue to take that share in the manner provided in California Probate Code section 240.

(b) If the property is not completely disposed of by the preceding provisions, twenty thousand dollars ($20,000) to each of the living brothers and sisters of the trustors and the remainder to GUIDE DOGS FOR THE BLIND OF MARIN, INC., of San Rafael, California.

(c) If the property is not completely disposed of by the preceding provisions, the trustee shall pay over and deliver the undisposed portion outright as follows: One-half (1/2) to the heirs of the deceased spouse and one-half (1/2) to the heirs of the surviving spouse.

5. Furthermore, the amendment to the Goodall Family Trust dated 1999, a document which opposing counsel failed to include in their motion papers, clearly states that K. Michael Goodall is the trustee of the trust, substituting in the place of his father, Kenneth F. Goodall, who had died. Thus, when his mother, Rachel A. Goodall, subsequently died, Michael became the surviving trustee.

6. This document shows that Mike Goodall inherited the property. Thus, the entire assets of the trust is in the Estate of Mike Goodall. The only way that Guide Dogs for the Blind could have gotten their hands on the house and the money would have been for Mike Goodall to have died before his parents did. However, that did not happen, as his father died in 1994 and his mother died in 1999. Mike died on October 5, 2010.

7. This relationship is confirmed by the drafting attorney, whose affidavit is included as Exhibit B. This affidavit states in paragraph 2: "Under the terms of the trust, a copy of which is attached hereto as Exhibit A, their son Michael was made their outright beneficiary after the death of the survivor of them (page 13, paragraph 6.3(a)) and Michael was their successor trustee."

8. The affidavit goes further to state in paragraph 8: "In January 1999 Rachel executed a second amendment to the Goodall Trust in

which she named Michael to act with her as co-trustee of the survivors trust."

9. The documents filed in this case further show that at the time of the death of Rachel Goodall on June 7, 1999, there was no money in the trust. However, the bank used strong-arm tactics to contact other financial institutions including USAA Investment Management of San Antonio Texas and demanded that they transfer the funds held by Rachel Goodall there, which amounted to $1.6 million, to Bank of America. In reality, Bank of America had no right to those funds.

10. Counsel for Bank of America stated in open court on May 25, 2011 that they plan to donate the entire Goodall Family Trust to Guide Dogs for the Blind of Marin County, which would leave the legitimate heirs of Mike Goodall with nothing, zero. Guide Dogs for the Blind is basically a scam operation which has amassed a huge fortune by aggressively soliciting vulnerable old people to leave their houses to them on the pretext of helping the poor blind people. Guide Dogs is the richest charity in Marin County. They have houses and property all over the county, which they have acquired by aggressively soliciting elderly people to leave their houses to them. The latest Form 990 filed by Guide Dogs for the Blind Inc. shows that donations to them for the prior year was $23,806,307 and their net assets are $269,714,615. That is two

hundred sixty nine million dollars! A copy of that Form 990 is attached hereto as Exhibit C.

11. Their business consists of giving lessons to animal-loving volunteers, teaching them how train guide dogs. There is no way they could possibly need two hundred sixty nine million dollars in tax exempt money just to give a few lessons to a few dogs. Clearly, nobody in their right mind would leave their estate to Guide Dogs for the Blind if they knew this true situation. I shall be contacting the Attorney General's office asking for an investigation of the obviously illegal practices of Guide Dogs for the Blind.

12. I have found out the reason that James R. Hastings advised Kenneth and Rachel to leave their money to Guide Dogs for the Blind if Michael Goodall died before they did, which was that Guide Dogs for the Blind pays a substantial commission or finders fee to estate planners of around 10%. Thus, according to the estimated value of this estate at $2.5 million, James R. Hastings stands to receive $250,000 for bringing in this donation, which he may have to split with the attorneys for the Bank of America, who are fighting this case now.

13. For these reasons, the motion by Bank of America should be denied. In addition, the San Francisco case is duplicative of a

case going on in Marin County Probate Court, PR1100596. That case was filed in January 2011, three months before the case in this court was filed, and concerns the same estate. The Bank of America is not doing well up there and therefore is engaging in forum shopping by filing this case here.

13. They obviously feel they will get a better break from a San Francisco judge than a Marin County judge. They even challenged me in this. "Try that on Judge Wiss and see what happens" one of the attorney's for Manatt, Phelps and Phillips said to me.

14. This sort of thing brings the courts into disrepute and therefore this case in San Francisco should be dismissed and Bank of America should be told to file in Marin County where this case belongs.

July 29, 2011

Samuel H. Sloan

Exhibit A

The Real Goodall Family Trust dated 1990

THE GOODALL TRUST

ARTICLE ONE

INTRODUCTION

1.1. Declaration. This trust declaration is made by KENNETH F. GOODALL and RACHEL A. GOODALL, both of Marin County, California, who are herein referred to as "the trustors" or "the trustee," depending on the context. The term "trustee," as used herein, also refers to each successor trustee who is serving as a trustee of a trust created under this instrument. This trust shall be known as the GOODALL TRUST.

ARTICLE TWO

THE TRUST ESTATE

2.1. Definition of Trust Estate. The property described in any schedule that is part of this instrument, the property hereafter transferred to any trust created under this instrument, and the income and proceeds attributable to all such property shall constitute the "trust estate," which shall be held in trust, administered, and distributed according to the terms of this instrument.

2.2. Initial Trust Corpus. The trust estate shall be comprised initially of the property described in the "Schedule of Community Property Assets," which is attached hereto and made a

EXHIBIT A

A

part of this trust instrument. The property described in that schedule is the trustors' community property.

2.3. Character of Property Retained. All property that now is or hereafter becomes part of the trust estate shall retain its character as community property, quasi-community property, or separate property, as the case may be, despite the transfer in trust.

2.4. Trustee's Powers in Community Property. Notwithstanding any other provision of this instrument, during the joint lifetimes of the trustors, the trustee shall not have powers beyond those granted either spouse under California Civil Code sections 5125 and 5127.

ARTICLE THREE

RIGHTS RESERVED TO TRUSTORS

3.1. Additions to the Trust Estate. A trustor or any other person may make inter vivos or testamentary transfers of property to the trustee. That additional property transferred by any other person shall become part of the trust estate upon written acceptance of it by the trustee.

3.2. Power of Revocation While Both Trustors Are Living. During the trustors' joint lifetimes, the trust may be revoked, in whole or in part, as provided in this paragraph.

(a) Community Property. Either trustor acting alone, or both of the trustors acting jointly, shall have the power to revoke the portion of the trust estate that is the trustors' community property. Upon revocation, the trustee shall pay to either trustor or to both trustors, as the trustors' community property, the community property portion of the trust estate that has been revoked.

(b) Separate Property and Quasi-Community Property. A trustor whose separate property or quasi-community property comprises any portion of the trust estate shall have the power to revoke that portion of the trust estate. Upon revocation, the trustee shall pay to the revoking trustor, as his or her separate or quasi-community property, the separate property or quasi-community property portion of the trust estate that has been revoked.

3.3. Power of Amendment While Both Trustors Are Living. During the trustors' joint lifetimes, the trust may be amended, in whole or in part, by both trustors acting jointly.

3.4. Power of Revocation and Power of Amendment After Death of First Trustor to Die. After the death of the first trustor to die, the surviving trustor shall have the power to revoke or amend, in whole or in part, the Survivor's Trust. All other trusts created under this instrument shall become irrevocable and shall not be subject to amendment after the death of the first trustor to die.

3.5. Method of Revocation or Amendment. The revocation or amendment of a trust created under this instrument shall be effective only if made in a writing that is signed by the person or persons having the power of revocation or amendment and delivered to the trustee. An exercise of the power of amendment substantially affecting the duties, rights, and liabilities of the trustee shall be effective only if agreed to by the trustee in writing.

3.6. Incompetent Trustor May Not Act. A power reserved to a trustor under this article may not be exercised by that trustor or by any other person or fiduciary, including the conservator of that trustor's estate or that trustor's attorney in fact designated in a durable power of attorney under the Uniform Durable Power of Attorney Act, if that trustor is incompetent (as defined in Article Nine) at the pertinent time. A power under this article that is exercisable only by the joint action of the trustors may not be exercised if either trustor is incompetent at the pertinent time. However, the incompetence of one trustor shall not prevent a competent trustor from exercising a power that is exercisable by the competent trustor acting alone.

ARTICLE FOUR

DISTRIBUTIONS DURING TRUSTORS' JOINT LIVES

4.1. Payment of Income During Trustors' Joint Lives. So long as both trustors are living, the trustee shall pay the net income of the trust as specified in this paragraph.

(a) Community Property. The trustee shall pay to either trustor or both trustors or apply for the trustors' benefit the entire net income from the trust community property, in monthly or other convenient installments (but not less often than annually) as either or both of the trustors and the trustee may agree upon from time to time.

(b) Separate Property and Quasi-Community Property. The trustee shall pay to or apply for the benefit of a trustor whose separate property or quasi-community property comprises part of the trust estate the entire net income from that separate property or quasi-community property, in monthly or other convenient installments (but not less often than annually) as that trustor and the trustee may agree upon from time to time.

4.2. Discretionary Payment of Principal by Trustee During Trustors' Joint Lives. So long as both trustors are living, the trustee shall pay trust principal, at any time or times, as specified in this paragraph.

(a) Community Property. The trustee shall pay to either trustor or both trustors or apply for the trustors' benefit so much of the principal of the trust community property as the trustee deems proper for the comfort, welfare, and happiness of the trustor or trustors.

(b) Separate Property and Quasi-Community Property. The trustee shall pay to or apply for the benefit of a trustor whose separate property or quasi-community property comprises part of the trust estate so much of the principal of that separate property or quasi-community property as the trustee deems proper for that trustor's comfort, welfare, and happiness.

(c) Consideration of Other Resources When Distributing Principal. In exercising discretion under subparagraphs (a) and (b) of this paragraph, the trustee shall give the consideration that the trustee deems proper to all other income and resources then readily available for use by the trustor or trustors, as the case may be, for the stated purposes and that are then known to the trustee. All decisions of the trustee regarding payments under subparagraph (a) or (b), if any, are within the trustee's discretion and shall be final and incontestable by anyone.

4.3. Trustors' Right to Withdraw Principal. So long as both trustors are living, the trustors shall have the right to withdraw trust principal, at any time or times, as specified in this paragraph.

(a) Community Property. Either trustor acting alone, if he or she is not incompetent (as defined in Article Nine) at the pertinent time, or both of the trustors acting jointly, if at least one of them is not incompetent at the pertinent time, shall have the right to withdraw any amount of trust principal that is the trustors' community property, by delivering a signed writing to the trustee.

(b) Separate Property and Quasi-Community Property. A trustor whose separate property or quasi-community property comprises part of the trust estate, if not incompetent (as defined in Article Nine) at the pertinent time, shall have the right to withdraw any amount of the principal of that separate property or quasi-community property, by delivering a signed writing to the trustee.

4.4. Trustors' Obligation for Community Property Received or Withdrawn. Net income of the trust community property paid to either trustor or both trustors pursuant to the provisions of this article and principal of the trust community property distributed to or withdrawn by either trustor or both trustors pursuant to the provisions of this article shall remain the trustors' community property. A trustor who receives such net income or principal shall have the same obligations respecting that property as he or she would have with regard to all community property generally.

ARTICLE FIVE
DIVISION INTO SHARES AND INITIAL DISTRIBUTIONS
AFTER DECEASED SPOUSE'S DEATH

5.1. Definitions. In this article and subsequent articles of this instrument, the first trustor to die is referred to as "the deceased spouse" and the other trustor is referred to as "the surviving spouse."

5.2. Trustee's Power to Defer Division or Distribution. Whenever the trustee is directed to divide any part of the trust estate or distribute trust assets upon the death of either trustor, the trustee may, in the trustee's discretion, defer actual division or distribution for a period not exceeding six (6) months after that trustor's death. The ability of the trustee to delay division or distribution shall not affect the vesting of interests in the respective shares, which shall be as of the date of death.

5.3. Division Into Three Shares After Death of Deceased Spouse. Upon the death of the deceased spouse, the trustee shall divide the trust estate, including any additions made to the trust by reason of the deceased spouse's death, such as from the deceased spouse's estate or policies of life insurance on his or her life, into three separate shares, designated "the survivor's share," "the marital deduction share," and "the credit shelter share," to be held, administered, or distributed as set forth below.

5.4. Payment of Death Taxes, Debts, and Expenses. After the death of the deceased spouse, upon receipt by the trustee of a written statement from the personal representative of the deceased spouse's estate requesting that the trustee pay death taxes, debts, and expenses (as defined in Article Nine), with respect to assets of any trust under this instrument or other taxable property or transfers, the trustee shall pay out of the trust estate, either directly or to the personal representative, any amounts requested by the personal representative for those purposes. The trustee may rely upon the personal representative's statement and shall not be liable for any act or omission by the personal representative in protesting or failing to protest the legality, propriety, or amount of the death taxes, debts, or expenses. The trustee shall pay as much of the federal estate tax as possible with any "flower bonds" (United States Treasury obligations acceptable at par value in payment of federal estate tax) that are part of the trust estate, but only to the extent of the deceased spouse's interest in those bonds. Payment of death taxes and payment of expenses shall be charged to the credit shelter share, except for any death taxes that are attributable to a disclaimer of property under this instrument by the surviving spouse, which shall be paid from the Disclaimer Trust. Payment of any debts allocable against the separate property of the deceased spouse shall be charged against the credit shelter share. Debts allocable against community property shall be allocated to the survivor's share and the credit shelter share in accordance with California law in effect at the date of the deceased spouse's death, so long as charges against the survivor's share do not exceed the value of community property allocable to that share. The trustee shall not pay death taxes, debts, and expenses or other obligations of the deceased spouse or the deceased spouse's estate from proceeds of insurance policies on the deceased spouse's life if making those payments would be the sole cause of the proceeds being includable in the deceased spouse's gross estate for federal estate tax purposes.

5.5. Survivor's Share Allocated to Survivor's Trust. The survivor's share, as determined in this paragraph, shall be held, administered, and distributed by the trustee according to the terms set forth in Article Six applicable to the Survivor's Trust, for the benefit of the surviving spouse. The survivor's share shall consist of the portion of the trust estate that is comprised of the surviving spouse's one-half (1/2) interest in the trustors' community property, the surviving spouse's one-half (1/2) interest in the deceased spouse's quasi-community property, all of the surviving spouse's separate property, and all of the surviving spouse's quasi-community property.

5.6. Credit Shelter Share Allocated to Credit Shelter Trust. The credit shelter share, as determined in this paragraph, shall be held, administered, and distributed by the trustee according to the terms set forth in Article Six applicable to the Credit Shelter Trust. The credit shelter share shall consist of a pecuniary gift from the trust estate other than the survivor's share (as defined in the preceding paragraph) that is the largest amount, if any, of property that can pass free of federal estate tax by reason of (1) the unified credit available to the deceased spouse's estate; and (2) the credit for state death taxes, to the extent that the use of that credit does not result in or increase any death tax payable to any state. Any qualified disclaimer made by the surviving spouse shall be disregarded in determining this amount. The trustors recognize that the amount of this pecuniary gift may be affected by a number of considerations, including:

(a) The net value of all property disposed of by this instrument or otherwise that is included in the deceased spouse's gross estate for federal estate tax purposes and that does not qualify for the federal estate tax marital or charitable deduction;

(b) The value of all property disposed of by the deceased spouse that constitutes "adjusted taxable gifts";

(c) All charges to principal that are deductible under Internal Revenue Code section 2053 but that are not deducted in computing the federal estate tax liability for the deceased spouse's gross estate; and

(d) Actions of the deceased spouse's executor in exercising certain tax elections.

The trustors recognize that because of the above factors no property may pass pursuant to this provision.

5.7. Marital Deduction Share Distributed Outright. The marital deduction share shall consist of the balance of the trust estate, and shall be distributed outright to the surviving spouse.

5.8. Allocation of Assets. In allocating assets between the marital deduction share and the credit shelter share, the trustee shall allocate the assets in the trust estate that qualify for the marital deduction between the marital deduction share and the credit shelter share in cash or in kind, or partly in each, on a prorata or a nonprorata basis, and in undivided interests or not, but subject to the following:

(a) Qualification for Marital Deduction. Only assets that qualify for the marital deduction shall be allocated to the marital deduction share.

(b) Allocations in Kind. Assets allocated in kind shall be valued for purposes of allocation on the date or dates of distribution.

(c) Foreign Death Tax Credit. Assets that qualify for the foreign death tax credit shall be allocated to the marital deduction share only if other trust property is insufficient to fund the marital deduction share.

5.9. Intention That Disposition of Marital Deduction Share Qualify for Marital Deduction. The trustors intend that the disposition of the marital deduction share qualify for the federal estate tax marital deduction and that the trustee take no action or exercise any power that may impair that deduction. The trustors incorporate in this instrument the provisions of California Probate Code section 21522.

5.10. Disclaimer of Property by Surviving Spouse. Any property or portion thereof that is disclaimed by the surviving spouse shall be held, administered, or distributed by the trustee according to the terms set forth in Article Six applicable to the Disclaimer Trust.

ARTICLE SIX

DISPOSITIVE PROVISIONS OF TRUSTS CREATED AFTER DECEASED SPOUSE'S DEATH

6.1. Survivor's Trust. The property allocated to the Survivor's Trust shall be held, administered, and distributed for the benefit of the surviving spouse according to the following terms and conditions:

(a) Payment of Income. The trustee shall pay to or apply for the benefit of the surviving spouse, so long as the surviving spouse lives, the entire net income of the trust, in monthly or other convenient installments (but not less often than annually) as the surviving spouse and the trustee may agree upon from time to time.

(b) Discretionary Payment of Principal by Trustee. At any time or times during the trust term, the trustee shall pay to or apply for the benefit of the surviving spouse so much of the principal of the trust as the trustee deems proper for the surviving spouse's comfort, welfare, and happiness. In exercising discretion, the trustee shall give the consideration that the trustee deems proper to all other income and resources then readily available to the surviving spouse for use for these purposes and that are then known to the trustee. All decisions of the trustee regarding payments under this subparagraph, if any, are within the trustee's discretion and shall be final and incontestable by anyone.

(c) Right of Surviving Spouse to Withdraw Principal. The trustee shall pay to the surviving spouse as much of the trust principal as the surviving spouse may from time to time demand in a signed writing delivered to the trustee.

(d) General Power of Appointment. Upon the death of the surviving spouse, all of the trust property (including the trust principal, all net income then held by the trustee, and all income then accrued but not collected by the trustee) shall be paid over and delivered to any entity or entities, person or persons, and upon any trust, terms and conditions, or to or in favor of the estate of the surviving spouse, as the surviving spouse may direct by will, provided only that no exercise of this power of appointment shall be effective unless it refers to this instrument and expressly indicates an intention to exercise this power of appointment. The trustee may rely upon any instrument admitted to probate as the last will of the surviving spouse in carrying out the terms of the power of appointment and shall not be liable for any good-faith act in reliance upon that will, even if for any reason it is later determined to be invalid with respect to its purported exercise of this power of appointment. If the trustee receives no notice of the existence of a will of the surviving spouse within six (6) months after the death of the surviving spouse, the trustee may distribute the trust assets and income as though this power of appointment had not been exercised and shall in that event be conclusively presumed to have acted in good faith, even if a valid will is thereafter discovered.

(e) Payment of Death Taxes, Debts, and Expenses. On the death of the surviving spouse and subject to any power of appointment exercised by him or her, the trustee may, in the trustee's discretion, pay out of the income or principal or partly from the income and partly from the principal of the Survivor's Trust, the death taxes, debts, and expenses (as defined in Article Nine) arising on the death of the surviving spouse.

(f) Default Provision. In default of the power of appointment, or to the extent that an attempt to exercise the power was ineffectual, the entire remaining principal, all net income then held by the trustee, and all income then accrued but not collected by the trustee, after any payment of taxes, debts, and expenses pursuant to the applicable provisions of this instrument, shall be disposed of in the manner specified in the paragraph below entitled "Disposition of Credit Shelter Trust Upon Death of Surviving Spouse," although the property disposed of pursuant to this subparagraph shall not be considered to be part of the Credit Shelter Trust.

6.2. Disposition of Credit Shelter Trust Until Death of Surviving Spouse. The property allocated to the Credit Shelter Trust shall be held, administered, and distributed until the death of the surviving spouse according to the following terms and conditions:

(a) Discretionary Payment of Income and Principal by Trustee. At any time or times, the trustee shall pay to or apply

for the benefit of the surviving spouse so much of the net income and principal of the trust as the trustee deems proper for the health, education, support, and maintenance of the surviving spouse. In exercising discretion, the trustee shall give the consideration that the trustee deems proper to all other income and resources then readily available to the surviving spouse for use for these purposes and that are then known to the trustee. All decisions of the trustee regarding payments under this subparagraph, if any, are within the trustee's discretion and shall be final and incontestable by anyone. Any net income not expended under the foregoing provisions of this subparagraph shall be accumulated and added to the principal of the trust.

(b) Right of Surviving Spouse to Withdraw Principal. The surviving spouse shall have the power to withdraw from the principal of the trust each calendar year those amounts as shall not exceed the greater of five thousand dollars ($5,000) or five (5) percent of the assets, valued as of the end of the calendar year. The surviving spouse shall exercise this power by a written instrument signed by him or her and delivered to the trustee. This power is noncumulative and to the extent it is not exercised by the end of the calendar year, it shall lapse. This power shall exist each year until the death of the surviving spouse.

6.3. Disposition of Credit Shelter Trust Upon Death of Surviving Spouse. Upon the death of the surviving spouse, the property in the Credit Shelter Trust shall be disposed of as follows:

(a) To KENNETH MICHAEL GOODALL, by right of representation, those issue to take that share in the manner provided in California Probate Code section 240.

(b) If the property is not completely disposed of by the preceding provisions, twenty thousand dollars ($20,000.00) to each of the living brothers and sisters of the trustors and the remainder to GUIDE DOGS FOR THE BLIND OF MARIN, INC., of San Rafael, California.

(c) If the property is not completely disposed of by the preceding provisions, the trustee shall pay over and deliver the undisposed portion outright as follows: one-half (1/2) to the heirs of the deceased spouse and one-half (1/2) to the heirs of the surviving spouse.

6.4. Disclaimer Trust. The property allocated to the Disclaimer Trust shall be held, administered, and distributed

according to the following terms and conditions:

(a) Payment of Income. The trustee shall pay to or apply for the benefit of the surviving spouse the entire net income of the trust, in monthly or other convenient installments (but not less often than annually) as the surviving spouse and the trustee may agree upon from time to time.

(b) Payment of Principal. At any time or times, the trustee shall pay to or apply for the benefit of the surviving spouse so much of the principal of the trust as the trustee deems proper for the health, education, support, and maintenance of the surviving spouse. In exercising discretion, the trustee shall give the consideration that the trustee deems proper to all other income and resources then readily available to the surviving spouse for use for these purposes and that are then known to the trustee.

(c) Distribution of Remainder. Upon the death of the surviving spouse, the remaining trust property (including all income then accrued but uncollected and all net income then remaining in the hands of the trustee) shall be disposed of in the manner specified in the preceding paragraph, entitled "Disposition of Credit Shelter Trust Upon Death of Surviving Spouse," although the property disposed of pursuant to this subparagraph shall not be considered to be part of the Credit Shelter Trust.

ARTICLE SEVEN

OFFICE OF TRUSTEE

7.1. Remaining Trustor-Trustee Serves Alone. Upon the death of the deceased spouse, or if before that time either trustor resigns as trustee, is removed pursuant to judicial procedure, becomes incompetent (as defined in Article Nine), or for any reason fails or ceases to act as trustee, the remaining trustor-trustee shall serve as sole trustee.

7.2. Successor Trustees. Upon the death of the remaining trustor-trustee, or if the remaining trustor-trustee resigns as trustee, is removed pursuant to judicial procedure, becomes incompetent, or for any reason fails or ceases to act as trustee,

KENNETH MICHAEL GOODALL shall become the trustee. If KENNETH MICHAEL GOODALL is not qualified for appointment as trustee, or if he later dies, resigns, is removed pursuant to judicial procedure, or for any reason fails or ceases to act as trustee, SECURITY PACIFIC BANK shall serve as the corporate sole trustee.

7.3. Waiver of Bond of Individual Trustees. No bond shall be required of any individual who serves as a trustee under this instrument.

7.4. Trustee's Right and Method of Resignation. Any trustee may resign at any time, without giving a reason for the resignation, by executing a signed written instrument and delivering it to any other trustee then acting, to the successor trustee designated in the manner provided in this article, to the trustors, if living, and if either trustor is deceased, to the trust beneficiaries. A resignation shall be effective upon written acceptance of the trust by the successor trustee.

7.5. Trustee's Liability. The trustee shall not be liable to any person with an interest in the trust for acts or omissions of the trustee, except those resulting from willful misconduct or gross negligence. This standard shall also apply regarding the trustee's liability for acts or omissions of any co-trustee, predecessor trustee, or agent employed by the trustee.

7.6. Compensation of Corporate Trustee. A corporate trustee shall be entitled to reasonable compensation for services rendered in accordance with its fee schedule in effect from time to time for inter vivos trusts.

the trustee deems advisable, and acquire every kind of investment, real, personal, or mixed, including but not limited to improved and unimproved real property, corporate and government (whether local, state, or federal) obligations of every kind, stocks (both preferred and common), and shares of mutual funds of any character; and (2) retain as an investment for the trust in the same form received by the trustee any property given to the trustee from any source. The trustee is under no duty to diversify the investments of the trust. This paragraph shall be construed as expanding the standards set forth in California Probate Code section 16040.

8.3. Power of Trustee with Regard to Accounts. Initially there will be two persons acting as co-trustees for this Trust. In order to make payments from the Trust without undue complications, the trustees will need to open bank, investment, securities brokerage, margin, and similar accounts in which either trustee may be the signatory. This provision specifically gives to the co-trustees the power to open as many accounts as needed (checking, savings, certificates of deposit, money market accounts, investment, etc.) and open such accounts so that deposits and withdrawals may be made with the signature of only one trustee. This includes the power to open an account where either trustee or only one may sign on the account. The initial trustees are specifically vested with the power and authority to open, operate and maintain these accounts and to use the other powers provided in this trust, such as the power to buy and sell on margin, hypothecate, borrow upon, purchase and/or sell as the sole trustee

7.7. Compensation of Individual Trustees. Each individual who is a trustee under this instrument shall be entitled to reasonable compensation for fiduciary services rendered. The trustee may pay these fees from the funds of the pertinent trust as an expense of trust administration, without court order.

ARTICLE EIGHT

POWERS OF TRUSTEE

8.1. General Powers of Trustee. In order to carry out the purposes of this trust, the trustee shall have all of the powers enumerated herein and, except as limited by any provision of this instrument, all powers now or hereafter granted to a trustee by law. Except as limited by a more specific provision of this instrument, the trustee shall have the power to:

(a) Sell, exchange, transfer, convey, lease without limitation as to term, borrow upon, and hypothecate all or any part of the trust property;

(b) Retain, maintain, repair, divide, partition, improve, and otherwise manage any trust property;

(c) Insure trust property against damage or loss, and against liability with respect to third persons, at the expense of the trust, with the carriers and coverages that the trustee deems advisable;

(d) Enforce the rights of the trust with respect to any mortgage, deed of trust, pledge, or similar security device held in trust; enforce, at a foreclosure sale (whether judicial or nonjudicial) or other sale, the rights of the trust in secured property; make bids upon and purchase, at trust expense, any property that is subject to security device; and accept a deed in lieu of foreclosure as full or complete satisfaction of the secured debt;

(e) Commence or defend, at the expense of the trust, legal actions relating to the trust or any trust property as the trustee deems advisable;

(f) Compromise, submit to arbitration, settle, or release (with or without consideration) or otherwise adjust any claims in favor of or against the trust;

(g) Hold trust property in the name of a nominee or nominees, with or without disclosing the trust character of such property (including securities in such condition that ownership may pass upon delivery), or in the name of the trustee as trustee;

(h) Exercise any and all rights and powers of an owner of stocks or securities; vote and give proxies; pay assessments or other charges; exercise or not exercise, as the trustee deems advisable, subscriptions, conversion rights, or other rights or options that may devolve upon holders of stocks or securities; and enter into shareholder agreements;

(i) Participate in any plans or proceedings for foreclosure or consolidations, merger, liquidation, or other reorganization of any corporation or organization having securities that are held as trust property and, in connection therewith, deposit securities with and transfer title or securities upon the terms that the trustee deems advisable to any protective or other committee established in connection with any such plan or proceeding;

(j) Subdivide and resubdivide trust real property and sign applications, maps, and other documents incidental thereto; to dedicate trust real property for public purposes, with or without consideration; grant and impose upon trust real property, conditions, covenants, easements, restrictions, rights of way, and other servitudes; borrow against trust real property; and do such other acts as may appear to the trustee advisable in connection with the exercise of any of the powers described in this subparagraph.

(k) Receive additions to the trust from any source at any time;

(l) Borrow money for any trust purpose on such terms and conditions as the trustee deems advisable and obligate the trust to repay the borrowing;

(m) Employ attorneys, investment counsel, accountants, bookkeepers, or other persons to render services regarding all matters pertaining to the trusts, and pay from trust property the reasonable compensation of such persons for their services.

8.2. <u>Trustee's Power to Invest and Retain Trust Property</u>.

The trustee shall have the power to (1) invest trust property as deems appropriate.

8.4. Trustee's Power Regarding Unproductive Property. The trustee may retain or acquire unproductive or underproductive property. California Probate Code section 16311 shall not apply to any trust created under this instrument.

8.5. Retention of Residence. After the deceased spouse's death, the trustee may retain in any trust or trusts provided for under this instrument, for the personal use of the surviving spouse, any property occupied by the trustors as a principal place of residence at the time of the deceased spouse's death, for as long as the surviving spouse desires to occupy the residence. The trustee shall pay from the trust estate all expenses associated with the maintenance and upkeep of such property. On the written request of the surviving spouse, the trustee may sell the residence and replace it with other property of comparable or lower value suitable as a residence for the surviving spouse. If the surviving spouse becomes subject to a conservatorship of the estate or person, the conservator shall be empowered to act for the surviving spouse.

8.6. Combining Multi-Trust Property. Each trust created under this instrument shall constitute a separate trust and be administered accordingly; however, the assets of all of the trusts may be combined for bookkeeping purposes and held for the trust beneficiaries without physical division into separate trusts until time of distribution.

8.7. Spendthrift Clause. To the maximum extent permitted by

law, the interests of each trust beneficiary under this instrument are not transferable by voluntary or involuntary assignment or by operation of law and shall be free from the claims of creditors and from attachment, execution, bankruptcy, and other legal process. If any such transfer is made or attempted by or against a trust beneficiary, all further trust payments of income or principal or both to that beneficiary (and any right of that beneficiary to such payments) shall be suspended for a period of time or indefinitely (but in no case for longer than the term of the trust) as the trustee determines. In lieu of payments to the beneficiary, the trustee may apply so much of the trust income or principal or both to which the beneficiary would otherwise be entitled as the trustee deems necessary for the beneficiary's education and support. All trust income (to which the beneficiary would otherwise be entitled) not so applied shall in the discretion of the trustee be accumulated and added to trust principal at such time or times as the trustee deems proper.

8.8. Division or Distribution in Cash or Kind. Except to the extent that any provisions in this instrument that specify the allocation of assets involving the marital deduction conflict with this paragraph, the trustee, in order to satisfy a pecuniary gift or to distribute or divide trust assets into shares or partial shares, may distribute or divide such assets in kind, or divide undivided interests in such assets, or sell all or any part of such assets and distribute or divide the property in cash, in kind, or partly in cash and partly in kind. Property distributed to satisfy a pecuniary gift under this instrument shall be valued at its fair market value at the time of distribution.

8.9. Payments on Behalf of Minors or Persons Under Disability. If at any time any beneficiary is a minor or it appears to the trustee that any beneficiary is disabled, incompetent, or for any other reason not able to receive payments or make intelligent or responsible use of the payments, then the trustee, in lieu of making direct payments to the beneficiary, may make payments to the beneficiary's conservator or guardian; to the beneficiary's custodian under the Uniform Gifts to Minors Act or Uniform Transfers to Minors Act of any state; to one or more suitable persons as the trustee deems proper, such as a relative of the beneficiary or a person residing with the beneficiary, to be used for the beneficiary's benefit; to any other person, firm, or agency for services rendered or to be rendered for the beneficiary's assistance or benefit; or to accounts in the beneficiary's name with financial institutions. The receipt of payments by any of the foregoing shall constitute a sufficient acquittance of the trustee for all purposes.

8.10. Trustee's Duty to Account. The trustee shall not be required to render periodic accounts to any person, but shall render accounts at the termination of a trust and upon a change of trustee, to the persons and in the manner required by law.

8.11. Written Notice to Trustee. Until the trustee receives written notice of any death or other event upon which the right to payments from any trust may depend, the trustee shall incur no liability for disbursements made in good faith to persons whose interests may have been affected by that event.

8.12. No Early Termination of Trust Without Prior Court Authorization. California Probate Code section 15408(b) shall not apply to any trust under this instrument, and except as otherwise provided in this instrument, the trustee may not terminate a trust before the trust term expires unless prior court authorization is obtained.

ARTICLE NINE

CONCLUDING PROVISIONS

9.1. Perpetuities Savings Clause. Unless sooner terminated, each trust created by this instrument shall terminate twenty-one (21) years after the later of (1) the death of the last to die of the trustors' issue who are living at the death of the surviving spouse, or (2) the death of the surviving spouse. If a trust is terminated because of the preceding sentence, the trustee shall distribute the trust property outright pro rata, to the persons who are then entitled or eligible to receive trust income (or if there are no such persons, outright in a manner that the trustee believes will give effect to the trustors' intent in creating the trust).

9.2. Period of Survivorship. For the purposes of this instrument, a beneficiary shall not be deemed to have survived a trustor if that beneficiary dies within sixty (60) days after the trustor's death.

9.3. Severability Clause. If any provision of this

instrument is invalid, that provision shall be disregarded and shall not affect any of the other provisions.

9.4. Captions. The captions appearing in this instrument are for convenience of reference only and shall have no significance in the construction or interpretation of this instrument.

9.5. Definition of Heirs. Any reference to a trustor's "heirs" in the dispositive provisions of this instrument shall be construed as referring to those persons who are entitled to that trustor's property under the laws of intestate succession in effect at the time of execution of this instrument.

9.6. Definitions of Issue, Child, and Children. The terms "issue," "child," and "children," when used in the dispositive provisions of this instrument, shall be given the meanings accorded those terms in Part 2 of Division 1 of the California Probate Code in effect at the time of execution of this instrument.

9.7. Definition of Incompetent. For all purposes under this instrument, a person shall be deemed "incompetent" if and so long as a conservator of his or her person or estate duly appointed by a court of competent jurisdiction is serving, or upon certification by two physicians (licensed to practice under the laws of the state where the person is domiciled) that the person is unable properly to care for himself or herself, for his or her person, or for his or her property.

9.8. Definition of Death Taxes, Debts, and Expenses. As used in this instrument, the term "death taxes, debts, and expenses" shall include the following:

(a) All estate, inheritance, succession, and similar taxes (including any interest and penalties) that become payable by reason of a trustor's death or by any person on account of that person's interest in that trustor's estate, but excluding any federal or state tax imposed on any "generation-skipping transfer," and excluding any addition to the federal estate tax for any "excess retirement accumulation" under Internal Revenue Code section 4980A.

(b) All costs, expenses of litigation, counsel fees, or other charges that the trustee incurs in connection with the determination of the amount of the taxes, interest, or penalties referred to in subparagraph (a) of this paragraph; and

(c) Legally enforceable debts, funeral expenses, expenses of last illness, and administration and property expenses.

9.9. California Trust Law to Apply. California law shall govern the validity, interpretation, and administration of any trust created under this instrument, regardless of the domicile of any trustee or beneficiary.

ARTICLE TEN

EXECUTION

10.1. Execution. We, and each of us, certify that we have read the foregoing trust declaration and that it correctly states the terms and conditions under which the trust estate is to be held, managed, and disposed of by the trustees. We approve of the trust declaration in all particulars, and as the trustees named in the trust declaration, accept the trusts provided for in the declaration.

10.2. Executed on SEP 12 1990 at San Anselmo, California.

Kenneth F. Goodall
KENNETH F. GOODALL

Rachel A. Goodall
RACHEL A. GOODALL

Exhibit B

Affidavit by drafting counsel stating "Under the terms of the trust, a copy of which is attached hereto as Exhibit A, their son Michael was made their outright beneficiary after the death of the survivor of them (page 13, paragraph 6.3(a)) and Michael was their successor trustee."

The affidavit goes further to state in paragraph 8: "In January 1999 Rachel executed a second amendment to the Goodall Trust in which she named Michael to act with her as co-trustee of the survivors trust."

MARTIN J. MALKIN
SBN 95455
1000 Fourth Street, Suite 875
San Rafael, CA 94901
(415) 459-2000
FAX (415) 459-3668

JAMES R. HASTINGS
SBN 79066
18 San Rafael Ave.
San Anselmo, Ca. 94960
(415) 459-6635
FAX (415) 459-6756

Attorneys for Bank of America

FILED
San Francisco County Superior Court
MAR 21 2000
ALAN CARLSON, Clerk
BY: [signature]
Deputy Clerk

SUPERIOR COURT OF CALIFORNIA

COUNTY OF SAN FRANCISCO

In Re: The Goodall Trust

NO. 273030

DECLARATION OF JAMES R. HASTINGS IN OPPOSITION TO PETITION TO REMOVE TRUSTEE

Date: March 27, 2000
Time: 9:30 AM
Department: Probate (Room 204)

I, James R. Hastings, declare:

1. I am an attorney at law licensed to practice in all courts of this state. I drafted the relevant testamentary instruments of Rachel A. Goodall and Kenneth F. Goodall, including their wills and their trust. Their major beneficiary was their son Kenneth Michael ("Michael").

2. In 1990 Mr and Mrs. Goodall requested me to draft a revocable living trust as their main testamentary instrument. Under the terms of the trust, a copy of which is attached hereto as **EXHIBIT A**, their son Michael was made their outright beneficiary after the death of the survivor of them (page 13 paragraph 6.3(a)), and Michael was their successor trustee.

3. On August 24, 1994 Mr. and Mrs. Goodall executed their Declaration of Trust

Law Offices of
MARTIN J. MALKIN
1000 Fourth Street, Suite 875
San Rafael, CA 94901
TEL: (415) 459-2000 - FAX: (415) 459-3668

and their pour over wills, substantially modifying their 1990 estate plan. They were convinced that Michael was unable to handle money properly, that he should not be given access to substantial funds, or have influence over the person or entity controlling his funds. They explained that Michael stopped working in 1997 or 1998 and was living in their home.

4. As a consequence, they instructed me to draft the new trust instrument under which the estate would remain in trust after the death of the survivor of them, with the trustee granted liberal discretion regarding payments of income and principal to Michael. Under its terms, all decisions of the trustee regarding payments are within the trustee's discretion and are final and incontestable. Attached hereto as **EXHIBIT B** is a true copy of the 1994 trust. See section 6.5, page 19-20.

5. Because they wanted a strong trustee, not subject to influence by Michael, my clients chose Bank of America to act as their successor trustee. It was their desire that the trustee be completely independent of Michael, not subject to his influence.

6. Consistent therewith, Mr. and Mrs. Goodall also named Bank of America as successor executor of their pour over wills.

7. Kenneth Goodall died on September 10, 1994. I am aware that after his death Rachel Goodall had at least three meetings with Bank of America concerning the trust, the first one I also attended in late 1994 or early 1995.

8. In January 1999 Rachel Goodall executed a second amendment to the Goodall Trust in which she named Michael to act as co-trustee with her for the survivor's trust. Bank of America remained as trustee for the exemption trust. See **EXHIBIT C**.

9. Rachel L. Goodall died on June 7, 1999. According to her checking account records that I reviewed, on July 14, 1999 Michael withdrew $4,000 for his own use. Similarly, on July 8, 1999 he withdrew $6,500 from the account. I understand that he claims that he lent that money to a friend.

Law Offices of
MARTIN J. MALKIN
1000 Fourth Street, Suite 875
San Rafael, CA 94901
TEL: (415) 459-2000 - FAX: (415) 459-3668

10. Prior to his mother's death Michael drew $2,000 from his mother's account on March 23, 1999. On May 24, 1999, when Mrs. Goodall was a patient at the Guardian of Greenbrae, apparently at Michael's request, she endorsed a $3,500 check made payable to her for Michael's use.

11. On July 15, 1999 I met with Susan Scribner of Bank of America Trust Department and informed her that Michael had drawn at least $10,500 from Mrs. Goodall's account after her death.

12. In his initial meeting with Bank of America, Michael requested monthly payments equivalent to $30,000 to $36,000 a year.

13. I assisted Bank of America in marshaling the trust assets. It took several months before USAA Investment Management Company released the trust's funds. I understand that the bank did not receive the funds until December 9, 1999.

14. Prior to any motions being filed in this case, on December 9, 1999 the trustee distributed $12,500 to Michael, based on $2,500 a month retroactive to August. Since that date the trustee has paid Michael $2,500 in each of January, February, and March 2000. Thus, Michael's impatience with the trustee making regularly monthly payments was satisfied in December before his motions were filed.

15. It is my firm belief that Mr. and Mrs. Goodall had substantial trust and confidence in Bank of America to act for them in administering the trust for Michael' benefit. It was their desire that Bank of America serve as trustee and there is no reason why it should not continue to serve.

16. I am aware that Michael has no children, and that Mrs. Goodall has five living siblings.

Executed at San Anselmo, California on March 20, 2000.

Law Offices of
MARTIN J. MALKIN
1000 Fourth Street, Suite 875
San Rafael, CA 94901
TEL: (415) 459-2000 - FAX: (415) 459-3668

I declare under the penalty of perjury that the foregoing is true and correct.

James R. Hastings, Esq.

Law Offices of
MARTIN J. MALKIN
1000 Fourth Street, Suite 875
San Rafael, CA 94901
TEL.: (415) 459-2000 · FAX: (415) 459-3668

Exhibit C

Form 990 filed by Guide Dogs for the Blind Inc. shows that donations to them for the prior year was $23,806,307 and their net assets are $269,714,615.

efile GRAPHIC print - DO NOT PROCESS | As Filed Data - | DLN: 93493313007210

Form **990**

Department of the Treasury Internal Revenue Service

Return of Organization Exempt From Income Tax

Under section 501(c), 527, or 4947(a)(1) of the Internal Revenue Code (except black lung benefit trust or private foundation)

▶ The organization may have to use a copy of this return to satisfy state reporting requirements

OMB No 1545-0047

2009

Open to Public Inspection

0411

A For the 2009 calendar year, or tax year beginning 07-01-2009 and ending 06-30-2010

B Check if applicable
- ☐ Address change
- ☐ Name change
- ☐ Initial return
- ☐ Terminated
- ☐ Amended return
- ☐ Application pending

Please use IRS label or print or type. See Specific Instructions.

C Name of organization
Guide Dogs for the Blind Inc

Doing Business As

Number and street (or P O box if mail is not delivered to street address) PO Box 151200 | Room/suite

City or town, state or country, and ZIP + 4
San Rafael, CA 949151200

D Employer identification number
94-1196195

E Telephone number
(415) 499-4000

G Gross receipts $ 165,002,432

F Name and address of principal officer
KEN STUPI
PO Box 151200
San Rafael, CA 949151200

H(a) Is this a group return for affiliates? ☐ Yes ☑ No

H(b) Are all affiliates included? ☐ Yes ☐ No
If "No," attach a list (see instructions)

H(c) Group exemption number ▶

I Tax-exempt status ☑ 501(c) (3) ◀ (insert no) ☐ 4947(a)(1) or ☐ 527

J Website: ▶ http //www.guidedogs.com/

K Form of organization ☑ Corporation ☐ Trust ☐ Association ☐ Other ▶

L Year of formation 1942 | M State of legal domicile CA

Part I Summary

Activities & Governance

1 Briefly describe the organization's mission or most significant activities
Provide greater mobility for visually impaired persons by partnering them with guide dogs

2 Check this box ▶☐ if the organization discontinued its operations or disposed of more than 25% of its net assets

3	Number of voting members of the governing body (Part VI, line 1a)	3	18
4	Number of independent voting members of the governing body (Part VI, line 1b)	4	17
5	Total number of employees (Part V, line 2a)	5	330
6	Total number of volunteers (estimate if necessary)	6	951
7a	Total gross unrelated business revenue from Part VIII, column (C), line 12	7a	16,797
b	Net unrelated business taxable income from Form 990-T, line 34	7b	-63,740

			Prior Year	Current Year
Revenue	8	Contributions and grants (Part VIII, line 1h)	23,806,307	18,074,312
	9	Program service revenue (Part VIII, line 2g)	207,368	216,087
	10	Investment income (Part VIII, column (A), lines 3, 4, and 7d)	-14,538,397	7,420,740
	11	Other revenue (Part VIII, column (A), lines 5, 6d, 8c, 9c, 10c, and 11e)	-111,091	198,429
	12	Total revenue—add lines 8 through 11 (must equal Part VIII, column (A), line 12)	9,364,187	25,909,568
Expenses	13	Grants and similar amounts paid (Part IX, column (A), lines 1-3)	53,589	50,190
	14	Benefits paid to or for members (Part IX, column (A), line 4)		0
	15	Salaries, other compensation, employee benefits (Part IX, column (A), lines 5-10)	21,412,504	19,472,906
	16a	Professional fundraising fees (Part IX, column (A), line 11e)	12,000	12,000
	b	Total fundraising expenses (Part IX, column (D), line 25) ▶2,978,926		
	17	Other expenses (Part IX, column (A), lines 11a-11d, 11f-24f)	10,720,291	11,559,163
	18	Total expenses Add lines 13-17 (must equal Part IX, column (A), line 25)	32,198,384	31,094,259
	19	Revenue less expenses Subtract line 18 from line 12	-22,834,197	-5,184,691

			Beginning of Current Year	End of Year
Net Assets or Fund Balances	20	Total assets (Part X, line 16)	264,501,986	277,234,982
	21	Total liabilities (Part X, line 26)	8,457,699	7,520,307
	22	Net assets or fund balances Subtract line 21 from line 20	256,044,287	269,714,675

Part II Signature Block

Under penalties of perjury, I declare that I have examined this return, including accompanying schedules and statements, and to the best of my knowledge and belief, it is true, correct, and complete Declaration of preparer (other than officer) is based on all information of which preparer has any knowledge

Sign Here

▶ ****** | 2010-10-29
Signature of officer | Date

▶ KEN STUPI CHIEF FINANCIAL OFFICER
Type or print name and title

Paid Preparer's Use Only

Preparer's signature ▶ TAMARA L BONGI | Date | Check if self-employed ▶ ☐ | Preparer's identifying number (see instructions)

Firm's name (or yours if self-employed), address, and ZIP + 4 ▶ HOOD & STRONG LLP CPAS
100 FIRST STREET 14th FLOOR
SAN FRANCISCO, CA 94105

EIN ▶

Phone no ▶ (415) 781-0793

May the IRS discuss this return with the preparer shown above? (see instructions) ☑ Yes ☐ No

Exhibit D

Second Amendment to the Trust dated 1999 naming Mike Goodall as co-trustee with his mother, replacing his father who had died in 1994.

COPY

0413

SECOND AMENDMENT TO GOODALL TRUST

Preamble. RACHEL A. GOODALL is the settlor of GOODALL TRUST created under that certain declaration dated September 12, 1990, as amended August 24, 1994. RACHEL A. GOODALL is the trustee duly appointed and acting under and by terms of that declaration. In Section 3.3 of Article Three of that declaration, the settlor reserved the right to amend the trust "(d)uring the trustors' joint lifetimes ...." The surviving settlor now wishes to exercise her right of amendment and, to that end, does hereby amend that declaration in the terms stated below. The trustees hereby consent to the terms of this amendment.

1. Amendment of Section 7.1. of Article Seven. Section 7.1. of Article Seven of that declaration is amended to read as follows:

> 7.1. Remaining Settlor-Trustee Serves Alone. On the death of the deceased settlor, or if, for any reason, before that time either settlor ceases to act as trustee, no successor cotrustee shall be appointed to act with regards to the Bypass Trust. Rather, the remaining settlor trustee named in Article One shall have full power to act as trustee of the Bypass Trust and to complete the trust administration.
>
> After the death of the deceased settlor, at the discretion of the surviving settlor, KENNETH MICHAEL GOODALL, may be appointed to act as cotrustee with regards to the Survivors Trust. This appointment shall be confirmed by KENNETH MICHAEL GOODALL signing a

document, such as an Amendment to Declaration of Trust, in which he agrees to be bound by the terms of the trust.

2. Ratification of Other Terms of Trust. In every other respect, the settlor confirms and ratifies the terms of the trust as stated in that certain declaration dated September 12, 1990, as amended August 24, 1994.

3. Execution. We certify that we have read the foregoing declaration of trust, as amended, and that it correctly states the terms and conditions under which the trust estate is to be held, administered, and distributed. As trustees of the trusts created by this declaration of trust, we approve this declaration of trust, as amended, in all particulars, and agree to be bound by its terms and conditions. RACHEL A. GOODALL, as settlor of the trusts created by this declaration of trust, approves this declaration of trust in all particulars, and agrees to be bound by its terms and conditions.

Executed on JAN 19 1999 at Novato, California.

SETTLOR-TRUSTEE

Rachel A. Goodall

RACHEL A. GOODALL

TRUSTEE

K. Michael Goodall

KENNETH MICHAEL GOODALL

ACKNOWLEDGMENT

STATE OF CALIFORNIA)
) ss
COUNTY OF MARIN)

On JAN 19 1999, before me, a notary public in and for the State of California, personally appeared KENNETH MICHAEL GOODALL and RACHEL A. GOODALL, personally known to me (or proved to me on the basis of satisfactory evidence) to be the persons whose names are subscribed to the within instrument, and acknowledged to me that they executed the same in their individual capacities, and that by their signatures on the instrument, the persons executed the instrument.

WITNESS my hand and official seal.

Signature ______________________ (SEAL)

AFFIDAVIT OF SERVICE

I hereby state that I am not a party, I am over 18 years of age and I served a copy of this motion and the exhibits attached thereto on July 29, 2011 to the following:

James R. Hastings
1003 3rd Street
San Rafael, CA 94901

Bank of America
1000 4th St.
San Rafael, CA 94901

Gary D. Rothstein
Manatt, Phelps & Phillips, LLP
One Embarcadero Center, 30th Floor
San Francisco CA 94111

Roy Hoppe
461 Peachstone Terrace
San Rafael CA 94903

Frank Thornally
461 Peachstone Terrace
San Rafael CA 94903

Julia Bentley Lemons
Apt. 308
12800 Marion Lane W
Minnetonka, MN 55305-1368
Surviving Sibling of Rachel Goodall

Robert Bentley
Bradford Village #504
906 N Boulevard Street
Edmond, OK 73030
Surviving Sibling of Rachel Goodall

Helen Beth Bentley Perry
7926 Praver Drive W
Jacksonville,FL 32217
Surviving Sibling of Rachel Goodall

Clenda Fern Bentley Zinar
4536 Chatman Street
The Colony, TX 75056

Beverly Gale Bentley Young
2316 Trenton
McKinney, TX 75070

Vickie Bentley Hankins
14580 NE 6th
Choctaw, OK 73020

Jeffrey Bentley
4701 N Douglas Boulevard
Spencer, OK 73084

Chad Everett Bentley
1609 Teepee Trail
Kingsland, TX 78639

Jeanette Goodall Phillips
152 S 11th Street
Salina, Kansas 67401

Kristin Kane
University of California
Berkeley College of Engineering
College Relations
208 Mclaughlin Hall #1722
Berkeley, CA 9472A-1722

Guide Dogs for the Blind
Mr. Thomas Horton
Planned Potential Beneficiary Giving Director
Guide Dogs for the Blind, Inc.
350 Los Ranchitos Road
San Rafael, CA 94903

[signature]

Samuel Sloan
461 Peachstone Ter.
San Rafael, CA 94903
415-894-7201

Pro per administrator
of the Estate of Michael Goodall

Telephone 415-419-5980

FILED
SUPERIOR COURT
COUNTY OF SAN FRANCISCO
2011 AUG 12 AM 11:16
CLERK OF THE COURT
BY: [signature]
DEPUTY CLERK

SUPERIOR COURT OF THE STATE OF CALIFORNIA

COUNTY OF SAN FRANCISCO

In the Matter of the Trust for Michael created under the Goodall Trust dated September 12, 1990	Case No. PTR-99-273030 SUPPLEMENTAL OBJECTIONS TO PETITION FOR DETERMINATION OF BENEFICIARIES AND REQUEST FOR CONTINUANCE OF HEARING Hearing Date: August 23, 2011 Time: 9 AM Department: 204

BY FAX

Samuel Sloan (hereinafter Sloan), as the duly appointed administrator of the Estate of K. Michael Goodall, a beneficiary under the Goodall Trust, hereby objects to the Petition filed by Bank of America in this matter. The Petition should be denied and Sloan be permitted the opportunity to obtain counsel, conduct discovery and be further heard in this matter for the following reasons:

1. By the present petition, Bank of America seeks the Court's imprimatur to distribute a single asset of the trust (the Goodall residence in Marin County), but Sloan contends that such a distribution would be premature at this time, as there are other unmentioned and unaccounted for assets of the trust, serious questions as to the capacity of the Goodalls to understand the circular residual bequest to Guide Dogs for the Blind in the 1994 amendment and how that amendment would otherwise affect their son Michael during his lifetime, and, so as to the nature and extent of the claims which Michael Goodall's Estate may have to the assets of the trust.

2. The trust which is the subject of this petition began with the 1990 Goodall Trust executed by Kenneth F. Goodall (Mr. Goodall) and Rachel A. Goodall (Mrs. Goodall) on September 12, 1990, a true and correct copy of which is attached hereto as Exhibit A. Pursuant to the terms of that trust their son Kenneth Michael Goodall (Michael) was to receive the entire trust corpus upon the last of his parents to die (see Exhibit A, ¶ 6.3).

3. Bank of America has attached to its moving papers a purported amendment to the 1990 trust, dated September 24, 1994, which, rather than conveying the trust corpus to Michael upon the death of his parents, reserved the administration of a Trust for Michael to the Bank of America during Michael's lifetime and then upon his death a distribution to who knows whom. (As revealed in the petition filed by Bank of America, the dispositive provisions upon the death of Michael are ambiguous

and run in circles)

4. Sloan disputes the authenticity of the 1994 amendment and is informed and believes that it was purportedly was executed just 17 days before Mr. Goodall died of esophageal cancer (9/10/1994) and at a time when he was heavily medicated on painkillers and obviously neither of the Goodall's could have understood the circular provisions of the 1994 amendment.

5. Shortly before her death on June 7, 1999, Mrs. Goodall executed a further amendment to the trust appointing Michael as cotrustee, a true and correct copy of which is attached hereto as Exhibit B.

6. This action was commenced on or about December 21, 1999, when Michael filed a petition apparently for determination that an action to remove Bank of America as the trustee did not constitute a contest of the trust, which was apparently followed by petition to remove Bank of America. That petition was apparently denied without prejudice by minute order filed March 28, 2000. (This all is apparently true to Sloan as it is all based upon a mere reading of the Court's register of actions only, as the Court's file is unavailable to Sloan as described below)

7. Michael resided at the Goodall Residence (261 Peachstone Ter., San Rafael, CA) in Marin County until his death in August 5, 2010, during which period he received only modest monthly income payments from Bank of America in the amount of $2500 - $3000 (even in his last days when he was dying of cancer and his insurance would not pay for chemotherapy treatments), albeit that it is believed that the corpus of the trust,

exclusive of the Goodall Residence, was/is $1.6 million or more.

8. When Michael died, Sloan was appointed as administrator with will attached of Michael's estate in Marin County action number PTR 110-0596, *Estate of K Michael Goodall*, and received letters of administration on March 21, 2011 (Exhibit C hereto). According to his will dated June 15, 2004, it was Michael's wish to pass his entire estate to his two longtime (30yrs.+) friends, roommates, and caregivers, Roy Hoppe and Frank Thornally.

9. On April 21, 2011, Bank of America filed a petition in this San Francisco action seeking to confirm that the Goodall Residence was an asset of the trust; which was opposed by Sloan in pro per as administrator Michael's estate; and, on June 3, 2011, the Court granted Bank of America's petition. (The Court deleted, however, from the form of order prepared by Bank of America language declaring that the Sloan's claims were without merit (see Order filed June 3, 2011))

10. Thereafter on June 8, 2011, the present petition was filed by Bank of America for a determination of beneficiaries; to which Sloan filed objections in pro per because he had not been served with proper notice of the hearing and he requested a continuance so that he could obtain counsel; the Court ordered on July 11, 2011 that the hearing on that petition be continued to August 23, 2011.

11. Sloan has filed a petition in the Marin County Superior Court requesting that the Marin Court approve the proposed agreement between Sloan and attorney Sam Ware to represent Sloan as administrator of the Estate of Michael Goodall in this action, which the Marin Court has scheduled for

hearing on August 22, 2011, a true and correct copy of which is attached hereto as Exhibit D.

12. As part of their investigation into this matter, Sloan and Sam Ware have attempted to obtain a copy of the Court's file in this action, but have been advised by the clerk's office that the file is not available for viewing at this time and will not be available for viewing until two weeks following the hearing on the present petition on August 23, 2011.

13. As a further part of his investigation into this matter, Sloan has attempted to obtain an accounting of the trust assets. There are/were no annual accountings filed by Bank of America in this action, and Sloan has been unable to find any accounting records among the effects of Michael Goodall; although it will be noted that in February 2011, representatives of Bank of America removed all of Michael's effects and other personal property from the Goodall residence, and after Sloan demanded that the property be returned, Bank of America's representatives did not return Michael's papers regarding the trust which were known to earlier exist at the residence.

14. On August 1, 2011, Sloan, on behalf of Michael as beneficiary of the trust, made a demand of Bank of America as trustee to provide an accounting pursuant to Probate Code §16062, true and correct copy of which is attached hereto as Exhibit E. In response to that request, however, and contrary to the obligations of a trustee under Probate Code, counsel for Bank of America has advised Sloan that such an accounting will not be provided, true and correct copy of his e-mail being attached hereto as Exhibit F.

15. In support of its present petition, Bank of America has proffered the declaration of James Hastings as to the intent of Mr. and Mrs. Goodall with regard to the distribution of the trust assets after Michael's death. James Hastings purportedly drafted the 1990 trust, the 1994 amendment, the 1999 amendment, and Michael's will in 2004, and he also represented Bank of America in opposition to Michael's petition to have the Bank of America removed as trustee in 1999 - 2000.

16. Sloan believes that James Hastings has valuable information *well beyond his mere declaration* which should be thoroughly discovered before the Court considers his declaration as to the capacity and intent of Mr. and Mrs. Goodall; namely, he should have files with regard to the 1990 Goodall trust, and all amendments thereto, and a file regarding the preparation of Michael's will in 2004, and a file with regard to his representation of Bank of America against Michael when Michael petitioned to have Bank of America removed as trustee; and James Hastings should be thoroughly deposed on these matters and on all matters relevant to the Goodall trust before his opinions about anything should be considered by anyone.

17. Sloan submits that there is much more at stake here than merely a judicial determination as to who gets the Goodall Residence under the terms of the 1994 amendment, which is the ostensible limited purpose of Bank of America's petition. As described above, Sloan is informed and believes that the other assets of the trust total $1.6 million which have been managed by Bank of America without an accounting for years, and, Sloan contends that Michael's parents did not intend, by the 1994

amendment or otherwise, their only son have been so mistreated by Bank of America during his lifetime.

18. Sloan submits that he must be allowed the opportunity to hire legal counsel in order to adequately represent the interests of Michael's estate in this matter, and that this can not be accomplished until his petition to hire an attorney is heard in the Marin County Superior Court on August 22, 2011.

19. Sloan submits that he must be allowed the opportunity to review the Court's file in this action, beyond the mere register of actions, and investigate the pleadings filed back in 1999 and 2000 in order to determine what allegations were made in those earlier papers and proceedings, and how such allegations may relate back to and have a direct bearing on the rights of Michael's estate with regard to the Goodall trust.

20. Sloan submits further that he must be allowed the opportunity to obtain an accounting from the Bank of America before any trust assets are distributed to anyone, because Sloan believes that the estate has claims against the trust for unpaid benefits to Michael during his lifetime.

21. Sloan further submits that he must be allowed the opportunity to conduct discovery from, including, but not limited to, Bank of America, James Hastings and Guide Dogs for the Blind on all potential claims Michael's estate may have with respect to the Goodall trust, and that this discovery should be allowed to be completed before the Court further considers Bank of America's petition and approves a distribution of any trust assets to anyone.

PRAYER FOR RELIEF

WHEREFORE Sloan as the duly appointed administrator of the Estate of K. Michael Goodall prays for the following relief:

1. That the petition filed by Bank of America be dismissed by this Court;

2. That the assets of the Goodall Trust be distributed according to the 199[illegible] Goodall Trust to the Estate of K. Michael Goodall;

3. That Bank of America provide an accounting to the Estate of K. Michael Goodall as provided by the Probate Code;

4. Alternatively, that the Court order that the hearing on this petition be continued for no less than 120 days in order to allow Sloan the opportunity to obtain counsel and conduct appropriate discovery into matters relevant to Bank of America's petition and any and all matters related to any claims regarding the Goodall trust;

5. Such other and further relief as the Court deems just and proper.

I declare under penalty of perjury under the laws of the state of California that the foregoing is true and correct and that this declaration was executed on August 10, 2011.

Samuel H Sloan

Samuel Sloan

PROOF OF SERVICE

I certify and declare as follows:

I am over the age of 18 years, not a party to this action. My business address is 700 Larkspur Landing Circle #199, Larkspur, CA 94939. I am readily familiar with the business practices of my firm for the collection, processing and service of items with the United States Postal Service, express service providers (same day messenger and overnight) and facsimile transmission.

On the date set forth below, I served the foregoing documents described as Supp Obj to Petition on the parties in this action as follows:

__X__: BY FIRST CLASS MAIL — By placing [ ] the original [X] a true and correct copy thereof in each sealed envelope addressed as indicated below. Said sealed envelopes, with postage fully prepaid, were deposited with the United States Postal Service in San Francisco, California this same day in the ordinary course of business.

____: BY FEDERAL EXPRESS — By placing [ ] the original [ ] a true and correct copy thereof in each sealed envelope addressed as indicated below. Said envelopes were deposited for collection and processing by Federal Express, Priority Overnight Service, in San Francisco, California.

____: BY PERSONAL SERVICE: By placing [ ] the original [x] a true and correct copy thereof in each sealed envelope addressed as indicated below and causing said envelopes to be delivered by hand, by our firm's messenger, to the offices of the addressees indicated below.

____: BY FACSIMILE TRANSMISSION — The foregoing document was transmitted between 9:00 a.m. and 5:00 p.m. to the fax number indicated below each address.

____: BY EMAIL TRANSMISSION — The foregoing document was transmitted between 9:00 a.m. and 5:00 p.m. to the e-mail address indicated below.

See attached service list

I declare under penalty of perjury under the laws of the State of California that the foregoing statements are true and correct.

Executed August 11, 2011

Service List

Gary D. Rothstein
Manatt, Phelps & Phillips, LLP
One Embarcadero Center, 30th Floor
San Francisco CA 94111

Julia Bentley Lemons
Apt. 308
12800 Marion Lane W
Minnetonka, MN 55305-1368

Robert Bentley
Bradford Village #504
906 N Boulevard Street
Edmond, OK 73030

Helen Beth Bentley Perry
7926 Praver Drive W
Jacksonville, FL 32217

Clenda Fern Bentley Zinar
4536 Chatman Street
The Colony, TX 75056

Beverly Gale Bentley Young
2316 Trenton
McKinney, TX 75070

Vickie Bentley Hankins
14580 NE 6th
Choctaw, OK 73020

Jeffrey Bentley
4701 N Douglas Boulevard
Spencer, OK 73084

Chad Everett Bentley
1609 Teepee Trail
Kingsland, TX 78639

Jeanette Goodall Phillips
152 S 11th Street
Salina, Kansas 67401

Kristin Kane
University of California
Berkeley College of Engineering
College Relations
208 Mclaughlin Hall #1722
Berkeley, CA 9472A-1722

Guide Dogs for the Blind
Mr. Thomas Horton
Giving Director
Guide Dogs for the Blind, Inc.
350 Los Ranchitos Road
San Rafael, CA 94903

EXHIBIT A

THE GOODALL TRUST

ARTICLE ONE

INTRODUCTION

1.1. Declaration. This trust declaration is made by KENNETH F. GOODALL and RACHEL A. GOODALL, both of Marin County, California, who are herein referred to as "the trustors" or "the trustee," depending on the context. The term "trustee," as used herein, also refers to each successor trustee who is serving as a trustee of a trust created under this instrument. This trust shall be known as the GOODALL TRUST.

ARTICLE TWO

THE TRUST ESTATE

2.1. Definition of Trust Estate. The property described in any schedule that is part of this instrument, the property hereafter transferred to any trust created under this instrument, and the income and proceeds attributable to all such property shall constitute the "trust estate," which shall be held in trust, administered, and distributed according to the terms of this instrument.

2.2. Initial Trust Corpus. The trust estate shall be comprised initially of the property described in the "Schedule of Community Property Assets," which is attached hereto and made a

EXHIBIT A

A

part of this trust instrument. The property described in that schedule is the trustors' community property.

2.3. Character of Property Retained. All property that now is or hereafter becomes part of the trust estate shall retain its character as community property, quasi-community property, or separate property, as the case may be, despite the transfer in trust.

2.4. Trustee's Powers in Community Property. Notwithstanding any other provision of this instrument, during the joint lifetimes of the trustors, the trustee shall not have powers beyond those granted either spouse under California Civil Code sections 5125 and 5127.

ARTICLE THREE

RIGHTS RESERVED TO TRUSTORS

3.1. Additions to the Trust Estate. A trustor or any other person may make inter vivos or testamentary transfers of property to the trustee. That additional property transferred by any other person shall become part of the trust estate upon written acceptance of it by the trustee.

3.2. Power of Revocation While Both Trustors Are Living. During the trustors' joint lifetimes, the trust may be revoked, in whole or in part, as provided in this paragraph.

(a) Community Property. Either trustor acting alone, or both of the trustors acting jointly, shall have the power to revoke the portion of the trust estate that is the trustors' community property. Upon revocation, the trustee shall pay to either trustor or to both trustors, as the trustors' community property, the community property portion of the trust estate that has been revoked.

(b) Separate Property and Quasi-Community Property. A trustor whose separate property or quasi-community property comprises any portion of the trust estate shall have the power to revoke that portion of the trust estate. Upon revocation, the trustee shall pay to the revoking trustor, as his or her separate or quasi-community property, the separate property or quasi-community property portion of the trust estate that has been revoked.

3.3. Power of Amendment While Both Trustors Are Living. During the trustors' joint lifetimes, the trust may be amended, in whole or in part, by both trustors acting jointly.

3.4. Power of Revocation and Power of Amendment After Death of First Trustor to Die. After the death of the first trustor to die, the surviving trustor shall have the power to revoke or amend, in whole or in part, the Survivor's Trust. All other trusts created under this instrument shall become irrevocable and shall not be subject to amendment after the death of the first trustor to die.

3.5. Method of Revocation or Amendment. The revocation or amendment of a trust created under this instrument shall be effective only if made in a writing that is signed by the person or persons having the power of revocation or amendment and delivered to the trustee. An exercise of the power of amendment substantially affecting the duties, rights, and liabilities of the trustee shall be effective only if agreed to by the trustee in writing.

3.6. Incompetent Trustor May Not Act. A power reserved to a trustor under this article may not be exercised by that trustor or by any other person or fiduciary, including the conservator of that trustor's estate or that trustor's attorney in fact designated in a durable power of attorney under the Uniform Durable Power of Attorney Act, if that trustor is incompetent (as defined in Article Nine) at the pertinent time. A power under this article that is exercisable only by the joint action of the trustors may not be exercised if either trustor is incompetent at the pertinent time. However, the incompetence of one trustor shall not prevent a competent trustor from exercising a power that is exercisable by the competent trustor acting alone.

ARTICLE FOUR

DISTRIBUTIONS DURING TRUSTORS' JOINT LIVES

4.1. Payment of Income During Trustors' Joint Lives. So long as both trustors are living, the trustee shall pay the net income of the trust as specified in this paragraph.

(a) Community Property. The trustee shall pay to either trustor or both trustors or apply for the trustors' benefit the entire net income from the trust community property, in monthly or other convenient installments (but not less often than annually) as either or both of the trustors and the trustee may agree upon from time to time.

(b) Separate Property and Quasi-Community Property. The trustee shall pay to or apply for the benefit of a trustor whose separate property or quasi-community property comprises part of the trust estate the entire net income from that separate property or quasi-community property, in monthly or other convenient installments (but not less often than annually) as that trustor and the trustee may agree upon from time to time.

4.2. Discretionary Payment of Principal by Trustee During Trustors' Joint Lives. So long as both trustors are living, the trustee shall pay trust principal, at any time or times, as specified in this paragraph.

(a) Community Property. The trustee shall pay to either trustor or both trustors or apply for the trustors' benefit so much of the principal of the trust community property as the trustee deems proper for the comfort, welfare, and happiness of the trustor or trustors.

(b) Separate Property and Quasi-Community Property. The trustee shall pay to or apply for the benefit of a trustor whose separate property or quasi-community property comprises part of the trust estate so much of the principal of that separate property or quasi-community property as the trustee deems proper for that trustor's comfort, welfare, and happiness.

(c) Consideration of Other Resources When Distributing Principal. In exercising discretion under subparagraphs (a) and (b) of this paragraph, the trustee shall give the consideration that the trustee deems proper to all other income and resources then readily available for use by the trustor or trustors, as the case may be, for the stated purposes and that are then known to the trustee. All decisions of the trustee regarding payments under subparagraph (a) or (b), if any, are within the trustee's discretion and shall be final and incontestable by anyone.

4.3. Trustors' Right to Withdraw Principal. So long as both trustors are living, the trustors shall have the right to withdraw trust principal, at any time or times, as specified in this paragraph.

(a) Community Property. Either trustor acting alone, if he or she is not incompetent (as defined in Article Nine) at the pertinent time, or both of the trustors acting jointly, if at least one of them is not incompetent at the pertinent time, shall have the right to withdraw any amount of trust principal that is the trustors' community property, by delivering a signed writing to the trustee.

(b) Separate Property and Quasi-Community Property. A trustor whose separate property or quasi-community property comprises part of the trust estate, if not incompetent (as defined in Article Nine) at the pertinent time, shall have the right to withdraw any amount of the principal of that separate property or quasi-community property, by delivering a signed writing to the trustee.

4.4. Trustors' Obligation for Community Property Received or Withdrawn. Net income of the trust community property paid to either trustor or both trustors pursuant to the provisions of this article and principal of the trust community property distributed to or withdrawn by either trustor or both trustors pursuant to the provisions of this article shall remain the trustors' community property. A trustor who receives such net income or principal shall have the same obligations respecting that property as he or she would have with regard to all community property generally.

ARTICLE FIVE

DIVISION INTO SHARES AND INITIAL DISTRIBUTIONS

AFTER DECEASED SPOUSE'S DEATH

5.1. Definitions. In this article and subsequent articles of this instrument, the first trustor to die is referred to as "the deceased spouse" and the other trustor is referred to as "the surviving spouse."

5.2. Trustee's Power to Defer Division or Distribution. Whenever the trustee is directed to divide any part of the trust estate or distribute trust assets upon the death of either trustor, the trustee may, in the trustee's discretion, defer actual division or distribution for a period not exceeding six (6) months after that trustor's death. The ability of the trustee to delay division or distribution shall not affect the vesting of interests in the respective shares, which shall be as of the date of death.

5.3. <u>Division Into Three Shares After Death of Deceased Spouse</u>. Upon the death of the deceased spouse, the trustee shall divide the trust estate, including any additions made to the trust by reason of the deceased spouse's death, such as from the deceased spouse's estate or policies of life insurance on his or her life, into three separate shares, designated "the survivor's share," "the marital deduction share," and "the credit shelter share," to be held, administered, or distributed as set forth below.

5.4. <u>Payment of Death Taxes, Debts, and Expenses</u>. After the death of the deceased spouse, upon receipt by the trustee of a written statement from the personal representative of the deceased spouse's estate requesting that the trustee pay death taxes, debts, and expenses (as defined in Article Nine), with respect to assets of any trust under this instrument or other taxable property or transfers, the trustee shall pay out of the trust estate, either directly or to the personal representative, any amounts requested by the personal representative for those purposes. The trustee may rely upon the personal representative's statement and shall not be liable for any act or omission by the personal representative in protesting or failing to protest the legality, propriety, or amount of the death taxes, debts, or expenses. The trustee shall pay as much of the federal estate tax as possible with any "flower bonds" (United States Treasury obligations acceptable at par value in payment of federal estate tax) that are part of the trust estate, but only to the extent of the deceased spouse's interest in those bonds. Payment of death taxes and payment of expenses shall be charged to the credit shelter share, except for any death taxes that are attributable to a disclaimer of property under this instrument by the surviving spouse, which shall be paid from the Disclaimer Trust. Payment of any debts allocable against the separate property of the deceased spouse shall be charged against the credit shelter share. Debts allocable against community property shall be allocated to the survivor's share and the credit shelter share in accordance with California law in effect at the date of the deceased spouse's death, so long as charges against the survivor's share do not exceed the value of community property allocable to that share. The trustee shall not pay death taxes, debts, and expenses or other obligations of the deceased spouse or the deceased spouse's estate from proceeds of insurance policies on the deceased spouse's life if making those payments would be the sole cause of the proceeds being includable in the deceased spouse's gross estate for federal estate tax purposes.

5.5. Survivor's Share Allocated to Survivor's Trust. The survivor's share, as determined in this paragraph, shall be held, administered, and distributed by the trustee according to the terms set forth in Article Six applicable to the Survivor's Trust, for the benefit of the surviving spouse. The survivor's share shall consist of the portion of the trust estate that is comprised of the surviving spouse's one-half (1/2) interest in the trustors' community property, the surviving spouse's one-half (1/2) interest in the deceased spouse's quasi-community property, all of the surviving spouse's separate property, and all of the surviving spouse's quasi-community property.

5.6. <u>Credit Shelter Share Allocated to Credit Shelter Trust</u>. The credit shelter share, as determined in this paragraph, shall be held, administered, and distributed by the trustee according to the terms set forth in Article Six applicable to the Credit Shelter Trust. The credit shelter share shall consist of a pecuniary gift from the trust estate other than the survivor's share (as defined in the preceding paragraph) that is the largest amount, if any, of property that can pass free of federal estate tax by reason of (1) the unified credit available to the deceased spouse's estate; and (2) the credit for state death taxes, to the extent that the use of that credit does not result in or increase any death tax payable to any state. Any qualified disclaimer made by the surviving spouse shall be disregarded in determining this amount. The trustors recognize that the amount of this pecuniary gift may be affected by a number of considerations, including:

(a) The net value of all property disposed of by this instrument or otherwise that is included in the deceased spouse's gross estate for federal estate tax purposes and that does not qualify for the federal estate tax marital or charitable deduction;

(b) The value of all property disposed of by the deceased spouse that constitutes "adjusted taxable gifts";

(c) All charges to principal that are deductible under Internal Revenue Code section 2053 but that are not deducted in computing the federal estate tax liability for the deceased spouse's gross estate; and

(d) Actions of the deceased spouse's executor in exercising certain tax elections.

The trustors recognize that because of the above factors no property may pass pursuant to this provision.

5.7. Marital Deduction Share Distributed Outright. The marital deduction share shall consist of the balance of the trust estate, and shall be distributed outright to the surviving spouse.

5.8. Allocation of Assets. In allocating assets between the marital deduction share and the credit shelter share, the trustee shall allocate the assets in the trust estate that qualify for the marital deduction between the marital deduction share and the credit shelter share in cash or in kind, or partly in each, on a prorata or a nonprorata basis, and in undivided interests or not, but subject to the following:

(a) Qualification for Marital Deduction. Only assets that qualify for the marital deduction shall be allocated to the marital deduction share.

(b) Allocations in Kind. Assets allocated in kind shall be valued for purposes of allocation on the date or dates of distribution.

(c) Foreign Death Tax Credit. Assets that qualify for the foreign death tax credit shall be allocated to the marital deduction share only if other trust property is insufficient to fund the marital deduction share.

5.9. Intention That Disposition of Marital Deduction Share Qualify for Marital Deduction. The trustors intend that the disposition of the marital deduction share qualify for the federal estate tax marital deduction and that the trustee take no action or exercise any power that may impair that deduction. The trustors incorporate in this instrument the provisions of California Probate Code section 21522.

5.10. Disclaimer of Property by Surviving Spouse. Any property or portion thereof that is disclaimed by the surviving spouse shall be held, administered, or distributed by the trustee according to the terms set forth in Article Six applicable to the Disclaimer Trust.

ARTICLE SIX

DISPOSITIVE PROVISIONS OF TRUSTS CREATED

AFTER DECEASED SPOUSE'S DEATH

6.1. Survivor's Trust. The property allocated to the Survivor's Trust shall be held, administered, and distributed for the benefit of the surviving spouse according to the following terms and conditions:

(a) Payment of Income. The trustee shall pay to or apply for the benefit of the surviving spouse, so long as the surviving spouse lives, the entire net income of the trust, in monthly or other convenient installments (but not less often than annually) as the surviving spouse and the trustee may agree upon from time to time.

(b) Discretionary Payment of Principal by Trustee. At any time or times during the trust term, the trustee shall pay to or apply for the benefit of the surviving spouse so much of the principal of the trust as the trustee deems proper for the surviving spouse's comfort, welfare, and happiness. In exercising discretion, the trustee shall give the consideration that the trustee deems proper to all other income and resources then readily available to the surviving spouse for use for these purposes and that are then known to the trustee. All decisions of the trustee regarding payments under this subparagraph, if any, are within the trustee's discretion and shall be final and incontestable by anyone.

(c) Right of Surviving Spouse to Withdraw Principal. The trustee shall pay to the surviving spouse as much of the trust principal as the surviving spouse may from time to time demand in a signed writing delivered to the trustee.

(d) General Power of Appointment. Upon the death of the surviving spouse, all of the trust property (including the trust principal, all net income then held by the trustee, and all income then accrued but not collected by the trustee) shall be paid over and delivered to any entity or entities, person or persons, and upon any trust, terms and conditions, or to or in favor of the estate of the surviving spouse, as the surviving spouse may direct by will, provided only that no exercise of this power of appointment shall be effective unless it refers to this instrument and expressly indicates an intention to exercise this power of appointment. The trustee may rely upon any instrument admitted to probate as the last will of the surviving spouse in carrying out the terms of the power of appointment and shall not be liable for any good-faith act in reliance upon that will, even if for any reason it is later determined to be invalid with respect to its purported exercise of this power of appointment. If the trustee receives no notice of the existence of a will of the surviving spouse within six (6) months after the death of the surviving spouse, the trustee may distribute the trust assets and income as though this power of appointment had not been exercised and shall in that event be conclusively presumed to have acted in good faith, even if a valid will is thereafter discovered.

(e) Payment of Death Taxes, Debts, and Expenses. On the death of the surviving spouse and subject to any power of appointment exercised by him or her, the trustee may, in the trustee's discretion, pay out of the income or principal or partly from the income and partly from the principal of the Survivor's Trust, the death taxes, debts, and expenses (as defined in Article Nine) arising on the death of the surviving spouse.

(f) Default Provision. In default of the power of appointment, or to the extent that an attempt to exercise the power was ineffectual, the entire remaining principal, all net income then held by the trustee, and all income then accrued but not collected by the trustee, after any payment of taxes, debts, and expenses pursuant to the applicable provisions of this instrument, shall be disposed of in the manner specified in the paragraph below entitled "Disposition of Credit Shelter Trust Upon Death of Surviving Spouse," although the property disposed of pursuant to this subparagraph shall not be considered to be part of the Credit Shelter Trust.

6.2. Disposition of Credit Shelter Trust Until Death of Surviving Spouse. The property allocated to the Credit Shelter Trust shall be held, administered, and distributed until the death of the surviving spouse according to the following terms and conditions:

(a) Discretionary Payment of Income and Principal by Trustee. At any time or times, the trustee shall pay to or apply

for the benefit of the surviving spouse so much of the net income and principal of the trust as the trustee deems proper for the health, education, support, and maintenance of the surviving spouse. In exercising discretion, the trustee shall give the consideration that the trustee deems proper to all other income and resources then readily available to the surviving spouse for use for these purposes and that are then known to the trustee. All decisions of the trustee regarding payments under this subparagraph, if any, are within the trustee's discretion and shall be final and incontestable by anyone. Any net income not expended under the foregoing provisions of this subparagraph shall be accumulated and added to the principal of the trust.

(b) Right of Surviving Spouse to Withdraw Principal. The surviving spouse shall have the power to withdraw from the principal of the trust each calendar year those amounts as shall not exceed the greater of five thousand dollars ($5,000) or five (5) percent of the assets, valued as of the end of the calendar year. The surviving spouse shall exercise this power by a written instrument signed by him or her and delivered to the trustee. This power is noncumulative and to the extent it is not exercised by the end of the calendar year, it shall lapse. This power shall exist each year until the death of the surviving spouse.

6.3. Disposition of Credit Shelter Trust Upon Death of Surviving Spouse. Upon the death of the surviving spouse, the property in the Credit Shelter Trust shall be disposed of as follows:

(a) To KENNETH MICHAEL GOODALL, by right of representation, those issue to take that share in the manner provided in California Probate Code section 240.

(b) If the property is not completely disposed of by the preceding provisions, twenty thousand dollars ($20,000.00) to each of the living brothers and sisters of the trustors and the remainder to GUIDE DOGS FOR THE BLIND OF MARIN, INC., of San Rafael, California.

(c) If the property is not completely disposed of by the preceding provisions, the trustee shall pay over and deliver the undisposed portion outright as follows: one-half (1/2) to the heirs of the deceased spouse and one-half (1/2) to the heirs of the surviving spouse.

6.4. Disclaimer Trust. The property allocated to the Disclaimer Trust shall be held, administered, and distributed

according to the following terms and conditions:

(a) Payment of Income. The trustee shall pay to or apply for the benefit of the surviving spouse the entire net income of the trust, in monthly or other convenient installments (but not less often than annually) as the surviving spouse and the trustee may agree upon from time to time.

(b) Payment of Principal. At any time or times, the trustee shall pay to or apply for the benefit of the surviving spouse so much of the principal of the trust as the trustee deems proper for the health, education, support, and maintenance of the surviving spouse. In exercising discretion, the trustee shall give the consideration that the trustee deems proper to all other income and resources then readily available to the surviving spouse for use for these purposes and that are then known to the trustee.

(c) Distribution of Remainder. Upon the death of the surviving spouse, the remaining trust property (including all income then accrued but uncollected and all net income then remaining in the hands of the trustee) shall be disposed of in the manner specified in the preceding paragraph, entitled "Disposition of Credit Shelter Trust Upon Death of Surviving Spouse," although the property disposed of pursuant to this subparagraph shall not be considered to be part of the Credit Shelter Trust.

ARTICLE SEVEN

OFFICE OF TRUSTEE

7.1. Remaining Trustor-Trustee Serves Alone. Upon the death of the deceased spouse, or if before that time either trustor resigns as trustee, is removed pursuant to judicial procedure, becomes incompetent (as defined in Article Nine), or for any reason fails or ceases to act as trustee, the remaining trustor-trustee shall serve as sole trustee.

7.2. Successor Trustees. Upon the death of the remaining trustor-trustee, or if the remaining trustor-trustee resigns as trustee, is removed pursuant to judicial procedure, becomes incompetent, or for any reason fails or ceases to act as trustee,

=AAA (cont)

KENNETH MICHAEL GOODALL shall become the trustee. If KENNETH MICHAEL GOODALL is not qualified for appointment as trustee, or if he later dies, resigns, is removed pursuant to judicial procedure, or for any reason fails or ceases to act as trustee, SECURITY PACIFIC BANK shall serve as the corporate sole trustee.

7.3. Waiver of Bond of Individual Trustees. No bond shall be required of any individual who serves as a trustee under this instrument.

7.4. Trustee's Right and Method of Resignation. Any trustee may resign at any time, without giving a reason for the resignation, by executing a signed written instrument and delivering it to any other trustee then acting, to the successor trustee designated in the manner provided in this article, to the trustors, if living, and if either trustor is deceased, to the trust beneficiaries. A resignation shall be effective upon written acceptance of the trust by the successor trustee.

7.5. Trustee's Liability. The trustee shall not be liable to any person with an interest in the trust for acts or omissions of the trustee, except those resulting from willful misconduct or gross negligence. This standard shall also apply regarding the trustee's liability for acts or omissions of any co-trustee, predecessor trustee, or agent employed by the trustee.

7.6. Compensation of Corporate Trustee. A corporate trustee shall be entitled to reasonable compensation for services rendered in accordance with its fee schedule in effect from time to time for inter vivos trusts.

7.7. Compensation of Individual Trustees. Each individual who is a trustee under this instrument shall be entitled to reasonable compensation for fiduciary services rendered. The trustee may pay these fees from the funds of the pertinent trust as an expense of trust administration, without court order.

ARTICLE EIGHT

POWERS OF TRUSTEE

8.1. General Powers of Trustee. In order to carry out the purposes of this trust, the trustee shall have all of the powers enumerated herein and, except as limited by any provision of this instrument, all powers now or hereafter granted to a trustee by law. Except as limited by a more specific provision of this instrument, the trustee shall have the power to:

(a) Sell, exchange, transfer, convey, lease without limitation as to term, borrow upon, and hypothecate all or any part of the trust property;

(b) Retain, maintain, repair, divide, partition, improve, and otherwise manage any trust property;

(c) Insure trust property against damage or loss, and against liability with respect to third persons, at the expense of the trust, with the carriers and coverages that the trustee deems advisable;

(d) Enforce the rights of the trust with respect to any mortgage, deed of trust, pledge, or similar security device held in trust; enforce, at a foreclosure sale (whether judicial or nonjudicial) or other sale, the rights of the trust in secured property; make bids upon and purchase, at trust expense, any property that is subject to security device; and accept a deed in lieu of foreclosure as full or complete satisfaction of the secured debt;

(e) Commence or defend, at the expense of the trust, legal actions relating to the trust or any trust property as the trustee deems advisable;

(f) Compromise, submit to arbitration, settle, or release (with or without consideration) or otherwise adjust any claims in favor of or against the trust;

(g) Hold trust property in the name of a nominee or nominees, with or without disclosing the trust character of such property (including securities in such condition that ownership may pass upon delivery), or in the name of the trustee as trustee;

(h) Exercise any and all rights and powers of an owner of stocks or securities; vote and give proxies; pay assessments or other charges; exercise or not exercise, as the trustee deems advisable, subscriptions, conversion rights, or other rights or options that may devolve upon holders of stocks or securities; and enter into shareholder agreements;

(i) Participate in any plans or proceedings for foreclosure or consolidations, merger, liquidation, or other reorganization of any corporation or organization having securities that are held as trust property and, in connection therewith, deposit securities with and transfer title or securities upon the terms that the trustee deems advisable to any protective or other committee established in connection with any such plan or proceeding;

(j) Subdivide and resubdivide trust real property and sign applications, maps, and other documents incidental thereto; to dedicate trust real property for public purposes, with or without consideration; grant and impose upon trust real property, conditions, covenants, easements, restrictions, rights of way, and other servitudes; borrow against trust real property; and do such other acts as may appear to the trustee advisable in connection with the exercise of any of the powers described in this subparagraph.

(k) Receive additions to the trust from any source at any time;

(l) Borrow money for any trust purpose on such terms and conditions as the trustee deems advisable and obligate the trust to repay the borrowing;

(m) Employ attorneys, investment counsel, accountants, bookkeepers, or other persons to render services regarding all matters pertaining to the trusts, and pay from trust property the reasonable compensation of such persons for their services.

8.2. <u>Trustee's Power to Invest and Retain Trust Property</u>.

The trustee shall have the power to (1) invest trust property as the trustee deems advisable, and acquire every kind of investment, real, personal, or mixed, including but not limited to improved and unimproved real property, corporate and government (whether local, state, or federal) obligations of every kind, stocks (both preferred and common), and shares of mutual funds of any character; and (2) retain as an investment for the trust in the same form received by the trustee any property given to the trustee from any source. The trustee is under no duty to diversify the investments of the trust. This paragraph shall be construed as expanding the standards set forth in California Probate Code section 16040.

8.3. Power of Trustee with Regard to Accounts. Initially there will be two persons acting as co-trustees for this Trust. In order to make payments from the Trust without undue complications, the trustees will need to open bank, investment, securities brokerage, margin, and similar accounts in which either trustee may be the signatory. This provision specifically gives to the co-trustees the power to open as many accounts as needed (checking, savings, certificates of deposit, money market accounts, investment, etc.) and open such accounts so that deposits and withdrawals may be made with the signature of only one trustee. This includes the power to open an account where either trustee or only one may sign on the account. The initial trustees are specifically vested with the power and authority to open, operate and maintain these accounts and to use the other powers provided in this trust, such as the power to buy and sell on margin, hypothecate, borrow upon, purchase and/or sell as the sole trustee deems appropriate.

8.4. Trustee's Power Regarding Unproductive Property. The trustee may retain or acquire unproductive or underproductive property. California Probate Code section 16311 shall not apply to any trust created under this instrument.

8.5. Retention of Residence. After the deceased spouse's death, the trustee may retain in any trust or trusts provided for under this instrument, for the personal use of the surviving spouse, any property occupied by the trustors as a principal place of residence at the time of the deceased spouse's death, for as long as the surviving spouse desires to occupy the residence. The trustee shall pay from the trust estate all expenses associated with the maintenance and upkeep of such property. On the written request of the surviving spouse, the trustee may sell the residence and replace it with other property of comparable or lower value suitable as a residence for the surviving spouse. If the surviving spouse becomes subject to a conservatorship of the estate or person, the conservator shall be empowered to act for the surviving spouse.

8.6. Combining Multi-Trust Property. Each trust created under this instrument shall constitute a separate trust and be administered accordingly; however, the assets of all of the trusts may be combined for bookkeeping purposes and held for the trust beneficiaries without physical division into separate trusts until time of distribution.

8.7. Spendthrift Clause. To the maximum extent permitted by

law, the interests of each trust beneficiary under this instrument are not transferable by voluntary or involuntary assignment or by operation of law and shall be free from the claims of creditors and from attachment, execution, bankruptcy, and other legal process. If any such transfer is made or attempted by or against a trust beneficiary, all further trust payments of income or principal or both to that beneficiary (and any right of that beneficiary to such payments) shall be suspended for a period of time or indefinitely (but in no case for longer than the term of the trust) as the trustee determines. In lieu of payments to the beneficiary, the trustee may apply so much of the trust income or principal or both to which the beneficiary would otherwise be entitled as the trustee deems necessary for the beneficiary's education and support. All trust income (to which the beneficiary would otherwise be entitled) not so applied shall in the discretion of the trustee be accumulated and added to trust principal at such time or times as the trustee deems proper.

8.8. Division or Distribution in Cash or Kind. Except to the extent that any provisions in this instrument that specify the allocation of assets involving the marital deduction conflict with this paragraph, the trustee, in order to satisfy a pecuniary gift or to distribute or divide trust assets into shares or partial shares, may distribute or divide such assets in kind, or divide undivided interests in such assets, or sell all or any part of such assets and distribute or divide the property in cash, in kind, or partly in cash and partly in kind. Property distributed to satisfy a pecuniary gift under this instrument shall be valued at its fair market value at the time of distribution.

8.9. Payments on Behalf of Minors or Persons Under Disability. If at any time any beneficiary is a minor or it appears to the trustee that any beneficiary is disabled, incompetent, or for any other reason not able to receive payments or make intelligent or responsible use of the payments, then the trustee, in lieu of making direct payments to the beneficiary, may make payments to the beneficiary's conservator or guardian; to the beneficiary's custodian under the Uniform Gifts to Minors Act or Uniform Transfers to Minors Act of any state; to one or more suitable persons as the trustee deems proper, such as a relative of the beneficiary or a person residing with the beneficiary, to be used for the beneficiary's benefit; to any other person, firm, or agency for services rendered or to be rendered for the beneficiary's assistance or benefit; or to accounts in the beneficiary's name with financial institutions. The receipt of payments by any of the foregoing shall constitute a sufficient acquittance of the trustee for all purposes.

8.10. Trustee's Duty to Account. The trustee shall not be required to render periodic accounts to any person, but shall render accounts at the termination of a trust and upon a change of trustee, to the persons and in the manner required by law.

8.11. Written Notice to Trustee. Until the trustee receives written notice of any death or other event upon which the right to payments from any trust may depend, the trustee shall incur no liability for disbursements made in good faith to persons whose interests may have been affected by that event.

8.12. No Early Termination of Trust Without Prior Court Authorization. California Probate Code section 15408(b) shall not apply to any trust under this instrument, and except as otherwise provided in this instrument, the trustee may not terminate a trust before the trust term expires unless prior court authorization is obtained.

ARTICLE NINE

CONCLUDING PROVISIONS

9.1. Perpetuities Savings Clause. Unless sooner terminated, each trust created by this instrument shall terminate twenty-one (21) years after the later of (1) the death of the last to die of the trustors' issue who are living at the death of the surviving spouse, or (2) the death of the surviving spouse. If a trust is terminated because of the preceding sentence, the trustee shall distribute the trust property outright pro rata, to the persons who are then entitled or eligible to receive trust income (or if there are no such persons, outright in a manner that the trustee believes will give effect to the trustors' intent in creating the trust).

9.2. Period of Survivorship. For the purposes of this instrument, a beneficiary shall not be deemed to have survived a trustor if that beneficiary dies within sixty (60) days after the trustor's death.

9.3. Severability Clause. If any provision of this

instrument is invalid, that provision shall be disregarded and shall not affect any of the other provisions.

9.4. Captions. The captions appearing in this instrument are for convenience of reference only and shall have no significance in the construction or interpretation of this instrument.

9.5. Definition of Heirs. Any reference to a trustor's "heirs" in the dispositive provisions of this instrument shall be construed as referring to those persons who are entitled to that trustor's property under the laws of intestate succession in effect at the time of execution of this instrument.

9.6. Definitions of Issue, Child, and Children. The terms "issue," "child," and "children," when used in the dispositive provisions of this instrument, shall be given the meanings accorded those terms in Part 2 of Division 1 of the California Probate Code in effect at the time of execution of this instrument.

9.7. Definition of Incompetent. For all purposes under this instrument, a person shall be deemed "incompetent" if and so long as a conservator of his or her person or estate duly appointed by a court of competent jurisdiction is serving, or upon certification by two physicians (licensed to practice under the laws of the state where the person is domiciled) that the person is unable properly to care for himself or herself, for his or her person, or for his or her property.

9.8. Definition of Death Taxes, Debts, and Expenses. As used in this instrument, the term "death taxes, debts, and expenses" shall include the following:

(a) All estate, inheritance, succession, and similar taxes (including any interest and penalties) that become payable by reason of a trustor's death or by any person on account of that person's interest in that trustor's estate, but excluding any federal or state tax imposed on any "generation-skipping transfer," and excluding any addition to the federal estate tax for any "excess retirement accumulation" under Internal Revenue Code section 4980A.

(b) All costs, expenses of litigation, counsel fees, or other charges that the trustee incurs in connection with the determination of the amount of the taxes, interest, or penalties referred to in subparagraph (a) of this paragraph; and

(c) Legally enforceable debts, funeral expenses, expenses of last illness, and administration and property expenses.

9.9. California Trust Law to Apply. California law shall govern the validity, interpretation, and administration of any trust created under this instrument, regardless of the domicile of any trustee or beneficiary.

ARTICLE TEN

EXECUTION

10.1. Execution. We, and each of us, certify that we have read the foregoing trust declaration and that it correctly states the terms and conditions under which the trust estate is to be held, managed, and disposed of by the trustees. We approve of the trust declaration in all particulars, and as the trustees named in the trust declaration, accept the trusts provided for in the declaration.

10.2. Executed on SEP 12 1990 at San Anselmo, California.

Kenneth F. Goodall
KENNETH F. GOODALL

Rachel A. Goodall
RACHEL A. GOODALL

EXHIBIT B

SECOND AMENDMENT TO GOODALL TRUST

Preamble. RACHEL A. GOODALL is the settlor of GOODALL TRUST created under that certain declaration dated September 12, 1990, as amended August 24, 1994. RACHEL A. GOODALL is the trustee duly appointed and acting under and by terms of that declaration. In Section 3.3 of Article Three of that declaration, the settlor reserved the right to amend the trust "(d)uring the trustors' joint lifetimes ...." The surviving settlor now wishes to exercise her right of amendment and, to that end, does hereby amend that declaration in the terms stated below. The trustees hereby consent to the terms of this amendment.

1. Amendment of Section 7.1. of Article Seven. Section 7.1. of Article Seven of that declaration is amended to read as follows:

> 7.1. Remaining Settlor-Trustee Serves Alone. On the death of the deceased settlor, or if, for any reason, before that time either settlor ceases to act as trustee, no successor cotrustee shall be appointed to act with regards to the Bypass Trust. Rather, the remaining settlor trustee named in Article One shall have full power to act as trustee of the Bypass Trust and to complete the trust administration.
>
> After the death of the deceased settlor, at the discretion of the surviving settlor, KENNETH MICHAEL GOODALL, may be appointed to act as cotrustee with regards to the Survivors Trust This appointment shall be confirmed by KENNETH MICHAEL GOODALL signing a

Exht B

document, such as an Amendment to Declaration of Trust, in which he agrees to be bound by the terms of the trust.

2. Ratification of Other Terms of Trust. In every other respect, the settlor confirms and ratifies the terms of the trust as stated in that certain declaration dated September 12, 1990, as amended August 24, 1994.

3. Execution. We certify that we have read the foregoing declaration of trust, as amended, and that it correctly states the terms and conditions under which the trust estate is to be held, administered, and distributed. As trustees of the trusts created by this declaration of trust, we approve this declaration of trust, as amended, in all particulars, and agree to be bound by its terms and conditions. RACHEL A. GOODALL, as settlor of the trusts created by this declaration of trust, approves this declaration of trust in all particulars, and agrees to be bound by its terms and conditions.

Executed on JAN 19 1998 at Novato, California.

SETTLOR-TRUSTEE

Rachel A. Goodall

RACHEL A. GOODALL

TRUSTEE

K. Michael Goodall

KENNETH MICHAEL GOODALL

ACKNOWLEDGMENT

STATE OF CALIFORNIA)
) ss
COUNTY OF MARIN)

On JAN 19 1999, before me, a notary public in and for the State of California, personally appeared KENNETH MICHAEL GOODALL and RACHEL A. GOODALL, personally known to me (or proved to me on the basis of satisfactory evidence) to be the persons whose names are subscribed to the within instrument, and acknowledged to me that they executed the same in their individual capacities, and that by their signatures on the instrument, the persons executed the instrument.

WITNESS my hand and official seal.

Signature ______________________ (SEAL)

JAMES R. HASTINGS
Commission # [illegible]
Notary Public - California
Marin County
My Comm. Expires [illegible]

EXHIBIT C

DE-150

ATTORNEY OR PARTY WITHOUT ATTORNEY (Name, state bar number, and address):	TELEPHONE AND FAX NOS.:	FOR COURT USE ONLY
Samuel H. Sloan 461 Peachstone Terrace San Rafael CA 94903 samhsloan@gmail.com	415-894-7201	FILED MAR 2 1 2011 KIM TURNER, Court Executive Officer MARIN COUNTY SUPERIOR COURT By: S. Bond, Deputy
ATTORNEY FOR (Name):		
SUPERIOR COURT OF CALIFORNIA, COUNTY OF Marin STREET ADDRESS: 3501 Civic Center Drive MAILING ADDRESS: CITY AND ZIP CODE: San Rafael CA 94903 BRANCH NAME:		
ESTATE OF (Name): K. Michael Goodall DECEDENT		
LETTERS ☐ TESTAMENTARY ☐ OF ADMINISTRATION ☑ OF ADMINISTRATION WITH WILL ANNEXED ☐ SPECIAL ADMINISTRATION		CASE NUMBER: PR 1100596

LETTERS

1. ☑ The last will of the decedent named above having been proved, the court appoints (name): Samuel H. Sloan
   a. ☐ executor
   b. ☑ administrator with will annexed
2. ☐ The court appoints (name):
   a. ☐ administrator of the decedent's estate
   b. ☐ special administrator of decedent's estate
      (1) ☐ with the special powers specified in the Order for Probate
      (2) ☐ with the powers of a general administrator
      (3) ☐ letters will expire on (date):
3. ☑ The personal representative is authorized to administer the estate under the Independent Administration of Estates Act ☑ **with full authority**
   ☐ **with limited authority** (no authority, without court supervision, to (1) sell or exchange real property or (2) grant an option to purchase real property or (3) borrow money with the loan secured by an encumbrance upon real property).
4. ☐ The personal representative is not authorized to take possession of money or any other property without a specific court order.

WITNESS, clerk of the court, with seal of the court affixed.

(SEAL) SEAL

Date: MAR 2 1 2011

KIM TURNER

Clerk, by

S. BOND

(DEPUTY)

AFFIRMATION

1. ☐ PUBLIC ADMINISTRATOR: No affirmation required (Prob. Code, § 7621(c)).
2. ☑ INDIVIDUAL: **I solemnly affirm** that I will perform the duties of personal representative according to law.
3. ☐ INSTITUTIONAL FIDUCIARY (name):

   I solemnly affirm that the institution will perform the duties of personal representative according to law. I make this affirmation for myself as an individual and on behalf of the institution as an officer.
   (Name and title):

4. Executed on (date): MARCH 3, 2011
   at (place): SAN RAFAEL, California

Samuel H. Sloan
(SIGNATURE)

CERTIFICATION

I certify that this document is a correct copy of the original on file in my office and the letters issued the personal representative appointed above have not been revoked, annulled, or set aside, and are still in full force and effect.

(SEAL)

Date:

Clerk, by

(DEPUTY)

Exh C

EXHIBIT D

Samuel Sloan
461 Peachstone Ter.
San Rafael, CA 94903
415-894-7201

Pro per administrator
of the Estate of Michael Goodall

Telephone 415-894-7201

FILED

AUG 01 2011

KIM TURNER
Court Executive Officer
MARIN COUNTY SUPERIOR COURT

SUPERIOR COURT OF THE STATE OF CALIFORNIA

COUNTY OF MARIN

In the Matter of the Estate of K. Michael Goodall	Case No. PR 1100596 PETITION FOR AUTHORITY TO ENTER INTO CONTINGENCY FEE AGREEMENT [PROBATE CODE §10811 (c); CALIFORNIA RULES OF COURT 7.703 (d)] Hearing Date: August 22, 2011 Time: 8:30 AM Department: H

Samuel Sloan declares:

(1) I am the duly appointed administrator of the Estate of K. Michael Goodall;

(2) I have received notice that the Bank of America as trustee for the Kenneth F Goodall and Rachel A Goodall Trust has filed a petition *In the Matter of the Trust for Michael Created under the Goodall Trust Dated September 12, 1990*, in San

EXBT. D

Francisco County, probate action TR-99-273030, contending that the real property commonly known as 461 Peachstone Ter., San Rafael, CA, where Michael Goodall was living at the time of his death, should be distributed according to the terms of the Goodall Trust rather than according to the terms of K. Michael Goodall's will which is the subject of this Marin County probate proceedings, with the result that the beneficiaries of the will of K. Michael Goodall would receive nothing;

(3) I recently retained Sam Ware to represent me as administrator of the Estate of K. Michael Goodall to represent the interests of the Estate in that San Francisco proceeding, pursuant to the terms of the contingency fee agreement attached hereto as Exhibit A, and it is the purpose of this petition to obtain approval and ratification of that contingency fee agreement;

(4) Bank of America's petition in the San Francisco action had earlier been scheduled for July 11, 2011 but as I did not receive proper notice of that hearing I filed an objection in Pro per to that hearing date and the San Francisco Superior Court ordered that the hearing be continued to August 23, 2011;

(5) As the Estate of K Michael Goodall has no other assets and is therefore unable to pay Mr. Ware an hourly rate, Mr. Ware and I have agreed that he will represent the interests of the Estate in the San Francisco action on a contingency fee basis as set forth in Exhibit A hereto;

(6) I am informed and believe that Mr. Ware has been practicing for 30 years and has experience in litigating wills and trusts contests such as the Superior Court action;

(7) It is respectfully submitted that it is in the interests of the Estate to retain Mr. Ware to represent its interests according to the terms of the contingency fee agreement attached hereto as Exhibit A, and, accordingly,

WHEREFORE, petitioner asks this court to find that the proposed agreement complies with all the requirements Section 6147 of the Business and Professions Code, that the compensation provided for in the agreement is just and reasonable, and that the agreement is to the advantage of the estate and in the best interest of persons who are interested in the estate, and to make its order approving and ratifying said agreement and I may make payment to Sam Ware in accordance with its terms without further order of the court.

I declare under penalty of perjury under the laws of the State of California that the foregoing is true and correct and that this declaration was executed on July 30, 2011.

Samuel H. Ross

ATTORNEYS' RETAINER AGREEMENT (Contingency)

In July 2011, the following agreement was made between Samuel Sloan, for and as administrator of Estate of K Michael Goodall (hereinafter "Client") and Sam Ware (hereinafter "Attorney");

1. Client retains Attorney to represent Client with regard to recovering amounts from Bank of America and/or the Goodall Trust, including, but not limited to representing Client in San Francisco Superior Court action # 273030, entitled In the Matter of the Trust for Michael (hereinafter "the Action");

2. Client agrees to pay Attorney for his services from the amount recovered by voluntary payment, settlement, mediation, arbitration, judgment, or otherwise 33 1/3% of the value of the property recovered. If the Court should make an award of attorney's fees in the action, that award will be used to offset the % amount owing to Attorneys pursuant to this agreement. Client is aware that the fee for Attorney's services is not set by law, but is instead negotiable between attorney and client.

3. In addition to the fees for services described above, Client agrees to pay the costs and necessary disbursements incurred in any prosecution or settlement of the Action. Attorney may nonetheless advance such costs and disbursements for Client's benefit as needed.

4. Client agrees that the costs and disbursements so advanced will be repaid to Attorney by subtracting them from the

total amount of the recovery. The amount of recovery for purposes of computing the attorneys' fees for services set forth in paragraph 2 above will be the total recovery prior to the costs and disbursements being repaid to Attorney.

5. Client agrees that Attorney may retain his share out of the amount finally collected by suit, settlement, judgment or otherwise.

6. Client empowers Attorney to institute such legal action(s) as may be advisable in his judgment.

7. Client agrees that if Client makes any settlement without the knowledge of Attorney, that Client agrees to pay Attorney the fees and costs described herein.

8. If Client substitutes attorneys, except for misconduct or incapacity of said Attorney to act, Attorney shall be entitled to a reasonable fee, and in any event the costs herein stated and advanced.

9. It is further agreed that, before Attorney performs services that pertain to related matters not covered by this fee agreement, Attorney and Client will conduct further negotiations, and enter into further agreements, and Client will not be obligated to pay any compensation to Attorney that is not already set forth in this agreement, unless and until such further agreement is reached.

10. It is agreed that Attorney has made no guarantees regarding the successful termination of said Action, and all

expressions relative hereto are matters of his opinion only.

Client and Attorneys accept said retainer on the conditions hereinbefore enumerated.

Dated:____________

____
Samuel Sloan for and as
administrator of the Estate of
K Michael Goodall

Dated:____________

____
Sam Ware

EXHIBIT E

Samuel H. Sloan
461 Peachstone Terrace
San Rafael CA 94903

415-419-5980
917-659-3397
samhsloan@gmail.com

August 1, 2011

Bank of America Trust Department
c/o Gary Rothstein
Manatt, Phelps & Phillips
One Embarcadero Center 30th Floor
San Francisco, CA 94111

Re: Estate of Goodall
Marin Action CR 110-0596
and San Francisco Action 273030

Dear Sir/Mdm.:

As the duly appointed administrator of the Estate of Michael Goodall demand is hereby made that you provide an accounting for all trust activity in the Goodall trust from the date of the death of Rachel Goodall (6/7/99) to the present.

I find no accounting filed in San Francisco action number 99-273030, In Re the Goodall Trust or elsewhere.

As you will recall, back in February of this year, a representative of Bank of America entered the house at 461 Peachstone Terrace and removed all its contents. Among what has been returned to the house and to me, I do not find any papers related to the trust.

Sincerely,

Samuel H. Sloan

cc: Gary Rothstein
Manatt, Phelps & Phillips
One Embarcadero Center 30th floor
San Francisco, CA 94111

Exh F

EXHIBIT F

From: Rothstein, Gary <GRothstein@manatt.com>
Date: 2011/8/1
Subject: RE: Demand is that you provide an accounting for all trust activity in the Goodall Trust
To: samhsloan@gmail.com

Sam,

As you know, there is a proceeding pending in the San Francisco Probate Court to determine the beneficiaries of the Trust for Michael under the Goodall Trust to whom the Trust assets shall pass. The hearing of the Bank of America's Petition (as the Trustee of the Trust for Michael) in that regard is set for August 23, 2011. At present, there is no determination that Michael Goodall's Estate is a beneficiary of the Trust for Michael. Consequently, you, as the Administrator of Michael Goodall's Estate, do not presently have standing to request an accounting from the Trustee. If Michael Goodall's Estate ultimately is determined by the Probate Court to be a beneficiary of the Trust for Michael, you, as Administrator, would have standing to request an accounting from the Trustee at that time.

Sincerely,

Gary

Gary D. Rothstein
Counsel
manatt¦phelps¦phillips

San Francisco Office:
One Embarcadero Center, 30th Floor
San Francisco, CA 94111
Direct Phone: 415.291.7431
Direct Fax: 415.291.7479

Los Angeles Office:
11355 W. Olympic Blvd.
Los Angeles, CA 90064
Direct Phone: 310.312.4115
Direct Fax: 310.914.5880

email: grothstein@manatt.com

Please consider the environment before printing this email.

CONFIDENTIALITY NOTICE: This e-mail transmission, and any documents, files or previous e-mail messages attached to it, may contain confidential information that is legally privileged. If you are not the intended recipient, or a person responsible for delivering it to the intended recipient, you are hereby notified that any disclosure, copying, distribution or use of any of the information contained in or attached to this message is STRICTLY PROHIBITED. If you have received this transmission in error, please immediately notify us by reply e-mail at

Exh F.

MANATT, PHELPS & PHILLIPS, LLP
GARY D. ROTHSTEIN (Bar No. CA 143157)
EUGENE L. HAHM (Bar No. CA 167596)
One Embarcadero Center, 30th Floor
San Francisco, CA 94111
Telephone: (415) 291-7400
Facsimile: (415) 291-7474

Attorneys for Petitioner,
BANK OF AMERICA, N.A.

SUPERIOR COURT OF THE STATE OF CALIFORNIA

FOR THE COUNTY OF SAN FRANCISCO

In the Matter of the Trust for Michael created under the Goodall Trust dated September 12, 1990.	Case No. PTR-99-273030 **PETITIONER BANK OF AMERICA, N.A.'S REPLY IN SUPPORT OF PETITION FOR DETERMINATION OF THE BENEFICIARIES TO WHOM TRUST PROPERTY SHALL PASS UPON TERMINATION OF TRUST** Hearing Date: August 23, 2011 Time: 9:00 A.M. Dept.: Room 204 (Probate)

Introduction

The Petition for Determination of the Beneficiaries to Whom Trust Property Shall Pass Upon Termination of Trust (the "Petition") seeks only one thing: a determination by this Court of the beneficiaries to whom the assets of the Trust for Michael shall pass now that the Trust for Michael is terminating as a result of Michael Goodall's ("Michael") death. *That determination of beneficiaries is the sole issue before this Court at this time.*

Sam Sloan, the administrator of Michael's estate, challenges the relief sought in the Petition, but none of the arguments set forth in either the (i) Further Probate Opposition/Objection to Petition For Determination of the Beneficiaries to Whom Trust Property Shall Pass Upon Termination of Trust (the "Further Opposition") or (ii) Supplemental Objections to Petition for Determination of Beneficiaries and Request for Continuance of Hearing (the "Supplemental Objections") supports his challenge.

In his Further Opposition, Mr. Sloan accuses Petitioner and its attorneys of attempting to perpetrate a fraud on this Court by Petitioner concealing that the Goodall's 1990 Trust document is the operative document. But as shown below, and contrary to Mr. Sloan's unfounded allegations of misconduct, it is clear that the 1994 Restatement is the effective trust document.

Mr. Sloan's Supplemental Objections seemingly abandon his contention that the 1990 Trust is the operative instrument. Instead, the Supplemental Objections raise numerous unsubstantiated issues that are *irrelevant* to the Court's current determination, including the following:

- Whether Petitioner must provide accountings to Mr. Sloan, in his capacity as the Administrator of Michael's Estate, prior to there being a determination by this Court that Michael Goodall's Estate is a beneficiary of the Trust for Michael.
- Whether the monthly distributions to Michael during his lifetime from the Trust for Michael were sufficient in amount in light of the broad discretion provided to Petitioner with respect to distributions.

- Whether the settlors had the capacity to understand their estate plan as provided for in the 1994 Restatement of their trust.
- Whether certain accounts previously held at USAA Investment Management are assets of the Trust for Michael.
- Whether Michael Goodall ever was a co-trustee of a trust under the Goodall Trust.

In short, the Supplemental Objections adopt the "kitchen sink" approach, arguing numerous irrelevant trust issues to cloud the only issue currently before the Court, all in a procedurally improper attempt to further delay the Court's determination of the limited issue raised by the Petition.

Petitioner believes that this Court can rule at this time with respect to the determination of the proper beneficiaries of the Trust for Michael (the "Beneficiary Issue"), as prayed for in the Petition. In doing so, the Court need not consider any of the foregoing irrelevant issues raised in the Further Opposition and Supplemental Objections. If Mr. Sloan wishes to have this Court make determinations with respect to issues pertaining to the effect of the settlors' capacity on the validity of the 1994 Restatement, the trustee accountings, and the distributions to Michael, he should have raised those issues in separate pleadings rather than in the Further Opposition and Supplemental Objections.

Reply

1. **Mr. Sloan's Allegations in the Further Opposition that the 1990 Trust is the Operative Trust Document are Without Merit.** The Further Opposition accuses Petitioner (and its counsel) of having conducted this case on a "fraudulent basis" by suggesting to this Court that the 1994 Restatement is the Goodalls' operative trust instrument, and of "using false documents to bamboozle" this court as to the true nature of the Goodall Trust. To the contrary, Petitioner has not attempted to "bamboozle" anyone; the record evidence clearly demonstrates that the 1994 Restatement is the operative trust document.

a. **The 1990 Goodall Trust Document Is Not the Effective Trust Document**. The Further Opposition alleges that the settlors' "real 1990 trust" document is the

Declaration of Trust for the Goodall Trust dated September 12, 1990 (the "1990 Trust Document") (Further Opposition, page 2, line 23). Mr. Sloan bases his argument on a quote from a Declaration of James R. Hasting in Opposition to Petition to Remove Trustee, which was filed in connection with a proceeding to remove the trustee of the Trust for Michael commenced by Michael Goodall in this matter in 2000 (the "Prior Proceeding"). Specifically, Mr. Sloan quotes from Paragraph 2 of Mr. Hastings' Declaration, which states as follows:

> "In 1990 Mr. and Mrs. Goodall requested me to draft a revocable living trust as their main testamentary instrument. Under the terms of the trust...their son Michael was made their outright beneficiary after the death of the survivor of them (page 13 paragraph 6.3(a))...." (Further Opposition, page 4, lines 19-25; also, Exhibit B to Further Opposition, page 4, lines 19-25)

Although the 1990 Trust Document did provide for an outright distribution of the Goodall Trust assets to Michael after his parents died, for the reasons explained below, the 1990 Trust Document is not the effective trust instrument.

b. **The 1994 Restatement Is the Effective Trust Document**. The 1994 Restatement is the operative trust instrument.

i. **The 1994 Restatement Itself Confirms that It Amended the 1990 Trust Document in its Entirety**. The 1994 Restatement amended the 1990 Trust Document *in its entirety* and thereby supplanted all of the provisions of the 1990 Trust Document. In this regard, the 1994 Restatement commences as follows:

> "Preamble. KENNETH F. GOODALL and RACHEL A. GOODALL are the settlors of GOODALL TRUST created under that certain declaration dated September 12, 1990....In Section 3.3 of Article Three of that declaration, the settlors reserved the right to amend the trust '(d)uring the trustors' joint lifetimes....' The settlors now wish to exercise their right of amendment and, to that end, do hereby amend that declaration in the terms stated below....
>
> 1. Amendment of the Declaration of Trust. *The entirety of the declaration is amended* to read as the attached 'THE GOODALL TRUST' which will be dated this date." (emphasis added) (the initial page to Exhibit 1 to the Petition)

Furthermore, Paragraph 2 of the Second Amendment to Goodall Trust dated January 19, 1999 confirmed that the 1994 Restatement (not the 1990 Trust Document) is the operative trust instrument, as follows:

> "Ratification of Other Terms of Trust. In every other respect, the settlor confirms and ratifies the terms of the trust as stated in that certain declaration dated September 12, 1990, *as amended August 24, 1994*." (emphasis added) [1]

ii. **Mr. Hastings' Declaration in the Prior Proceeding Confirms that the 1994 Restatement is the Effective Trust Document**. Paragraphs 3 and 4 of Mr. Hastings' Declaration, which Mr. Sloan fails to bring to the Court's attention in his Further Opposition, explain the origins of the 1994 Restatement, as follows:

> "3. On August 24, 1994 Mr. and Mrs. Goodall executed their Declaration of Trust...substantially modifying their 1990 estate plan. They were convinced that Michael was unable to handle money properly, that he should not be given access to substantial funds, or have influence over the person or entity controlling his funds. They explained that Michael stopped working in 1997 or 1998 and was living in their home.
>
> 4. As a consequence, they instructed me to draft the new trust instrument under which the estate would remain in trust after the death of the survivor of them, with the trustee granted liberal discretion regarding payments of income and principal to Michael. Under its terms, all decisions of the trustee regarding payments are within the trustee's discretion and are final and incontestable...." (Exhibit B to Opposition, page 1, line 26 to page 2, line 11)

Thus, Paragraphs 3 and 4 of Mr. Hastings' Declaration clearly evidence that Kenneth and Rachel Goodall intended the 1994 Restatement to replace the provision in the 1990 Trust Document that previously provided for an outright distribution to Michael after they passed away.

iii. **Michael Goodall Acknowledged that the 1994 Restatement is the Effective Trust Document and that Section 6.3(d) of the 1994 Restatement Controls the Disposition of the Trust for Michael Following Michael's Death**. Mr. Sloan's assertion that the 1990 Trust Document is the effective trust instrument is inconsistent with Michael's own understanding of his parents' trust. In initiating the Prior Proceeding, Michael himself acknowledged in his Petition for Removal of Trustee (a copy of which is attached hereto as Exhibit 1 and incorporated herein) that his parents intended Section

[1] Contrary to Mr. Sloan's allegation (Further Opposition, page 4, lines 1-3), a copy of the Second Amendment is attached at the end of Exhibit 1 to the Petition.

6.3(d) under the 1994 Restatement to dispose of the assets of the Trust for Michael at his death. He stated in his Petition:

> "K. Michael Goodall is the only child of the trustors and the lifetime beneficiary of the trust (§6.3). The primary remainder beneficiary is Guide Dogs For The Blind of Marin, Inc. (§6.3(d))" (Petition for Removal of Trustee, page 2, lines 1-4)

The foregoing acknowledgement necessarily pertained to the 1994 Restatement because (i) Section 6.3 of the 1990 Trust Amendment provided for an outright bequest to Michael Goodall and (ii) the 1990 Trust Amendment did not contain a Section 6.3(d).

2. **The Supplemental Objections Attempt to Inject Extraneous Issues that are not Relevant to the Court's Ruling on the Petition**. In his Supplemental Objections, Mr. Sloan appears to abandon his contentions that the 1990 Trust represents the effective trust document. Instead, Mr. Sloan attempts to raise additional probate issues to justify his request for further delay in the Court's adjudication of this Petition. None of those issues, however, are germane to the limited issue raised by the Petition and should not form the basis for any further delay.

a. **Allegations That the Petitioner Failed to Provide Accountings to Mr. Sloan are Irrelevant and Should Have Been Raised in a Separate Petition**. Mr. Sloan asserts that he demanded an accounting from Petitioner, that Petitioner had an obligation to provide such accountings to Mr. Sloan as the Administrator of Michael's Estate, and that Petitioner advised Sloan that such an accounting will not be provided. (Supplemental Objections, page 5, lines 9-28; page 6, lines 26-27; page 7, lines 15-19; page 8, lines 9-10) The Beneficiary Issue is the only issue raised by the Petition and, therefore, is the only issue presently to be resolved by this Court. Whether or not Petitioner had a duty as trustee of the Trust for Michael to provide Mr. Sloan with any accountings (the "Accounting Issue") is irrelevant to this Court's determination of the Beneficiary Issue. Furthermore, because the Accounting Issue is irrelevant to the only issue before the Court, it was improper for Mr. Sloan to raise the Accounting Issue in the Supplemental Objections. If Mr. Sloan wishes this Court to determine whether Petitioner must provide him with accountings, he should bring such issue before this Court by filing a separate petition seeking that relief.

b. **Allegations That the Monthly Distributions to Michael During Michael's Lifetime Were Not Sufficient in Amount are Irrelevant and Should Have Been Raised in a Separate Petition.** Mr. Sloan asserts that monthly distributions in the amount of $2,500 to $3,000 to Michael during his lifetime from the Trust for Michael were inappropriately small. (Supplemental Objections, page 3, line 22 to page 4, line 1; page 6, line 27 to page 7, line 2; page 7, lines 15-19) The Beneficiary Issue is the only issue raised by the Petition and, therefore, is the only issue presently to be resolved by this Court. Whether or not Petitioner should have made larger monthly distributions to Michael from the Trust for Michael during Michael's lifetime (the "Distribution Issue") is irrelevant to this Court's determination of the Beneficiary Issue. Furthermore, because the Distribution Issue is irrelevant to the only issue before the Court, it was improper for Mr. Sloan to raise the Distribution Issue in the Supplemental Objections. If Mr. Sloan wishes this Court to determine whether Petitioner should have made larger distributions to Michael, he should bring such issue before this Court by filing a separate petition seeking such relief.

c. **Allegations That the Settlors may have Lacked the Capacity to Understand the Dispositive Plan in the 1994 Restatement are Irrelevant and Should Have Been Raised in a Separate Pleading**. Mr. Sloan alleges that the Goodalls may have lacked the capacity to understand the dispositive plan contained in the 1994 Restatement. (Supplemental Objections, page 2, lines 7-10; page 3, lines 2-7; page 6, lines 1-20; page 8, lines 6-8) The Beneficiary Issue is the only issue raised by the Petition and, therefore, is the only issue presently to be resolved by this Court. Whether or not the settlors lacked the testamentary capacity to understand the dispositive plan contained in the 1994 Restatement (the "Capacity Issue") is irrelevant to this Court's determination of the Beneficiary Issue. Furthermore, because the Capacity Issue is irrelevant to the only issue before the Court, it was improper for Mr. Sloan to raise the Capacity Issue in the Supplemental Objections. If Mr. Sloan wishes a determination by this Court with respect to whether the 1994 Restatement is invalid as the Goodalls' operative testamentary document because they may have lacked the capacity to understand the dispositive plan provided for by the 1994 Restatement, he should bring such issue before this Court by filing a separate pleading seeking such relief.

3. **San Francisco is the Proper Venue for this Trust Petition**. As described in the Petition, the principal place of administration of the Trust for Michael is San Francisco, California. Therefore, venue in this county is proper under Calif. Prob. Code §17005.

This Court previously has acknowledged on multiple occasions that San Francisco is the proper venue for proceedings involving the administration of the Goodall Trust and the Trust for Michael; first with respect to the Prior Proceeding in 2000, and recently with respect to this Court issuing its Order Confirming Real Property as an Asset of the Trust (filed by this Court in this matter on June 3, 2011). Notwithstanding the foregoing, the Further Opposition declares that "[t]he San Francisco case is duplicative of a case going on in Marin County Probate Court, PR1100596. That case was filed in January 2011, three months before the case in this court was filed, and concerns the same estate." (Further Opposition, page 7, line 28 to page 8, line 3). The Further Opposition continues: "...Bank of America should be told to file in Marin County where this case belongs." (Further Opposition, page 7, lines 14-16) The present Petition and the proceeding in Marin County to which Mr. Sloan refers (the "Marin Probate Proceeding") are not duplicative. The Petition seeks a determination of this Court as to the proper beneficiaries under the Trust for Michael. As such, the Petition is a trust matter, the proper venue of which is the principal place of administration (i.e., San Francisco). In contrast, the Marin Probate Proceeding is a proceeding for the administration of Michael's probate Estate. There is no proceeding pending in the Marin Probate Proceeding by which that Court is asked to determine the proper beneficiaries to whom the assets of the Trust for Michael are to be distributed and, as explained above, the Marin County Superior Court would not be the proper venue for such a trust proceeding.

Mr. Sloan also asserts that Petitioner's alleged forum-shopping is the "sort of thing [that] brings the courts into disrepute." (Further Opposition, page 7, lines 3-14) Not so; as explained above, San Francisco is the proper venue for the determination of this trust-related Petition.

For the foregoing reasons, Petitioner respectfully requests that the Court reject the Further Opposition and Supplemental Objections as being without merit, and grant the Petition as prayed.

Dated: August 19, 2011 BANK OF AMERICA, N.A.

By: Jacquel Hutchings
Jacquel Hutchings
Its: Assistant Vice-President and Trust Officer

Dated: August 19, 2011 MANATT, PHELPS & PHILLIPS, LLP

By: Gary D. Rothstein
Gary D. Rothstein
Attorneys for Petitioner
BANK OF AMERICA, N.A.

VERIFICATION

I am Assistant Vice-President and Trust Officer of Bank of America, N.A., the petitioner in the above-entitled action; I have read the foregoing **REPLY TO: (1) THE FURTHER PROBATE OPPOSITION/OBJECTION TO PETITION FOR DETERMINATION OF THE BENEFICIARIES TO WHOM TRUST PROPERTY SHALL PASS UPON TERMINATION OF TRUST; AND (2) SUPPLEMENTAL OBJECTIONS TO PETITION FOR DETERMINATION OF BENEFICIARIES AND REQUEST FOR CONTINUANCE OF HEARING** and know the contents thereof; and I certify that the same is true of my own knowledge, except as to those matters which are therein stated upon my information and belief, and as to those matters I believe them to be true.

I declare, under penalty of perjury under the laws of the State of California, that the foregoing is true and correct, and that this Verification was executed on this ____ day of ________, 2011, at ____________, ________.

[signature]
Jacquel Hutchings

EXHIBIT 1

ROBERT J. ROTHMAN, A PROFESSIONAL CORPORATION
ROBERT J. ROTHMAN, ESQ. (SBN 47108)
601 California Street, Suite 800
San Francisco, CA 94108
Telephone: (415) 392-3661
Fax: (415) 982-7372

Attorney for K. Michael Goodall, Beneficiary

FILED
San Francisco County Superior Court
FEB 14 2000
ALAN CARLSON, Clerk
BY: [signature]
Deputy Clerk

SUPERIOR COURT OF THE STATE OF CALIFORNIA

IN AND FOR THE CITY AND COUNTY OF SAN FRANCISCO

In Re The Goodall Trust	Case No. 273030 PETITION FOR REMOVAL OF TRUSTEE Date: MAR 27 2000 Time: 9:30 a.m. Dept. Probate Room: 204

Petitioner K. Michael Goodall, alleges:

1. Kenneth F. Goodall and Rachel A. Goodall, the parents of petitioner established a trust known as the Goodall Trust. A copy of the same together with the First and Second Amendments was attached as Exhibit A to petitioner's motion filed December 21, 1999.

2. K. Michael Goodall is the only child of the trustors and the lifetime beneficiary of the trust (§ 6.3). The primary remainder beneficiary is Guide Dogs For The Blind of Marin, Inc. (§ 6.3(d)).

3. Pursuant to § 7.2 of the Goodall Trust, Bank of America's named as successor-trustee. Petitioner was informed and believes and accordingly alleges that Bank of America, NT&SA is a corporation with its principal place of business in the City and County of San Francisco and pursuant to Probate Code § 17005 San Francisco and is the proper venue.

4. Kenneth Goodall predeceased his wife, Rachel Goodall, and Rachel Goodall died on June 7, 1999. Because Michael Goodall was receiving no income distributions from the trust he retained counsel and contacted the attorney for the trust, J.R. Hastings and Bank of America in September. No response was forthcoming and no income distributions were made despite the severe economic problems experienced by the beneficiary. Finally a meeting was set up on November 2, 1999 and the Bank of America admitted that they still had not gathered any of the assets. K. Michael Goodall, disturbed by the situation, after considering the same and reviewing the matter further requested Bank of America to resign in favor of Karen Anderson and Estate Minders, a well known professional

trustee. Attached to petitioner's motion of December 21, 1999 is K. Michael Goodall's attorney letter to Bank of America of November 11, 1999 (Exhibit B). A second letter was sent out on November 17, 1999, and Bank of America has refused to resign. A copy of that letter is attached as Exhibit C to petitioner's motion of December 21, 1999.

5. The Trust is for the benefit of the beneficiaries and not for the benefit of the Trustee. The sole income beneficiary has requested the Bank of America to resign. The remainder beneficiaries have no opposition. Bank of America's refusal to resign accordingly is troubling in light of the wishes of the beneficiaries of the Trust.

6. The nominated successor-trustee is Estate Minders, principal Karen Anderson. Estate Minders and Karen Anderson is well known to this court as an experienced and well regarded professional trustee. Ms. Anderson herself has extensive experience in the trust field, working at the Trust Department of Crocker Bank in Oakland, Trust Department of California Canadian Bank and head of Barclay's Personal Trust Department. Estate Minders, Inc., has been in existence since 1987. If for any reason the court believes that a corporate trustee is to be preferred, then petitioner nominates Union Bank

of California, N.A. Prior to the hearing on these issues, the Consent To Act As Trustee will be filed by each of the trustees.

WHEREFORE, petitioner prays as follows:

1. That Bank of America be removed as successor-trustee.

2. That Karen Anderson of Estate Minders be appointed as successor-trustee; or in the alternate, that Union Bank of California N.A. be appointed as successor-trustee.

3. The Bank of America be ordered to turn over to the successor-trustee all assets in its possession and account for the same.

4. Such other and further relief as the court deems proper.

Dated: December 19, 1999

ROBERT J. ROTHMAN,
A PROFESSIONAL CORPORATION

By: ______________________
ROBERT J. ROTHMAN
Attorney for Petitioner
K. Michael Goodall

goodall\Pet.Removal

VERIFICATION

I, the undersigned, declare:

I, K. MICHAEL GOODALL, am the petitioner of the estate. This document is true of my own knowledge, except as to the matters that are stated in it as to information and belief, and as to those matters I believe them to be true.

I declare under penalty of perjury under the laws of the State of California that the foregoing is true and correct.

Executed on this 12-19-99 day of December 1999 at San Rafael, California.

Dated: December 19, 1999 K. Michael Goodall
K. MICHAEL GOODALL

Goodall\Verif

PROOF OF SERVICE

I, Julie McGuire, declare as follows:

I am employed in San Francisco County, San Francisco, California. I am over the age of eighteen years and not a party to this action. My business address is MANATT, PHELPS & PHILLIPS, LLP, One Embarcadero Center, 30th Floor, San Francisco, California 94111. On August 19, 2011, I served the within:

PETITIONER BANK OF AMERICA, N.A.'S REPLY IN SUPPORT OF PETITION FOR DETERMINATION OF THE BENEFICIARIES TO WHOM TRUST PROPERTY SHALL PASS UPON TERMINATION OF TRUST

on the interested parties in this action addressed as follows:

Please see attached Service List

☒ **(BY MAIL)** By placing such document(s) in a sealed envelope, with postage thereon fully prepaid for first class mail, for collection and mailing at Manatt, Phelps & Phillips, LLP, San Francisco, California following ordinary business practice. I am readily familiar with the practice at Manatt, Phelps & Phillips, LLP for collection and processing of correspondence for mailing with the United States Postal Service, said practice being that in the ordinary course of business, correspondence is deposited in the United States Postal Service the same day as it is placed for collection.

☒ **(BY ELECTRONIC MAIL)** By transmitting such document(s) electronically from my e-mail address, JMcGuire@manatt.com at Manatt, Phelps & Phillips, LLP, San Francisco, California, to the person(s) at the electronic mail addresses listed above. The transmission was reported as complete and without error.

I declare under penalty of perjury under the laws of the State of California that the foregoing is true and correct and that this declaration was executed on August 19, 2011, at San Francisco, California.

Julie McGuire

300682126.1

Service List

Name	Address	Relationship
Samuel H. Sloan (Adult) (via U.S. and Email - samhsloan@gmail.com)	461 Peachstone Terrace San Rafael, CA 94903	Administrator of the Estate of Kenneth Michael Goodall
Julia Bentley Lemons (Adult)	Apt. 308 12800 Marion Lane W Minnetonka, MN 55305-1368	Surviving Sibling of Rachel Goodall; Heir of Rachel Goodall
Robert Bentley (Adult)	Bradford Village #504 906 N Boulevard Street Edmond, OK 73030	Surviving Sibling of Rachel Goodall; Heir of Rachel Goodall
Helen Beth Bentley Perry (Adult)	7926 Praver Drive W Jacksonville, FL 32217	Surviving Sibling of Rachel Goodall; Heir of Rachel Goodall
Glenda Fern Bentley Zinar (Adult)	4536 Chatman Street The Colony, TX 75056	Heir of Rachel Goodall
Beverly Gale Bentley Young (Adult)	2316 Trenton McKinney, TX 75070	Heir of Rachel Goodall
Vickie Bentley Hankins (Adult)	14580 NE 6th Choctaw, OK 73020	Heir of Rachel Goodall
Jeffrey Bentley (Adult)	4701 N Douglas Boulevard Spencer, OK 73084	Heir of Rachel Goodall
Chad Everett Bentley (Adult)	1609 Teepee Trail Kingsland, TX 78639	Heir of Rachel Goodall
Jeanette Goodall Phillips (Adult)	152 S 11th Street Salina, Kansas 67401	Heir of Kenneth Goodall
Kristin Kane (Adult)	University of California, Berkeley College of Engineering College Relations 208 McLaughlin Hall #1722 Berkeley, CA 94720-1722	Potential Heir
Guide Dogs for the Blind	Mr. Thomas Horton, Planned Giving Director Guide Dogs for the Blind, Inc. 350 Los Ranchitos Road San Rafael, CA 94903	Potential Beneficiary

John L. McDonnell, Jr., Esq. Reed Smith, LLP (via U.S. and Email - jmcdonnell@reedsmith.com)	1999 Harrison Street Suite 2400 Oakland, CA 94612-3572	Counsel for Guide Dogs for the Blind, Inc.
Sam Ware, Esq. Attorney at Law (via U.S. and Email - sam@samware.us.com)	700 Larkspur Landing Circle, #199 Larkspur, CA 94939	Counsel for Samuel H. Sloan

James R. Hastings (SBN 079066)
J. R. HASTINGS LAW CORPORATION
1003 Third Street
San Rafael, CA 94901-3107
(415) 459-6635 (tel)
(415) 459-6756 (fax)

Attorney for ROY HOPPE and
FRANK THORNALLY

FILED
SUPERIOR COURT
COUNTY OF SAN FRANCISCO

2011 AUG 19 AM 11:57

CLERK OF THE COURT
BY: [signature]
DEPUTY CLERK

FILED BY FAX

SUPERIOR COURT OF CALIFORNIA

COUNTY OF SAN FRANCISCO

In the Matter of the Trust for Michael created under the Goodall Trust dated September 12, 1990.	CASE NO. PTR-99-273030 **DECLARATION OF JAMES R. HASTINGS FAMILY AND ESTATE PLANNING ATTORNEY FOR THE GOODALLS** Hearing: August 22, 2011 Time: 9:00 a.m. Dept.: Probate, Rm. 204

I, JAMES R. HASTINGS, declare as follows:

1. I am an attorney licensed to practice law in the States of California, Colorado, Nevada and the District of Columbia. I am the principal in the LAW OFFICE OF J.R. HASTINGS. Except as otherwise stated, I have personal knowledge of the matter stated herein, if called and sworn as a witness could and would testify.

2. I was the family and estate planning counsel of Kenneth F. Goodall, from on or about August of 1990 until his death on September 10, 1994. I was the family and estate planning counsel for Rachel A. Goodall from on or about August of 1990 until her death on June 7, 1999. I was the trust administration attorney for the Trust Department of the Bank of America from on or about July 19, 1999 through on or about December of 2000. I was the family and estate planning counsel for the son of

Kenneth F. Goodall and Rachel A. Goodall, K. Michael Goodall, from on or about July of 1999 until his death on October 5 of 2010. Regarding the Last Will of K. Michael Goodall, dated January 15, 2004, I was the estate attorney for the named executors Ray Hoppe and Frank Thornally from on or about October of 2010 until on or about January 2011.

3. I will present a chronology in this declaration, but before I do so I state that these are truths which may be pertinent to the issues before the court:

a. On their own volition, Kenneth F. Goodall and Rachel A. Goodall chose Guide Dogs for the Blind in San Rafael, California, as the residuary beneficiary of their estate. K. Michael Goodall understood he had no right to the residuary estate of Kenneth F. Goodall and Rachel A. Goodall, and he understood that he had no power to direct the residuary benefits of their estate.

b. I did not, nor has anyone in my employ, ever received or had an agreement with Guide Dogs for the Blind for any remuneration resulting from the fact that Kenneth F. Goodall and Rachel A. Goodall named Guide Dogs for the Blind as a residuary beneficiary. Further, there has not been nor is there any agreement for any remuneration in the past, in the present or in the future.

c. The operative document defining the distribution of the estate of Kenneth F. Goodall and the operative document defining the distribution of the estate of Rachel A. Goodall is the Declaration of the Goodall Trust dated August 24, 1994, an amended and restated declaration of the original trust dated September 12, 1990. Accordingly, this amended and restated declaration replaced in its entirety the declaration of September 12, 1990; however, the trust retains the original date, though it had been amended and restated.

4. I first met Kenneth F. Goodall on or about 1980 as I employed him to make door signs for my office. After his retirement as a Lieutenant Colonel in the United States Air Force, Kenneth F. Goodall established a sign making business out of his garage. Subsequently, I met Rachel A. Goodall, a homemaker. Mr. and Mrs. Goodall were very honorable, religious, good and wonderful people.

5. Kenneth F. Goodall and Rachel A. Goodall had one son, J. Michael Goodall, born approximately 1950. K. Michael Goodall was gifted in many ways, including being a chess master. Unfortunately, his parents found him subject to the undue influence of others, resulting in caution in their ultimate estate plan.

6. On or about August 1990, after employing Kenneth F. Goodall to make signs for me, Kenneth F. Goodall and Rachel A. Goodall visited me for estate planning advice and preparation. During the estate planning consultations with Mr. and Mrs. Goodall, they directed me as to their desires for the disposition of their estate. These desires were reflected in the document entitled the Goodall Trust, which was signed by Kenneth F. Goodall and Rachel A. Goodall, their signatures notarized by me, on September 12, 1990. Though the document speaks for itself, after the first death this declaration contemplated the estate being divided into two parts, one part for the survivor, a Survivor's Trust, and one part representing the deceased's estate, a Credit Shelter Trust. The document provided at paragraph 6.3(a) that the residuary beneficiary of both of those trusts would be K. Michael Goodall, if living, and if

not, paragraph 6.3(b) gave gifts to family members and the residual estate to Guide Dogs for the Blind.

7. On or about late July or early August of 1994, Kenneth F. Goodall and Rachel A. Goodall again visited me for advice and document preparation concerning their estate plan. During the discussions they told me of the changes they wished to make to their estate plan. Those changes were recorded in the amended and restated declaration of trust dated August 24, 1994, a document signed by them, of which I acted as the Notary Public. This document retained the division of the estate at the first death, creating a Survivor's Trust and a Bypass ("Credit Shelter") Trust. The document revised the gift in paragraph 6.3(a) from a direct gift to their son, K. Michael Goodall, to a gift of a lifetime trust for K. Michael Goodall, this trust memorialized in Section 6.5. As indicated in a separate declaration signed by me and filed in this court, the Goodalls intended the ultimate distribution of the Trust for Michael to be the residuary beneficiary named in 6.3(b), Guide Dogs for the Blind. (Please see the attached Exhibit A.)

8. At no time did I suggest that the Guide Dogs for the Blind as the residuary beneficiary for the Goodalls; instead, the selection of Guide Dogs for the Blind as residuary beneficiary was communicated to me by them.

9. At no time have I received any remuneration for the fact that the Guide Dogs for the Blind is named as a residuary beneficiary in the trust declarations for the Goodalls. Neither has my staff. There has not been, is not now and will not be in the future any agreement for

remuneration from the Guide Dogs for the Blind for assisting the Goodalls to name them in their trust documents.

10. Kenneth F. Goodall died on September 10, 1994. When he died the declaration of the Goodall Trust dated August 24, 1994 was the operative document used for the trust administration of his estate. Similarly, the Last Will of Kenneth F. Goodall dated August 24, 1994, was lodged with the Clerk of the Court of Marin County, the distribution of this Last Will being a pour-over to the Goodall Trust dated August 24, 1994. During the subsequent trust administration several investment accounts were transferred to the Bypass Trust of the Goodall Trust, and the remainder of the assets, including the family home at 461 Peachstone Terrace, San Rafael, California, remained in the Goodall Trust as the Survivor's Trust. A Trustee's Deed transferring 461 Peachstone Terrace to the Survivor's Trust of the Goodall Trust was signed on June 8, 1995 and recorded on September 11, 1995 by the Marin County Recorder on September 11, 1995, as Document No. 95-042772.

11. Rachel A. Goodall died on June 7, 1999. When she died the Declaration of the Goodall Trust dated August 24, 1994 was the operative document used for the trust administration of her estate. Similarly, the Last Will of Rachel A. Goodall dated August 24, 1994, was lodged with the Clerk of the Court of Marin County, the distribution of this Last Will being a pour-over to the Goodall Trust dated August 24, 1994.

12. During the trust administration of the Estate of Rachel A. Goodall all assets of the Bypass Trust and the Survivor's Trust were passed to Bank of America, as trustee, and placed into the Trust for Michael as directed by the Declaration of Trust dated August 24, 1994. As a part

of that distribution a Notice Regarding Real Property, Affidavit of Death of Trustee and Acceptance of Office of Successor Trustee dated July 15, 1999, was recorded by the Marin County Recorder on October 26 of 2000. This document transferred the trusteeship and the ownership of 461 Peachstone Terrace, San Rafael, California, to the Bank of America Trust Department.

13. On or about July of 1999 K. Michael Goodall visited me for advice and documents concerning his estate plan. During that visit K. Michael Goodall informed me that he had no children, had not had any marriages and that his assets included personal property, his automobile and a bank account. The primary operative documents for K. Michael Goodall's estate plan were the Advance Health Care Directive and the Power of Attorney for Asset Management, documents assisting him should he become incapacitated. A will was completed, though K. Michael Goodall understood he did not have any assets which would ever require a probate, to ensure personal property and his minimal bank account would be properly handled at his passing.

14. Subsequently, I handled several general matters for K. Michael Goodall, including questions concerning his debts, problems with his license through the Department of Motor Vehicles, questions concerning debt relief and transmission of his Advance Health Care Directive to medical authorities during emergencies. Subsequently, as well, K. Michael Goodall revisited me on or about December of 2003 or early January of 2004 and refreshed all of his documents, which were the Advance Health Care Directive, property power of attorney and Last Will. In the Last Will he named two friends, Roy Hoppe and Frank Thornally, as

initial executors, and Bank of America as the subsequent executor. During our discussions and at the signing of both of his Last Wills, I clearly understood that K. Michael Goodall understood he has no residuary interest or power of appointment in the estate of his parents as comprised of the Trust for Michael of the Goodall Trust, the trust managed by the Bank of America following the death of his mother.

I declare under penalty of perjury that the foregoing declaration is true and correct and I executed same on August 18, 2011 at San Rafael, California.

Dated: August 18, 2011

JAMES R. HASTINGS, Declarant

EXHIBIT A

MANATT, PHELPS & PHILLIPS, LLP
GARY D. ROTHSTEIN (Bar No. CA 143157)
SUZANNE C. FARLEY (Bar No. CA 256693)
One Embarcadero Center, 30th Floor
San Francisco, CA 94111
Telephone: (415) 291-7400
Facsimile: (415) 291-7474

Attorneys for Petitioner,
BANK OF AMERICA, N.A.

SUPERIOR COURT OF THE STATE OF CALIFORNIA

FOR THE COUNTY OF SAN FRANCISCO

In the Matter of the Trust for Michael created under the Goodall Trust dated January 19, 1999.	Case No. **DECLARATION IN SUPPORT OF PETITION FOR DETERMINATION OF THE BENEFICIARIES TO WHOM TRUST PROPERTY SHALL PASS UPON TERMINATION OF TRUST** Hearing Date: Time: Dept.:

I, James Raymond Hastings, hereby declare as follows:

1. I am an active member of the State Bar of California and the principal in the Law Offices of J. R. Hastings. Except as otherwise stated, I have personal knowledge of the matters stated herein, and if called and sworn as a witness could and would testify competently thereto.

2. Bank of America, N.A. has filed a Petition for Determination of the Beneficiaries to Whom Trust Property Shall Pass Upon Termination of Trust (the "Petition"), in this matter.

3. I was estate planning counsel for Kenneth F. Goodall ("Kenneth") and Rachel A. Goodall ("Rachel") in connection with the Goodall Trust. I was responsible for the drafting of the Amendment to Goodall Trust dated August 24, 1994, and the Second Amendment

to Goodall Trust dated January 19, 1999 (collectively, the "Amendments").

4. In connection with the preparation of the Amendments, I discussed with Kenneth and Rachel how they wanted to dispose of the Goodall Trust estate upon their deaths and the death of their only child, Michael. It was my understanding based on that discussion that Rachel and Kenneth intended the balance of the trust established for the benefit of Michael ("the Trust for Michael") remaining at Michael's death to be distributed pursuant to Section 6.3(d) of the Goodall Trust, as follows: twenty thousand dollars to each of Rachel's then-living brothers and sisters, and the remainder to Guide Dogs for the Blind of Marin. Section 6.3(e) of the Goodall Trust, which states that the assets should be distributed one-half to Kenneth's heirs and one-half to Rachel's heirs, was intended to apply only if upon Michael's death there were no beneficiaries to take under Section 6.3(d) of the Goodall Trust.

5. The Petition seeks an order to determine the proper beneficiaries of the Trust for Michael in light of Michael's death and the resulting termination of the Trust for Michael. I have reviewed said Petition and believe that the determination sought by the Petition accurately reflects the intentions of Kenneth and Rachel.

I declare under penalty of perjury under the Laws of the State of California that the foregoing is true and correct.

Executed at San Rafael, California, on January 10, ~~2010~~ xxx 2011.

By: ______________________
James Raymond Hastings

Manatt, Phelps & Phillips, LLP
Attorneys At Law
San Francisco

POS-050/EFS-050

ATTORNEY OR PARTY WITHOUT ATTORNEY (Name, State Bar number, and address):	FOR COURT USE ONLY
JAMES R. HASTINGS (SBN 079066) J.R. HASTINGS LAW CORPORATION 1003 THIRD STREET SAN RAFAEL, CA 94901-3107 TELEPHONE NO.: (415) 459-6635 FAX NO. (Optional): (415) 459-6756 E-MAIL ADDRESS (Optional): jrhastings@pacbell.net ATTORNEY FOR (Name): ROY HOPPE AND FRANK THORNALLY	
SUPERIOR COURT OF CALIFORNIA, COUNTY OF SAN FRANCISCO STREET ADDRESS: 400 McALLISTER STREET, RM 204 MAILING ADDRESS: CITY AND ZIP CODE: SAN FRANCISCO, CA 94102-4514 BRANCH NAME: PROBATE	
PLAINTIFF/PETITIONER: IN THE MATTER OF GOODALL TRUST	CASE NUMBER: PTR-99-273030
DEFENDANT/RESPONDENT:	JUDICIAL OFFICER:
PROOF OF ELECTRONIC SERVICE	DEPT.: PROBATE

1. I am at least 18 years old and **not a party to this action.**

   a. My residence or business address is *(specify)*:
   1003 THIRD STREET
   SAN RAFAEL, CA 94901-3107

   b. My electronic service address is *(specify)*:
   jrhastings@pacbell.net

2. I electronically served the following documents *(exact titles)*:
   DECLARATION OF JAMES R. HASTINGS FAMILY AND ESTATE PLANNING ATTORNEY FOR THE GOODALLS

   ☐ The documents served are listed in an attachment. *(Form POS-050(D)/EFS-050(D) may be used for this purpose.)*

3. I electronically served the documents listed in 2 as follows:

   a. Name of person served: SAM H. SLOAN
   On behalf of *(name or names of parties represented, if person served is an attorney)*:

   b. Electronic service address of person served: SAMHSLOAN@GMAIL.COM

   c. On *(date)*: AUGUST 19, 2011

   d. At *(time)*: 10:00 AM

   ☐ The documents listed in item 2 were served electronically on the persons and in the manner described in an attachment. *(Form POS-050(P)/EFS-050(P) may be used for this purpose.)*

Date: AUGUST 19, 2011

I declare under penalty of perjury under the laws of the State of California that the foregoing is true and correct.

RENEE MOORE ▶ Renee Moore

(TYPE OR PRINT NAME OF DECLARANT) (SIGNATURE OF DECLARANT)

Form Approved for Optional Use
Judicial Council of California
POS-050/EFS-050 [Rev. January 1, 2011]

PROOF OF ELECTRONIC SERVICE
(Proof of Service/Electronic Filing and Service)

Cal. Rules of Court, rule 2.251
www.courts.ca.gov

GOODALL

James R. Hastings, Esq. (SBN 079066)
J. R. HASTINGS LAW CORPORATION
1003 Third Street
San Rafael, CA 94901-3107
(415) 459-6635 (tel)
(415) 459-6756 (fax)

Attorney for
ROY HOPPE AND FRANK THORNALLY

SUPERIOR COURT OF CALIFORNIA

COUNTY OF SAN FRANCISCO

In The Matter of the Trust for Michael created Under the Goodall Trust dated January 19, 1999	CASE NO. PTR-99-273030 PROOF OF SERVICE

--SEE ATTACHED--

PROOF OF TRANSMISSION BY FAX

(California Rules of Court, rule 2.304)

In re the Matter of the Trust for Michael Created Under the Goodall Trust dated January 19, 1999

At the time of transmission, I was at least 18 years of age and not a party to this action. I am a resident of or employed in the county where the mailing occurred. My business address 1003 Third Street, San Rafael, CA 94901. On August 19, 2011 at 9:45am I transmitted the within

DECLARATION OF JAMES R. HASTINGS, FAMILY AND ESTATE PLANNING ATTORNEY FOR THE GOODALLS

on each person named below by fax machine, under California Rules of Court, rule 2.304. The fax machine I used complied with California Rules of Court, rule 2.301 and no error was reported by the machine. Under California Rules of Court, rule 2.304, I caused the machine to print a record of the transmission, a copy of which is attached to this declaration. enclosing a copy in an envelope addressed as shown below and depositing the sealed envelope with the United States Postal Service on **August 19, 2011**, at San Rafael, California:

GARY D. ROTHSTEIN, ESQ.
MANATT, PHELPS & PHILLIPS, LLP
ONE EMBARCADERO AVENUE, 30TH FLOOR
SAN FRANCISCO, CA 94111
FAX NO: (415) 291-7474

I declare under penalty of perjury under the laws of the State of California that the foregoing is true and correct.

Dated: **August 19, 2011**

Renee Moore

TRANSMIT CONFIRMATION REPORT

0503

NO.	:	003
RECEIVER	:	415 291 7474
TRANSMITTER	:	J. R. HASTINGS CORP.
DATE	:	AUG 19'11 9:43
DURATION	:	05'43
MODE	:	STD
PAGES	:	12
RESULT	:	OK

MINI-MINUTES FOR AUG-23-2011 9:00 AM FOR

Appearances: Gary Rothstein for Bank of America (Trustee). John McDonnell, Jr. for Guide Dogs. Sam Ware for and with Sam Sloan. James Hastings drafter of the Goodall Trust also present.

Mr. Ware stated that he has an executed Substitution of Attorney, and requested more time to look into the matter and have the opportunity to conduct discovery. The matter was continued to November 15, 2011 at 9:00 a.m., in Dept. 204 for status of a hearing on the Petition to Determine Beneficiaries.

Judge: Mary E. Wiss. Reporter: Diana Chen, CSR#11312. Clerk: Rosie Noguera. Bailiff: Deputy F. Smith.

MC-050

ATTORNEY OR PARTY WITHOUT ATTORNEY (Name, State Bar number, and address):
Sam Ware (105005)
700 Larkspur Landing Cir. #199
Larkspur CA 94939

TELEPHONE NO.: 415 464 4872 FAX NO. (Optional):
E-MAIL ADDRESS (Optional): sam@samware.us
ATTORNEY FOR (Name): Samuel Sloan

SUPERIOR COURT OF CALIFORNIA, COUNTY OF San Francisco
STREET ADDRESS: 400 MacAllister Street
MAILING ADDRESS:
CITY AND ZIP CODE: San Francisco CA 94102
BRANCH NAME:

CASE NAME:
In Matter of Goodall Trust

FOR COURT USE ONLY

FILED
San Francisco County Superior Court
NOV 1 0 2011
CLERK OF THE COURT
BY: Norma Rivera

SUBSTITUTION OF ATTORNEY—CIVIL
(Without Court Order)

CASE NUMBER:
PTR 99 273030

THE COURT AND ALL PARTIES ARE NOTIFIED THAT (name): Samuel Sloan makes the following substitution:

1. **Former legal representative** [✓] Party represented self [ ] Attorney (name):
2. **New legal representative** [ ] Party is representing self* [✓] Attorney
   a. Name: Sam Ware b. State Bar No. (if applicable): 105005
   c. Address (number, street, city, ZIP, and law firm name, if applicable):
   700 Larkspur Landing Cir. #199, Larkspur CA 94939

BY FAX

   d. Telephone No. (include area code): 415 464 4872
3. The party making this substitution is a [ ] plaintiff [ ] defendant [ ] petitioner [✓] respondent [ ] other (specify):

***NOTICE TO PARTIES APPLYING TO REPRESENT THEMSELVES**

- Guardian
- Conservator
- Trustee
- Personal Representative
- Probate fiduciary
- Corporation
- Guardian ad litem
- Unincorporated association

If you are applying as one of the parties on this list, you may NOT act as your own attorney in most cases. Use this form to substitute one attorney for another attorney. SEEK LEGAL ADVICE BEFORE APPLYING TO REPRESENT YOURSELF.

NOTICE TO PARTIES WITHOUT ATTORNEYS
A party representing himself or herself may wish to seek legal assistance. Failure to take timely and appropriate action in this case may result in serious legal consequences.

4. I consent to this substitution
   Date: 8/23/2011
   Samuel Sloan (TYPE OR PRINT NAME) ▶ Samuel H Sloan (SIGNATURE OF PARTY)

5. [✓] I consent to this substitution
   Date: 8/23/2011
   Samuel Sloan (TYPE OR PRINT NAME) ▶ Samuel H Sloan (SIGNATURE OF FORMER ATTORNEY)

6. [✓] I consent to this substitution.
   Date: 8/23/2011
   Sam Ware (TYPE OR PRINT NAME) ▶ (SIGNATURE OF NEW ATTORNEY)

(See reverse for proof of service by mail)

PROOF OF SERVICE

I certify and declare as follows:

I am over the age of 18 years, not a party to this action. My business address is 700 Larkspur Landing Circle #199, Larkspur, CA 94939. I am readily familiar with the business practices of my firm for the collection, processing and service of items with the United States Postal Service, express service providers (same day messenger and overnight) and facsimile transmission.

On the date set forth below, I served the foregoing documents described as substitution of attorneys and notice of deposition on the parties in this action as follows:

__X__: BY FIRST CLASS MAIL — By placing [ ] the original [X] a true and correct copy thereof in each sealed envelope addressed as indicated below. Said sealed envelopes, with postage fully prepaid, were deposited with the United States Postal Service in San Francisco, California this same day in the ordinary course of business.

____: BY FEDERAL EXPRESS — By placing [ ] the original [ ] a true and correct copy thereof in each sealed envelope addressed as indicated below. Said envelopes were deposited for collection and processing by Federal Express, Priority Overnight Service, in San Francisco, California.

____: BY PERSONAL SERVICE: By placing [ ] the original [x] a true and correct copy thereof in each sealed envelope addressed as indicated below and causing said envelopes to be delivered by hand, by our firm's messenger, to the offices of the addressees indicated below.

____: BY FACSIMILE TRANSMISSION — The foregoing document was transmitted between 9:00 a.m. and 5:00 p.m. to the fax number indicated below each address.

____: BY EMAIL TRANSMISSION — The foregoing document was transmitted between 9:00 a.m. and 5:00 p.m. to the e-mail address indicated below.

See attached service list

I declare under penalty of perjury under the laws of the State of California that the foregoing statements are true and correct.

Executed October 3, 2011

Service List

Gary D. Rothstein
Manatt, Phelps & Phillips, LLP
One Embarcadero Center, 30th Floor
San Francisco CA 94111

John L McDonnell
Reed Smith
1999 Harrison St. # 2400
Oakland, CA 94612

Julia Bentley Lemons
Apt. 308
12800 Marion Lane W
Minnetonka, MN 55305-1368

Robert Bentley
Bradford Village #504
906 N Boulevard Street
Edmond, OK 73030

Helen Beth Bentley Perry
7926 Praver Drive W
Jacksonville, FL 32217

Clenda Fern Bentley Zinar
4536 Chatman Street
The Colony, TX 75056

Beverly Gale Bentley Young
2316 Trenton
McKinney, TX 75070

Vickie Bentley Hankins
14580 NE 6th
Choctaw, OK 73020

Jeffrey Bentley
4701 N Douglas Boulevard
Spencer, OK 73084

Chad Everett Bentley
1609 Teepee Trail
Kingsland, TX 78639

Jeanette Goodall Phillips
152 S 11th Street
Salina, Kansas 67401

Kristin Kane
University of California
Berkeley College of Engineering
College Relations
208 Mclaughlin Hall #1722
Berkeley, CA 9472A-1722

Mr. Thomas Horton
Guide Dogs for the Blind, Inc.
350 Los Ranchitos Road
San Rafael, CA 94903

SAM WARE (State Bar No. 105005)
700 Larkspur Landing Circle, #199
Larkspur, CA 94939
Telephone 415-464-4872
E-mail sam@samware.us
Attorney for Sam Sloan, administrator of Estate of Michael Goodall

FILED
Superior Court of California
County of San Francisco
DEC 14 2011
CLERK OF THE COURT
BY: [signature] Deputy Clerk

SUPERIOR COURT OF THE STATE OF CALIFORNIA

COUNTY OF SAN FRANCISCO

In the Matter of the Trust for Michael created under the Goodall Trust dated September 12, 1990	Case No. PTR-99-273030 Separate Statement in Support of Motion to Compel Production of Documents and Further Deposition Hearing Date: JAN. 12, 2012 Time: 2:15 P.M. Department: 204 JUDGE: PETER J. BUSCH

The Estate of Michael submits the following Separate Statement in support of its motion to compel:

Subpoenaed Documents Request 1: Any and all writings, as defined in Evidence Code §250, which include e-mails, which in any way relate to … Kenneth F Goodall.

Objection to the Discovery Request: James R Hasting objects to Demand Number 1 on the grounds that the category of documents sought fails to specifically describe each individual item and fails to reasonably particularized the category of items to be produced as required by CCP Section 2020.510(a)(2). He further objects to the extent that this request seeks documents protected by the attorney-client privilege and/or work product doctrine and that the request as written is overbroad, vague and ambiguous, and thus incomprehensible.

Argument: At his deposition Hastings testified that he has only four files: the Goodall estate planning file, the Kenneth Goodall's trust administration file, the Rachel Goodall's trust administration file, and the Michael Goodall will file.

It is submitted that there is nothing uncertain or overbroad about what was requested in the deposition subpoena. Hastings has only four files related to the Goodalls and the Estate of Michael asked that he bring those files to his deposition and he did not.

With regard to the objections of lawyer-client privilege and/or attorney work product doctrine, Hastings objections are not specifically related to any documents so the most that can be argued this point is, first, that the lawyer-client privilege is not applicable to these proceedings pursuant to Evidence Code §975 and 960.

> There is no privilege under this article as to a communication relevant to an issue between parties all of whom claim through a deceased client, regardless of whether the claims are by testate or intestate succession, nonprobate transfer, or inter vivos transaction. Evidence Code §957

> There is no privilege under this article as to a communication relevant to an issue concerning the intention of a client, now deceased, with respect to a deed of conveyance, will, or other writing, executed by the client, purporting to affect an interest in property. Evidence Code §960

Further, with regard to the lawyer-client privilege claim, and also with regard to the attorney work product claim, Hastings has waived such privileges by the contents of the declaration is filed in this action.

On the subject of waiver as to the lawyer-client privilege claim, Evidence Code §912 provides in pertinent part:

> (a) Except as otherwise provided in this section, the right of any person to claim the privilege provided by Section 954 (lawyer-client privilege)… is waived with respect to a communication protected by the privilege if any holder of the privilege, without coercion, has disclosed a significant part of the communication… Evidence Code §912.

With regard to the attorney work product claim, this principle of waiver has been applied by extension under case law as well. *Wells Fargo Bank v Superior Court* (2000) 22 Cal 4th 201, 214.

The Estate of Michael presented these authorities to Hastings lawyer prior to Hastings deposition but to no avail. (Sam Ware Declaration, Exhibit E) but to no avail.

The subpoenaed documents should be ordered produced and Hastings ordered to submit to a further deposition so that he may be effectively cross examined on these documents and on the contents of this declaration which describes events going back 20 years.

Subpoenaed Documents Request 2: Any and all writings, as defined in Evidence Code §250, which include e-mails, which in any way relate to … Rachel A Goodall.

Objection to the Discovery Request: James R Hasting objects to Demand Number 1 on the grounds that the category of documents sought fails to specifically describe each individual item and fails to reasonably particularized the category of items to be produced as required by CCP Section 2020.510(a)(2). He further objects to the extent that this request seeks documents protected by the attorney-client privilege and/or work product doctrine and that the request as written is overbroad, vague and ambiguous, and thus incomprehensible.

Argument: At his deposition Hastings testified that he has only four files: the Goodall estate planning file, the Kenneth Goodall's trust administration file, the Rachel Goodall's trust administration file, and the Michael Goodall will file.

It is submitted that there is nothing uncertain or overbroad about what was requested in the deposition subpoena. Hastings has only four files related to the Goodalls and the Estate of Michael asked that he bring those files to his deposition and he did not.

With regard to the objections of lawyer-client privilege and/or attorney work product doctrine, Hastings objections are not specifically related to any documents so the most that can be argued this point is, first, that the lawyer-client privilege is not applicable to these proceedings pursuant to Evidence Code §975 and 960.

> There is no privilege under this article as to a communication relevant to an issue between parties all of whom claim through a deceased client, regardless of whether the claims are by testate or intestate succession, nonprobate transfer, or inter vivos transaction. Evidence Code §957

> There is no privilege under this article as to a communication relevant to an issue concerning the intention of a client, now deceased, with respect to a deed of conveyance, will, or other writing, executed by the client, purporting to affect an interest in property. Evidence Code §960

Further, with regard to the lawyer-client privilege claim, and also with regard to the attorney work product claim, Hastings has waived such privileges by the contents of the declaration is filed in this action.

On the subject of waiver as to the lawyer-client privilege claim, Evidence Code §912 provides in pertinent part:

> (a) Except as otherwise provided in this section, the right of any person to claim the privilege provided by Section 954 (lawyer-client privilege)… is waived with respect to a communication protected by the privilege if any holder of the privilege, without coercion, has disclosed a significant part of the communication… Evidence Code §912.

With regard to the attorney work product claim, this principle of waiver has been applied by extension under case law as well. *Wells Fargo Bank v Superior Court* (2000) 22 Cal 4th 201, 214.

The Estate of Michael presented these authorities to Hastings lawyer prior to Hastings deposition but to no avail. (Sam Ware Declaration, Exhibit E) but to no avail.

The subpoenaed documents should be ordered produced and Hastings ordered to submit to a further deposition so that he may be effectively cross examined on these documents and on the contents of this declaration which describes events going back 20 years.

Subpoenaed Documents Request 3: Any and all writings, as defined in Evidence Code §250, which include e-mails, which in any way relate to … K Michael Goodall.

Objection to the Discovery Request: James R Hasting objects to Demand Number 1 on the grounds that the category of documents sought fails to specifically describe each individual item and fails to reasonably particularized the category of items to be produced as required by CCP Section 2020.510(a)(2). He further objects to the extent that this request seeks documents protected by the attorney-client privilege and/or work product doctrine and that the request as written is overbroad, vague and ambiguous, and thus incomprehensible.

Argument: At his deposition Hastings testified that he has only four files: the Goodall estate planning file, the Kenneth Goodall's trust administration file, the Rachel Goodall's trust administration file, and the Michael Goodall will file.

It is submitted that there is nothing uncertain or overbroad about what was requested in the deposition subpoena. Hastings has only four files related to the Goodalls and the Estate of Michael asked that he bring those files to his deposition and he did not.

With regard to the objections of lawyer-client privilege and/or attorney work product doctrine, Hastings objections are not specifically related to any documents so the most that can be argued this point is, first, that the lawyer-client privilege is not applicable to these proceedings pursuant to Evidence Code §975 and 960.

> There is no privilege under this article as to a communication relevant to an issue between parties all of whom claim through a deceased client, regardless of whether the claims are by testate or intestate succession, nonprobate transfer, or inter vivos transaction. Evidence Code §957

> There is no privilege under this article as to a communication relevant to an issue concerning the intention of a client, now deceased, with respect to a deed of conveyance, will, or other writing, executed by the client, purporting to affect an interest in property. Evidence Code §960

Further, with regard to the lawyer-client privilege claim, and also with regard to the attorney work product claim, Hastings has waived such privileges by the contents of the declaration is filed in this action.

On the subject of waiver as to the lawyer-client privilege claim, Evidence Code §912 provides in pertinent part:

> (a) Except as otherwise provided in this section, the right of any person to claim the privilege provided by Section 954 (lawyer-client privilege)… is waived with respect to a communication protected by the privilege

> if any holder of the privilege, without coercion, has disclosed a significant part of the communication… Evidence Code §912.

With regard to the attorney work product claim, this principle of waiver has been applied by extension under case law as well. *Wells Fargo Bank v Superior Court* (2000) 22 Cal 4th 201, 214.

The Estate of Michael presented these authorities to Hastings lawyer prior to Hastings deposition but to no avail. (Sam Ware Declaration, Exhibit E) but to no avail.

The subpoenaed documents should be ordered produced and Hastings ordered to submit to a further deposition so that he may be effectively cross examined on these documents and on the contents of this declaration which describes events going back 20 years.

Additionally, the lawyer-client privilege and attorney work product doctrine have no application to Michael Goodall's file, because, after all, that is the property of his estate, and he is obliged to produce it pursuant to the Rules of Professional Conduct, Rule 3-700 (D).

Date: December 10, 2011

Attorneys for Estate of Michael

PROOF OF SERVICE

I certify and declare as follows:

I am over the age of 18 years, not a party to this action. My business address is 700 Larkspur Landing Circle #199, Larkspur, CA 94939. I am readily familiar with the business practices of my firm for the collection, processing and service of items with the United States Postal Service, express service providers (same day messenger and overnight) and facsimile transmission.

On the date set forth below, I served the foregoing documents described as a motion to compel and separate statement on the parties who have appeared in this action as follows:

__X__: BY FIRST CLASS MAIL — By placing [ ] the original [X] a true and correct copy thereof in each sealed envelope addressed as indicated below. Said sealed envelopes, with postage fully prepaid, were deposited with the United States Postal Service in San Francisco, California this same day in the ordinary course of business.

____: BY FEDERAL EXPRESS — By placing [ ] the original [ ] a true and correct copy thereof in each sealed envelope addressed as indicated below. Said envelopes were deposited for collection and processing by Federal Express, Priority Overnight Service, in San Francisco, California.

____: BY PERSONAL SERVICE: By placing [ ] the original [x] a true and correct copy thereof in each sealed envelope addressed as indicated below and causing said envelopes to be delivered by hand, by our firm's messenger, to the offices of the addressees indicated below.

____: BY FACSIMILE TRANSMISSION — The foregoing document was transmitted between 9:00 a.m. and 5:00 p.m. to the fax number indicated below each address.

____: BY EMAIL TRANSMISSION — The foregoing document was transmitted between 9:00 a.m. and 5:00 p.m. to the e-mail address indicated below.

Gary D. Rothstein
Manatt, Phelps & Phillips, LLP
One Embarcadero Center, 30th Floor
San Francisco CA 94111

John L McDonnell
Reed Smith
1999 Harrison St. # 2400
Oakland, CA 94612

Don Lesser
1010 B St. Suite 350
San Rafael, CA 94901

I declare under penalty of perjury under the laws of the State of California that the foregoing statements are true and correct.

Executed December 14, 2011

SAM WARE (State Bar No. 105005)
700 Larkspur Landing Circle, #199
Larkspur, CA 94939

Telephone 415-464-4872

E-mail sam@samware.us

Attorney for Sam Sloan, administrator of Estate of Michael Goodall

FILED
Superior Court of California
County of San Francisco
DEC 14 2011
CLERK OF THE COURT
BY: [signature] Deputy Clerk

SUPERIOR COURT OF THE STATE OF CALIFORNIA

COUNTY OF SAN FRANCISCO

In the Matter of the Trust for Michael created under the Goodall Trust dated September 12, 1990	Case No. PTR-99-273030 Notice of Motion and Motion to Compel Production of Documents and Further Deposition and Declaration of Sam Ware in Support Thereof and Memorandum of Points and Authorities Hearing Date: JAN. 12, 2012 Time: 2:15 P.M. Department: 204 JUDGE: PETER J. BUSCH

OK TO SET R.R.

To all parties and their attorneys of record into this honorable court,

Please take notice that on the date time and in the Department described above Respondent Sam Sloan on behalf of the Estate of Michael Goodall will bring a motion to compel production of documents from and a further deposition of James Hastings, a nonparty deponent, because he failed to produce documents as required by subpoena at his deposition held

November 14, 2011 (transcribed 12/2/2011), which documents are reasonably calculated to lead to the discovery of admissible evidence and, further, that it is necessary once those files are produced to re-depose Mr. Hastings in order that the Estate of Michael may conduct a meaningful cross-examination of Hastings on the subjects contained in the declaration which he filed in this action on or about August 18, 2011.

The grounds for said motion are that the deponent was served with a lawful subpoena (Exhibit A hereto), deponent's objections (Exhibit B hereto) were unfounded (see Separate Statement filed herewith) and his failure to produce documents at the deposition was without reasonable justification, supporting this motion pursuant to Code of Civil Procedure §2025.480 (a). The motion will be based upon this Notice of Motion and Motion, the attached Declaration of Sam Ware, the Separate Statement filed herewith and any and all other evidence and argument which may be presented at a hearing.

Date: December 10, 2011

Attorneys for Sam Sloan

MEMORANDUM OF POINTS AND AUTHORITIES

Underlying Facts

In this present action, the trustee of the Goodall Trust, Bank of America, seeks a declaration from the Court as to the proper residual beneficiary to whom it should distribute the assets of the Goodall Trust. The Trust was created first created by Kenneth and Rachel Goodall in 1990, and Michael Goodall was the residual beneficiary, but then the Trust was allegedly amended a few weeks before Kenneth Goodall's death in 1994.

The Estate of Michael Goodall is represented by Sam Sloan, the administrator of the Estate of Michael pending in Marin County, who was the son of Kenneth and Rachel Goodall.

The Estate of Michael contends that the Estate of Michael is the rightful residual beneficiary of the Goodall Trust and that the 1994 amendment did not change that.

James R Hastings was the attorney who drafted the Goodall trust and the amendments to that trust and he has filed a declaration with regard to the intentions of Kenneth Goodall and Rachel Goodall in creating and amending the trust and on numerous other matters as well. (A copy of that declaration is attached hereto as Exhibit C for the Court's ready reference) Hastings says that Kenneth and Rachel Goodall intended to change the trust in 1994 to make the residual beneficiary to Guide Dogs for the Blind, which the Estate of Michael disputes.

The Estate of Michael served Hastings with the subpoena attached hereto as Exhibit A, demanding that Hastings give a deposition and bring with them to that deposition any and all files relating to the Goodalls. (The deposition was originally noticed for October 21, 2011, and was served September 27, 2007, but it was continued several times for the convenience of Mr. Hastings and his attorney).

At his deposition Hastings testified that he had only four files related to the Goodalls (the Goodall estate planning file, the Kenneth Goodall trust administration file, the Rachel Goodall trust administration file and the Michael Goodall will file) but Hastings did not bring any of these files to his deposition (see declaration of Sam Ware and the deposition transcript, Exhibit D hereto). With regard to perhaps most important file, the estate planning file for Kenneth and Rachel Goodall, Hastings testified that he could not find it prior to his deposition.

The Applicable Law

A motion to compel can be used to force a recalcitrant nonparty witness to attend, testify at, or produce documents or tangible things at a deposition. CCP §2025.480(a); *Sears Roebuck and Company Versus National Fire Insurance Company* (2005) 131 Cal App 4th 1342, 1351. If the witness fails to produce documents and/or testify as to certain matters, the deposing party may complete the examination on other matters and then adjourned the deposition to move to compel production of documents and/or answer further questions without waiving its rights to seek further discovery. CCP §2025.460 (d).

The moving party must show that the discovery sought is within the scope of discovery, CCP §2025.480 (b) (i.e. that it is relevant to the subject matter of the action or reasonably calculated to lead to the discovery of admissible evidence. CCP §2017.010); that it has satisfied the meet and confer requirement, CCP §2025.480 (b) and it must include a Separate Statement of the discovery requests in dispute unless no response was given. California Rule Court, Rule 3.1345

The motion may be served on the nonparty deponent by mail if the nonparty deponent agreed on the deposition record to accept service by mail. California Rules of Court, Rule 3.1346

Argument

The Estate of Michael's discovery requests seeks

information that is relevant to the matter of this action and reasonably calculated to lead to discovery of admissible evidence. Hastings has submitted a declaration as to the intent of the Goodall pursuant to Probate Code §21102. Any and all files within Hastings possession created in the drafting of the trust and/or in the administration of the trust are reasonably likely to contain information relevant to the subject matter of the Goodalls' intent. Furthermore having these files available at his deposition is critical to a fair and effective cross-examination of Hastings on the subjects described in the declaration he has filed in this action which go back 20 years. A review of Hasting's declaration makes clear *in its specificity* that he must have referred to those files in the creation on his August 2011 declaration filed herein (Exhibit C), and even if he did not, he should have. The Estate of Michael should have the same files available to use in its cross examination of Hastings.

Hastings objections (Exhibit B) are addressed in the accompanying Separate Statement, and they should be overruled for the reasons stated therein.

With regard to Hastings claim that he could not find the Goodall Estate Planning File in order to bring it to his deposition, the Court should order that he go back and conduct an exhaustive search in order to find that file. Clearly, he had the file to refer not long ago in August 2011 when he filed his declaration and now is unable to find when the Estate of Michael seeks to cross-examine him on the contents of that file and his declaration, is highly suspect.

Finally, once the files are ordered produced, Hastings should submit to a further examination on the contents of those files as they relate to the Goodalls' intent the other matters raise in his declaration. Obviously, Hasting's involvement happened more than 20 years ago, and without the files, Hastings recollection cannot be trusted.

In short, either the Estate of Michael should have the benefit of the cross-examination of Hastings using his files or the Court should disregard his declaration altogether.

The Estate of Michael has met and conferred with Hastings on this discovery as described in the declaration of Sam Ware and Exhibits E, F and G hereto.

Hastings counsel agreed to accept service of this motion by mail as described in the attached Declaration of Sam Ware.

Date: December 8, 2011

Attorneys for Estate of Michael

DECLARATION OF SAM WARE

Sam Ware declares:

1. I am the attorney for Sam Sloan as the duly appointed administrator of the *Estate of Michael Goodall* pending in Marin County, action number PR 01100596;

2. Attached hereto as Exhibit A is a true and correct copy of the subpoena which was served upon James R Hastings;

3. Attached hereto as Exhibit B is a true and correct copy of Hasting's objections;

4. Attached hereto as Exhibit C is a true and correct copy of the Declaration filed by James Hastings in this action on or about August 18, 2011:

5. Attached hereto as Exhibit D is a true and correct copy of the mini script of the deposition of James Hastings taken November 14, 2011;

6. Attached hereto as Exhibit E is a true and correct copy of the letter I wrote to Hasting's counsel Don Lesser on November 11, 2011 prior to the deposition with regard to Hastings objections to producing the documents described in the subpoena;

7. Attached hereto as Exhibit F is a true and correct copy of the letter I sent to Hasting's counsel on December 2, 2011 with regard to bring this motion and attached hereto as Exhibit G a copy of his e-mail reply.

8. At the deposition of Hastings, his counsel Don Lesser agreed to accept service of this motion by mail (see Deposition, Exhibit D hereto 66:9-19).

9. At his deposition, Hastings testified that he has had four files related to the Goodalls, the estate planning file for Kenneth and Rachel Goodall, the trust administration file for Kenneth Goodall, the trust administration Rachel Goodall, and the will file for Michael Goodall, and he brought none of them. (See Exhibit D hereto)

I declare under penalty of perjury under the laws of the state of California that the foregoing is true and correct and that this declaration was executed on December 10, 2011

SUBP-020

ATTORNEY OR PARTY WITHOUT ATTORNEY (Name, State Bar number, and address):	FOR COURT USE ONLY
Sam Ware (105005) 700 Larkspur Landing Cir. # 199 Larkspur CA 94939 TELEPHONE NO.: 415 464 4872 FAX NO. (Optional): E-MAIL ADDRESS (Optional): ATTORNEY FOR (Name): Respondent Sam Sloan	
SUPERIOR COURT OF CALIFORNIA, COUNTY OF San Francisco STREET ADDRESS: 400 MacAllister St MAILING ADDRESS: CITY AND ZIP CODE: San Francisco CA 94102 BRANCH NAME:	EXHIBIT 1 Deponent Hastings Date 11-14-11 Rptr. CK WWW.DEPOBOOK.COM (3 pgs)
PLAINTIFF/PETITIONER: In the Matter of the Goodall Trust DEFENDANT/RESPONDENT:	
DEPOSITION SUBPOENA FOR PERSONAL APPEARANCE AND PRODUCTION OF DOCUMENTS AND THINGS	CASE NUMBER: PTR 99 273030

THE PEOPLE OF THE STATE OF CALIFORNIA, TO *(name, address, and telephone number of deponent, if known)*:
James R Hastings, 1003 Third Street, San Rafael CA 94901 459 6635

1. **YOU ARE ORDERED TO APPEAR IN PERSON TO TESTIFY AS A WITNESS in this action at the following date, time, and place:**

Date: 10/21/2011 Time: 10:00 am Address: 700 Larkspur Landing Cir. #199 Larkspur CA 94939

a. [ ] As a deponent who is not a natural person, you are ordered to designate one or more persons to testify on your behalf as to the matters described in item 4. (Code Civ. Proc., § 2025.230.)

b. [✓] You are ordered to produce the documents and things described in item 3.

c. [✓] This deposition will be recorded stenographically [ ] through the instant visual display of testimony and by [ ] audiotape [ ] videotape.

d. [ ] This videotape deposition is intended for possible use at trial under Code of Civil Procedure section 2025.620(d).

2. The personal attendance of the custodian or other qualified witness and the production of the original records are required by this subpoena. The procedure authorized by Evidence Code sections 1560(b), 1561, and 1562 will not be deemed sufficient compliance with this subpoena.

3. The documents and things to be produced and any testing or sampling being sought are described as follows:

described in attachment

[✓] Continued on Attachment 3.

4. If the witness is a representative of a business or other entity, the matters upon which the witness is to be examined are described as follows:

[ ] Continued on Attachment 4.

5. **IF YOU HAVE BEEN SERVED WITH THIS SUBPOENA AS A CUSTODIAN OF CONSUMER OR EMPLOYEE RECORDS UNDER CODE OF CIVIL PROCEDURE SECTION 1985.3 OR 1985.6 AND A MOTION TO QUASH OR AN OBJECTION HAS BEEN SERVED ON YOU, A COURT ORDER OR AGREEMENT OF THE PARTIES, WITNESSES, AND CONSUMER OR EMPLOYEE AFFECTED MUST BE OBTAINED BEFORE YOU ARE REQUIRED TO PRODUCE CONSUMER OR EMPLOYEE RECORDS.**

6. *At the deposition, you will be asked questions under oath. Questions and answers are recorded stenographically at the deposition; later they are transcribed for possible use at trial. You may read the written record and change any incorrect answers before you sign the deposition. You are entitled to receive witness fees and mileage actually traveled both ways. The money must be paid, at the option of the party giving notice of the deposition, either with service of this subpoena or at the time of the deposition. Unless the court orders or you agree otherwise, if you are being deposed as an individual, the deposition must take place within 75 miles of your residence or within 150 miles of your residence if the deposition will be taken within the county of the court where the action is pending. The location of the deposition for all deponents is governed by Code of Civil Procedure section 2025.250.*

DISOBEDIENCE OF THIS SUBPOENA MAY BE PUNISHED AS CONTEMPT BY THIS COURT. YOU WILL ALSO BE LIABLE FOR THE SUM OF $500 AND ALL DAMAGES RESULTING FROM YOUR FAILURE TO OBEY.

Date issued: 9-21-2011

(SIGNATURE OF PERSON ISSUING SUBPOENA)

Sam Ware Attorney

(TYPE OR PRINT NAME) (Proof of service on reverse) (TITLE)

Form Adopted for Mandatory Use Judicial Council of California SUBP-020 [Rev. January 1, 2009]

DEPOSITION SUBPOENA FOR PERSONAL APPEARANCE AND PRODUCTION OF DOCUMENTS AND THINGS

Code of Civil Procedure §§ 2020.510, 2025.220, 2025.230, 2025.250, 2025.620; Government Code, § 68097.1
www.courtinfo.ca.gov

A

A

SUBP-020

PLAINTIFF/PETITIONER: In the Matter of the Goodall Trust	CASE NUMBER: PTR 99 273030
DEFENDANT/RESPONDENT:	

PROOF OF SERVICE OF DEPOSITION SUBPOENA FOR PERSONAL APPEARANCE AND PRODUCTION OF DOCUMENTS AND THINGS

1. I served this *Deposition Subpoena for Personal Appearance and Production of Documents and Things* by personally delivering a copy to the person served as follows:
   a. Person served (name): JAMES R. HASTINGS
   b. Address where served: 42 W. OAK KNOLL, KENTFIELD, CA
   c. Date of delivery: SEPT 27, 2011
   d. Time of delivery: 5:55pm
   e. Witness fees and mileage both ways (*check one*):
      (1) ☐ were paid. Amount: .... $ ______
      (2) ☑ were not paid
      (3) ☐ were tendered to the witness's public entity employer as required by Government Code section 68097.2. The amount tendered was (*specify*): .... $ ______
   f. Fee for service: .... $ ______
2. I received this subpoena for service on (*date*):
3. Person serving:
   a. ☐ Not a registered California process server
   b. ☐ California sheriff or marshal
   c. ☐ Registered California process server
   d. ☐ Employee or independent contractor of a registered California process server
   e. ☑ Exempt from registration under Business and Professions Code section 22350(b)
   f. ☐ Registered professional photocopier
   g. ☐ Exempt from registration under Business and Professions Code section 22451
   h. Name, address, telephone number, and, if applicable, county of registration and number:
      JOHN M ROGERS
      1430 LINCOLN AVE.
      SAN RAFAEL, CA 94901
      415/258-1880

I declare under penalty of perjury under the laws of the State of California that the foregoing is true and correct.

Date: SEPTEMBER 29, 2011

▶ [signature]
(SIGNATURE)

(For California sheriff or marshal use only)
I certify that the foregoing is true and correct.

Date:

▶ ______
(SIGNATURE)

ATTACHMENT B

Any and all writings, as defined in Evidence Code §250, which include e-mails, which in any way relate to the following:

1. Kenneth F. Goodall

2. Rachel A. Goodall.

3. K. Michael Goodall

4. San Francisco action number PTR-99-273030

5. Marin probate action number PR 1100596

6. The declarations you filed in the actions described in #4 and #5 above

Don A. Lesser, SBN #112887
LESSER LAW GROUP
1010 B Street, Suite 350
San Rafael, California 94901
Telephone: (415) 453-7600
Facsimile: (415) 295-4122
E-mail: DLesser@LesserGroup.com

Attorney for Subpoenaed Witness
JAMES R. HASTINGS

Δ π EXHIBIT 2
Deponent Hastings
Date 11-4-11 Rptr. CK
WWW.DEPOBOOK.COM
(3 pages)

SUPERIOR COURT OF THE STATE OF CALIFORNIA

COUNTY OF SAN FRANCISCO

In the Matter of the Trust for Michael created under the Goodall Trust dated January 19, 1999.	CASE NO. PTR-99-273030 **OBJECTIONS TO ATTACHMENT 3 DEMAND FOR PRODUCTION OF DOCUMENTS AND THINGS INCLUDED WITHIN DEPOSITION SUBPOENA**

DEMANDING PARTY: RESPONDENT SAM SLOAN

RESPONDING PARTY: SUBPOENAED WITNESS JAMES R. HASTINGS

PLEASE TAKE NOTICE THAT pursuant to the provisions of Code of Civil Procedure section 2020.510 et seq., Subpoenaed Witness JAMES R. HASTINGS hereby objects to the that portion of the Deposition Subpoena set forth in Attachment 3, as follows:

1. James R. Hastings objects to Demand Number 1 on the grounds that the category of documents sought fails to specifically describe each individual item and fails to reasonably particularize the category of items to be produced as required by C.C.P. Section 2020.510 (a) (2). He further objects to the extent that this request seeks documents protected by the attorney-client privilege and/or work product doctrine and that the request as written is overbroad, vague and ambiguous, and thus incomprehensible.

2. James R. Hastings objects to Demand Number 2 on the grounds that the category of documents sought fails to specifically describe each individual item and fails to reasonably

B

B

particularize the category of items to be produced as required by C.C.P. Section 2020.510 (a) (2). He further objects to the extent that this request seeks documents protected by the attorney-client privilege and/or work product doctrine and that the request as written is overbroad, vague and ambiguous, and thus incomprehensible.

3. James R. Hastings objects to Demand Number 3 on the grounds that the category of documents sought fails to specifically describe each individual item and fails to reasonably particularize the category of items to be produced as required by C.C.P. Section 2020.510 (a) (2). He further objects to the extent that this request seeks documents protected by the attorney-client privilege and/or work product doctrine and that the request as written is overbroad, vague and ambiguous, and thus incomprehensible.

4. James R. Hastings objects to Demand Number 4 on the grounds that the category of documents sought fails to specifically describe each individual item and fails to reasonably particularize the category of items to be produced as required by C.C.P. Section 2020.510 (a) (2). He further objects to the extent that this request seeks documents protected by the attorney-client privilege and/or work product doctrine and that the request as written is overbroad, vague and ambiguous, and thus incomprehensible.

5. James R. Hastings objects to Demand Number 5 on the grounds that the category of documents sought fails to specifically describe each individual item and fails to reasonably particularize the category of items to be produced as required by C.C.P. Section 2020.510 (a) (2). He further objects to the extent that this request seeks documents protected by the attorney-client privilege and/or work product doctrine and that the request as written is overbroad, vague and ambiguous, and thus incomprehensible.

6. James R. Hastings will produce the declarations requested in Demand Number 6.

DATED: October 31, 2011

LESSER LAW GROUP

By: ______________________

Don A. Lesser
Attorneys for Subpoenaed Witness
James R. Hastings

PROOF OF SERVICE

I, the undersigned, declare: I am over the age of 18 years at the time of service, and am not a party to the within action. I am employed in the County of Marin. My business address is 1010 B Street, Suite 350, San Rafael, California 94901.

On this date, October 31, 2011, the following document(s) were served:

OBJECTIONS TO ATTACHMENT 3 DEMAND FOR PRODUCTION OF DOCUMENTS AND THINGS INCLUDED WITHIN DEPOSITION SUBPOENA

on the parties, through their attorneys of record, by means of service designated below:

Samuel G. Ware
700 Larkspur Landing Cir
Ste 199
Larkspur, CA 94939

☐ **(By Electronic Mail)** Copies of the above-documents were served via e-mail only (per agreement by the parties) unless otherwise indicated.

☐ **(By First Class Mail)** I caused each such envelope, with first-class postage thereon fully prepaid, to be deposited in the United States mail at San Rafael, California.

☒ **(By Personal Service)** I caused each such envelope to be personally delivered to each addressee.

☐ **(By U.S. Postal Express Mail)** I caused **each** such envelope with Express Mail postage thereon fully prepaid to be placed in the U.S. Post Office Express Mail depository at San Rafael, California.

☐ **(By Federal Express) I caused** each such envelope with shipping charges fully prepaid, to be delivered to a Federal Express pick-up box at San Rafael, California, for next business day delivery.

☐ **(By Facsimile)** I caused each such document to be sent via telecopier at the fax numbers listed for each party on the service list.

I declare under penalty of perjury that the foregoing is true and correct and that this Declaration was executed on October 31, 2011, at San Rafael, California.

DON LESSER

James R. Hastings (SBN 079066)
J. R. HASTINGS LAW CORPORATION
1003 Third Street
San Rafael, CA 94901-3107
(415) 459-6635 (tel)
(415) 459-6756 (fax)

Attorney for ROY HOPPE and
FRANK THORNALLY

EXHIBIT 3
Deponent Hastings
Date 11-14-11 Rptr. CK
(11 pages)

SUPERIOR COURT OF CALIFORNIA

COUNTY OF SAN FRANCISCO

In the Matter of the Trust for Michael created under the Goodall Trust dated January 19, 1999.	CASE NO. PTR-99-273030 **DECLARATION OF JAMES R. HASTINGS FAMILY AND ESTATE PLANNING ATTORNEY FOR THE GOODALLS** Hearing: August 22, 2011 Time: 9:00 a.m. Dept.: Probate, Rm. 204

I, JAMES R. HASTINGS, declare as follows:

1. I am an attorney licensed to practice law in the States of California, Colorado, Nevada and the District of Columbia. I am the principal in the LAW OFFICE OF J.R. HASTINGS. Except as otherwise stated, I have personal knowledge of the matter stated herein, if called and sworn as a witness could and would testify.

2. I was the family and estate planning counsel of Kenneth F. Goodall, from on or about August of 1990 until his death on September 10, 1994. I was the family and estate planning counsel for Rachel A. Goodall from on or about August of 1990 until her death on June 7, 1999. I was the trust administration attorney for the Trust Department of the Bank of America from on or about July 19, 1999 through on or about December of 2000. I was the family and estate planning counsel for the son of

Kenneth F. Goodall and Rachel A. Goodall, K. Michael Goodall, from on or about July of 1999 until his death on October 5 of 2010. Regarding the Last Will of K. Michael Goodall, dated January 15, 2004, I was the estate attorney for the named executors Ray Hoppe and Frank Thornally from on or about October of 2010 until on or about January 2011.

3. I will present a chronology in this declaration, but before I do so I state that these are truths which may be pertinent to the issues before the court:

a. On their own volition, Kenneth F. Goodall and Rachel A. Goodall chose Guide Dogs for the Blind in San Rafael, California, as the residuary beneficiary of their estate. K. Michael Goodall understood he had no right to the residuary estate of Kenneth F. Goodall and Rachel A. Goodall, and he understood that he had no power to direct the residuary benefits of their estate.

b. I did not, nor has anyone in my employ, ever received or had an agreement with Guide Dogs for the Blind for any remuneration resulting from the fact that Kenneth F. Goodall and Rachel A. Goodall named Guide Dogs for the Blind as a residuary beneficiary. Further, there has not been nor is there any agreement for any remuneration in the past, in the present or in the future.

c. The operative document defining the distribution of the estate of Kenneth F. Goodall and the operative document defining the distribution of the estate of Rachel A. Goodall is the Declaration of the Goodall Trust dated August 24, 1994, an amended and restated declaration of the original trust dated September 12, 1990. Accordingly, this amended and restated declaration replaced in its entirety the declaration of September 12, 1990; however, the trust retains the original date, though it had been amended and restated.

4. I first met Kenneth F. Goodall on or about 1980 as I employed him to make door signs for my office. After his retirement as a Lieutenant Colonel in the United States Air Force, Kenneth F. Goodall established a sign making business out of his garage. Subsequently, I met Rachel A. Goodall, a homemaker. Mr. and Mrs. Goodall were very honorable, religious, good and wonderful people.

5. Kenneth F. Goodall and Rachel A. Goodall had one son, J. Michael Goodall, born approximately 1950. K. Michael Goodall was gifted in many ways, including being a chess master. Unfortunately, his parents found him subject to the undue influence of others, resulting in caution in their ultimate estate plan.

6. On or about August 1990, after employing Kenneth F. Goodall to make signs for me, Kenneth F. Goodall and Rachel A. Goodall visited me for estate planning advice and preparation. During the estate planning consultations with Mr. and Mrs. Goodall, they directed me as to their desires for the disposition of their estate. These desires were reflected in the document entitled the Goodall Trust, which was signed by Kenneth F. Goodall and Rachel A. Goodall, their signatures notarized by me, on September 12, 1990. Though the document speaks for itself, after the first death this declaration contemplated the estate being divided into two parts, one part for the survivor, a Survivor's Trust, and one part representing the deceased's estate, a Credit Shelter Trust. The document provided at paragraph 6.3(a) that the residuary beneficiary of both of those trusts would be K. Michael Goodall, if living, and if

not, paragraph 6.3(b) gave gifts to family members and the residual estate to Guide Dogs for the Blind.

7. On or about late July or early August of 1994, Kenneth F. Goodall and Rachel A. Goodall again visited me for advice and document preparation concerning their estate plan. During the discussions they told me of the changes they wished to make to their estate plan. Those changes were recorded in the amended and restated declaration of trust dated August 24, 1994, a document signed by them, of which I acted as the Notary Public. This document retained the division of the estate at the first death, creating a Survivor's Trust and a Bypass ("Credit Shelter") Trust. The document revised the gift in paragraph 6.3(a) from a direct gift to their son, K. Michael Goodall, to a gift of a lifetime trust for K. Michael Goodall, this trust memorialized in Section 6.5. As indicated in a separate declaration signed by me and filed in this court, the Goodalls intended the ultimate distribution of the Trust for Michael to be the residuary beneficiary named in 6.3(b), Guide Dogs for the Blind. (Please see the attached Exhibit A.)

8. At no time did I suggest that the Guide Dogs for the Blind as the residuary beneficiary for the Goodalls; instead, the selection of Guide Dogs for the Blind as residuary beneficiary was communicated to me by them.

9. At no time have I received any remuneration for the fact that the Guide Dogs for the Blind is named as a residuary beneficiary in the trust declarations for the Goodalls. Neither has my staff. There has not been, is not now and will not be in the future any agreement for

remuneration from the Guide Dogs for the Blind for assisting the Goodalls to name them in their trust documents.

10. Kenneth F. Goodall died on September 10, 1994. When he died the declaration of the Goodall Trust dated August 24, 1994 was the operative document used for the trust administration of his estate. Similarly, the Last Will of Kenneth F. Goodall dated August 24, 1994, was lodged with the Clerk of the Court of Marin County, the distribution of this Last Will being a pour-over to the Goodall Trust dated August 24, 1994. During the subsequent trust administration several investment accounts were transferred to the Bypass Trust of the Goodall Trust, and the remainder of the assets, including the family home at 461 Peachstone Terrace, San Rafael, California, remained in the Goodall Trust as the Survivor's Trust. A Trustee's Deed transferring 461 Peachstone Terrace to the Survivor's Trust of the Goodall Trust was signed on June 8, 1995 and recorded on September 11, 1995 by the Marin County Recorder on September 11, 1995, as Document No. 95-042772.

11. Rachel A. Goodall died on June 7, 1999. When she died the Declaration of the Goodall Trust dated August 24, 1994 was the operative document used for the trust administration of her estate. Similarly, the Last Will of Rachel A. Goodall dated August 24, 1994, was lodged with the Clerk of the Court of Marin County, the distribution of this Last Will being a pour-over to the Goodall Trust dated August 24, 1994.

12. During the trust administration of the Estate of Rachel A. Goodall all assets of the Bypass Trust and the Survivor's Trust were passed to Bank of America, as trustee, and placed into the Trust for Michael as directed by the Declaration of Trust dated August 24, 1994. As a part

of that distribution a Notice Regarding Real Property, Affidavit of Death of Trustee and Acceptance of Office of Successor Trustee dated July 15, 1999, was recorded by the Marin County Recorder on October 26 of 2000. This document transferred the trusteeship and the ownership of 461 Peachstone Terrace, San Rafael, California, to the Bank of America Trust Department.

13. On or about July of 1999 K. Michael Goodall visited me for advice and documents concerning his estate plan. During that visit K. Michael Goodall informed me that he had no children, had not had any marriages and that his assets included personal property, his automobile and a bank account. The primary operative documents for K. Michael Goodall's estate plan were the Advance Health Care Directive and the Power of Attorney for Asset Management, documents assisting him should he become incapacitated. A will was completed, though K. Michael Goodall understood he did not have any assets which would ever require a probate, to ensure personal property and his minimal bank account would be properly handled at his passing.

14. Subsequently, I handled several general matters for K. Michael Goodall, including questions concerning his debts, problems with his license through the Department of Motor Vehicles, questions concerning debt relief and transmission of his Advance Health Care Directive to medical authorities during emergencies. Subsequently, as well, K. Michael Goodall revisited me on or about December of 2003 or early January of 2004 and refreshed all of his documents, which were the Advance Health Care Directive, property power of attorney and Last Will. In the Last Will he named two friends, Roy Hoppe and Frank Thornally, as

initial executors, and Bank of America as the subsequent executor. During our discussions and at the signing of both of his Last Wills, I clearly understood that K. Michael Goodall understood he has no residuary interest or power of appointment in the estate of his parents as comprised of the Trust for Michael of the Goodall Trust, the trust managed by the Bank of America following the death of his mother.

I declare under penalty of perjury that the foregoing declaration is true and correct and I executed same on August 18, 2011 at San Rafael, California.

Dated: August 18, 2011

JAMES R. HASTINGS, Declarant

EXHIBIT A

MANATT, PHELPS & PHILLIPS, LLP
GARY D. ROTHSTEIN (Bar No. CA 143157)
SUZANNE C. FARLEY (Bar No. CA 256693)
One Embarcadero Center, 30th Floor
San Francisco, CA 94111
Telephone: (415) 291-7400
Facsimile: (415) 291-7474

Attorneys for Petitioner,
BANK OF AMERICA, N.A.

SUPERIOR COURT OF THE STATE OF CALIFORNIA

FOR THE COUNTY OF SAN FRANCISCO

In the Matter of the Trust for Michael created under the Goodall Trust dated January 19, 1999.	Case No. **DECLARATION IN SUPPORT OF PETITION FOR DETERMINATION OF THE BENEFICIARIES TO WHOM TRUST PROPERTY SHALL PASS UPON TERMINATION OF TRUST** Hearing Date: Time: Dept.:

I, James Raymond Hastings, hereby declare as follows:

1. I am an active member of the State Bar of California and the principal in the Law Offices of J. R. Hastings. Except as otherwise stated, I have personal knowledge of the matters stated herein, and if called and sworn as a witness could and would testify competently thereto.

2. Bank of America, N.A. has filed a Petition for Determination of the Beneficiaries to Whom Trust Property Shall Pass Upon Termination of Trust (the "Petition"), in this matter.

3. I was estate planning counsel for Kenneth F. Goodall ("Kenneth") and Rachel A. Goodall ("Rachel") in connection with the Goodall Trust. I was responsible for the drafting of the Amendment to Goodall Trust dated August 24, 1994, and the Second Amendment

to Goodall Trust dated January 19, 1999 (collectively, the "Amendments").

4. In connection with the preparation of the Amendments, I discussed with Kenneth and Rachel how they wanted to dispose of the Goodall Trust estate upon their deaths and the death of their only child, Michael. It was my understanding based on that discussion that Rachel and Kenneth intended the balance of the trust established for the benefit of Michael ("the Trust for Michael") remaining at Michael's death to be distributed pursuant to Section 6.3(d) of the Goodall Trust, as follows: twenty thousand dollars to each of Rachel's then-living brothers and sisters, and the remainder to Guide Dogs for the Blind of Marin. Section 6.3(e) of the Goodall Trust, which states that the assets should be distributed one-half to Kenneth's heirs and one-half to Rachel's heirs, was intended to apply only if upon Michael's death there were no beneficiaries to take under Section 6.3(d) of the Goodall Trust.

5. The Petition seeks an order to determine the proper beneficiaries of the Trust for Michael in light of Michael's death and the resulting termination of the Trust for Michael. I have reviewed said Petition and believe that the determination sought by the Petition accurately reflects the intentions of Kenneth and Rachel.

I declare under penalty of perjury under the Laws of the State of California that the foregoing is true and correct.

Executed at San Rafael, California, on January 10, ~~2010.~~ 2011.

By: ______________________
James Raymond Hastings

POS-050/EFS-050

ATTORNEY OR PARTY WITHOUT ATTORNEY (Name, State Bar number, and address): JAMES R. HASTINGS (SBN 079066) J.R. HASTINGS LAW CORPORATION 1003 THIRD STREET SAN RAFAEL, CA 94901-3107 TELEPHONE NO.: (415) 459-6635 FAX NO. (Optional): (415) 459-6756 E-MAIL ADDRESS (Optional): jrhastings@pacbell.net ATTORNEY FOR (Name): ROY HOPPE AND FRANK THORNALLY	FOR COURT USE ONLY
SUPERIOR COURT OF CALIFORNIA, COUNTY OF SAN FRANCISCO STREET ADDRESS: 400 McALLISTER STREET, RM 204 MAILING ADDRESS: CITY AND ZIP CODE: SAN FRANCISCO, CA 94102-4514 BRANCH NAME: PROBATE	
PLAINTIFF/PETITIONER: IN THE MATTER OF GOODALL TRUST	CASE NUMBER: PTR-99-273030
DEFENDANT/RESPONDENT:	JUDICIAL OFFICER:
PROOF OF ELECTRONIC SERVICE	DEPT.: PROBATE

1. I am at least 18 years old and not a party to this action.
   a. My residence or business address is *(specify)*:
   1003 THIRD STREET
   SAN RAFAEL, CA 94901-3107
   b. My electronic service address is *(specify)*:
   jrhastings@pacbell.net

2. I electronically served the following documents *(exact titles)*:
   DECLARATION OF JAMES R. HASTINGS FAMILY AND ESTATE PLANNING ATTORNEY FOR THE GOODALLS

   ☐ The documents served are listed in an attachment. *(Form POS-050(D)/EFS-050(D) may be used for this purpose.)*

3. I electronically served the documents listed in 2 as follows:
   a. Name of person served: SAM H. SLOAN
   On behalf of *(name or names of parties represented, if person served is an attorney)*:
   b. Electronic service address of person served: SAMHSLOAN@GMAIL.COM
   c. On *(date)*: AUGUST 19, 2011
   d. At *(time)*: 10:00 AM

   ☐ The documents listed in item 2 were served electronically on the persons and in the manner described in an attachment. *(Form POS-050(P)/EFS-050(P) may be used for this purpose.)*

Date: AUGUST 19, 2011

I declare under penalty of perjury under the laws of the State of California that the foregoing is true and correct.

RENEE MOORE ▶ Renee Moore

(TYPE OR PRINT NAME OF DECLARANT) (SIGNATURE OF DECLARANT)

Form Approved for Optional Use
Judicial Council of California
POS-050/EFS-050 [Rev. January 1, 2011]

PROOF OF ELECTRONIC SERVICE
(Proof of Service/Electronic Filing and Service)

Cal. Rules of Court, rule 2.251
www.courts.ca.gov

GOODALL

3-11

0541

In re: Goodall Trust

PTR 99-273030

James Hastings

November 14, 2011

WEST COAST REPORTERS INC

117 Paul Drive, Suite A
San Rafael, CA 94903
(800) 979-2361

EXHIBIT D

D

SUPERIOR COURT OF THE STATE OF CALIFORNIA
FOR THE COUNTY OF SAN FRANCISCO

In the Matter of the
Trust for Michael created under the Goodall Trust dated January 19, 1999)

NO. PTR-99-273030

Deposition of
JAMES R. HASTINGS

NOVEMBER 14, 2011

DEPOSING ATTORNEY: SAM WARE, ESQ.

REPORTED BY: CINDY J. KAISER, CSR #7647

I N D E X

EXAMINATION BY		PAGE
MR. WARE		4

EXHIBITS

RESPONDENT'S FOR IDENTIFICATION	DESCRIPTION	
1	Deposition Subpoena for James R. Hastings	4
2	Objections to Attachment 3 Demand For Production	7
3	Declaration of James R. Hastings	15

--oOo--

Pursuant to Notice of Deposition, and on Monday, November 14, 2011, commencing at the hour of 2:03 p.m., at the Law Offices of Sam Ware, 700 Larkspur Landing Circle, #199, Larkspur, California, before me, CINDY J. KAISER, a Certified Shorthand Reporter and Deposition Officer of the State of California, there personally appeared

JAMES R. HASTINGS,

called as a witness by the Respondent, who having been duly sworn, was examined and testified as hereinafter set forth.

--oOo--

A P P E A R A N C E S

SAM WARE, Attorney at Law, LAW OFFICES OF SAM WARE, 700 Larkspur Landing Circle, #199, Larkspur, California 94939, appeared as counsel on behalf of the Respondent. (415) 464-4872.

DON A. LESSER, Attorney at Law, LESSER LAW GROUP, 101 B Street, Suite 350, San Rafael, California 94901, appeared as counsel on behalf of the Subpoenaed Witness, James R. Hastings. (415) 453-7600.

ALSO PRESENT: Sam Sloan.

--oOo--

EXAMINATION

(Respondent's Exhibit 1 was were marked for identification.)

BY MR. WARE:

Q. Mr. Hastings, would you state your name for the record, please.

A. James Hastings.

Q. My name is Sam Ware. I represent Sam Sloan, who is the administrator of the estate of Michael Goodall. Do you understand that?

A. I understand it, yes.

Q. Have you had your deposition taken before on any occasion?

A. Yes.

Q. How many times?

A. Once.

Q. How long ago was that?

A. Approximately nine years ago.

Q. Have you ever taken a deposition as an attorney?

A. Yes.

Q. How many times, would you say?

A. I don't know.

Q. More than 100?

A. I don't believe so.

Q. Are you generally familiar with the law with regard to depositions?
A. I don't think so.
Q. Okay. I'll give you my understanding of what a deposition is and we'll take it from there.
A deposition is an opportunity, it's a discovery device, it gives me an opportunity, representing Mr. Sloan, to ask you as a witness to the matters involving the Goodall trust, questions on that subject. If my question isn't clear, I'll ask you to tell me you don't understand, I'll try and clarify it. Your attorney has the right on your behalf and is duty bound to make objections as he sees fit. We'll take those objections as we go.
With regard to answering a question that I have posed and an objection has been made by your attorney, or another attorney in the room, if you understand the question, notwithstanding the objection, I'll expect you to answer it, unless your attorney instructs you not to answer the question, then that's a different matter to be taken up by the court.
Do you understand that?
A. Do I understand which?
Q. Do you understand that you're under oath?
A. Yes.

Q. Do you understand that this process is a process for me to gather information from you?
A. Yes.
Q. You're here pursuant to a subpoena, correct?
A. Yes.
Q. Let me show you what's been marked as Exhibit 1, and ask you to look at that document, please. Once you've had an opportunity to review that document, I have questions for you.
A. I've reviewed the document.
Q. Have you seen that document before?
A. This particular document? No.
Q. Have you seen a copy of that document before?
A. I believe so.
Q. When did you see that for the first time?
A. I don't know.
Q. Do you recall being served with a subpoena in this matter?
A. Yes.
Q. Do you recall that the subpoena that you were served with asks that you bring certain documents today?
A. Yes.
Q. Do you have any documents --
A. No.
Q. -- that you brought today? Why not?

MR. LESSER: Mr. Ware, as you know, we served some objections with respect to the documents on your office sometime ago. I won't take the time now to reiterate the objections, but I will tell you that Mr. Hastings, at my instruction, searched for documents that he understood to reflect the intentions of the settlors with respect to the trust that's at issue in this matter. He has done a search for those documents. You can certainly ask him about the search that he did, but that is the limit to which we believe Mr. Hastings is required to respond to the subpoena, pursuant to the court's order.
MR. WARE: Okay. That's fine.
This is next marked Number 2, and I'll ask you to take a look at that.
(Respondent's Exhibit 2 was marked for identification.)
MR. WARE: Those are the objections that I received.
Q. Mr. Hastings, have you ever seen a copy of Exhibit 2 before?
A. No.
Q. I'll represent to you, Mr. Hastings, that those are the objections to which your counsel has referred.
MR. WARE: Mr. Lesser, would you just confirm

that that's --
MR. LESSER: They are.
BY MR. WARE:
Q. Let me ask you something.
When you looked for documents which reflected the intentions of Kenneth Goodall, where did you look?
A. In all of the locations in my office where documents would be and in the particular files that would be related.
Q. That is related to the Goodall matter?
A. Yes.
Q. And how voluminous are those documents? Bankers box? Two bankers boxes? A couple files? What's the universe of documents with regard to the Goodalls that you looked at?
A. Less than a bankers box.
Q. Are they categorized by file, that is, Goodall trust 1990? Goodall trust 1994? How are those kept in your office?
A. Which is the question? You asked two questions.
Q. Can you give me a description of how those documents related to the Goodalls are kept in your office.
A. Some were in manila folders, some were in

Page 9

expandable folders, some were marked with file numbers and some aren't.
Q. How recently did you review those documents?
A. This weekend.
Q. Are they all kept in one place in your office?
A. Yes.
Q. In one box?
A. Well, apparently not.
Q. What does that mean to you?
A. There were some documents I could not locate.
Q. Documents which you thought existed, which you just couldn't find, is that what you're saying to me?
A. Yes.
Q. What documents did you expect to find that you did not find?
A. A file marked G 080-01.
Q. What does that number mean to you, in your record keeping practices?
A. It means it's the initial estate planning file for Mr. and Mrs. Goodall.
Q. G 080-01?
A. That's right.
Q. What files did you find there, in your office, when you were reviewing your files to see whether you had documents which reflected the intentions of the

Page 10

Goodalls?
A. G 080-05 and G 080-86 and G 181-01.
Q. Now, what sorts of documents are included within the dash 05 file?
A. Mr. Goodall's trust administration.
Q. The 06 number.
A. Mrs. Goodall's trust administration.
Q. And the G 181-01 file.
A. That's Michael Goodall's will.
Q. Then I'll focus, if I may, on the G 080-01. Does the G stand for Goodall?
A. Yes.
Q. I notice that the numbers jump from dash 01 to dash 05. Would you expect to find a 02, 3, 4 someplace?
A. No.
Q. The reason for that gap is what?
A. That's not the way I identify files.
Q. Now, the G 080-01 file, what would you expect that file to contain?
A. The initial paperwork concerning the estate plan of Mr. and Mrs. Goodall.
Q. Initial paperwork would include your notes regarding your discussions with them?
A. It may.
Q. And in your record keeping practices, would you

Page 11

expect that file to contain such notes?
A. Yes.
Q. Typically during the estate planning process, do you keep notes --
A. Yes.
Q. -- with regard to the client?
MR. LESSER: Let him finish the question before you answer.
MR. WARE: I paused, and I should have nodded. So there you have it. Thank you.
Q. Do you recall when it was you last saw that file?
A. No.
Q. Let's turn to the dash 05 file, which is Mr. Goodall's trust administration file.
A. Yes.
Q. What sorts of things would be contained within such a file, the trust administration file?
MR. LESSER: Well, you're asking him generally as a matter of custom and practice, or this particular client?
BY MR. WARE:
Q. Fine. This particular file, let's go for that. What sorts of documents did you find in there when you looked at it?

Page 12

A. The trust, the will.
Q. Anything else?
A. Any other estate planning documents which had become obsolete.
Q. Such as? Would you give me an example.
A. Power of attorney is obsolete at the death, any paperwork relating to the trust administration.
Q. And when you say "trust administration" in this instance, what did the trust administration of Kenneth Goodall's trust administration include?
A. That pieces of the process that are necessary to make the distributions required by the trust.
Q. Okay. With regard to the dash 06 file, that's Mrs. Goodall's trust administration file, what sorts of documents are in there?
A. The same sorts of documents as in Mr. Goodall's file.
Q. That is a copy of the trust, right?
A. Yes.
Q. Would there be a copy of the 1990 trust in there? Was there a copy of the 1990 trust in there?
A. I don't know.
Q. You don't recall?
A. I don't recall.
Q. Do you recall seeing a copy of the 1994 trust

in there? That's in the 06 file.
A. At this point you're making some sort of assumption as to when I looked at those files and I'm supposed to remember something about the files and I don't know what that assumption is, so I can't answer that question.
Q. Fine. My assumption is you looked at them over the weekend.
A. That's -- that's not a valid assumption.
Q. When was the last time you looked at the 05 file?
A. I don't know.
Q. Do you recall when it was you last looked in the 06 file?
A. I don't know.
Q. How about the 01 file, the G 181-01 file, Michael Goodall's file?
A. I don't know.
Q. When did you begin looking for the G 080-01 file in preparation for this deposition?
A. Several weeks before I hired Mr. Lesser, and I don't know when that is.
Q. So you began looking for it several weeks before hiring Mr. Lesser, you discovered that it wasn't where it was supposed to be?

A. That's not a valid statement.
Q. When did you first start looking for the G 080-01 file?
A. Several weeks before I hired Mr. Lesser. I don't know when that was. Someplace within the last three months.
Q. Within the last three months you discovered that it did not exist, when you looked for it at that time?
A. I can't answer that question, because it has a predicate in it that's not true.
Q. What's untrue about that question? What's the predicate that's not true there?
A. You're saying something does not exist.
Q. Where is it? Where's the file?
A. I do not know.
Q. Why not?
A. Because I can't find it.
Q. When was the last time you saw it?
A. I don't know.
Q. Was it that several weeks ago when you first started looking for the file, before you hired Mr. Lesser?
A. No.
Q. You couldn't find it then either?

A. Not that I recall.
MR. WARE: We'll mark this next.
(Respondent's Exhibit 3 was marked for identification.)
THE WITNESS: I looked at Exhibit 3.
BY MR. WARE:
Q. Have you ever seen that document before?
A. I've seen a similar document before, yes.
Q. You've seen a copy of that document before?
A. Yes.
Q. You've probably seen the original of that document before, right, because you prepared it?
A. Yes.
Q. Is that a complete copy of your declaration?
A. It appears.
Q. I beg your pardon, please.
A. It appears to be there.
Q. There's an attachment to it, an Exhibit A, that's referred to in the body of the document, correct?
A. That's true.
Q. You prepared Exhibit A, as well, correct?
A. Yes.
Q. When you prepared that Exhibit 3, did you have the G 080-01 file in front of you?
A. The question was too broad.

Q. What you're saying is the G 080-01 file is unavailable to us today, right?
A. Okay, you're talking about the 1 file?
Q. The 1 file, right. That's unavailable to you right? It's unavailable to us, right?
A. Yes.
Q. It's unavailable to you, right?
A. Yes.
Q. Have you ever given the file to Mr. Lesser, for example?
A. No.
Q. You looked for that file, the dash 01 file, and you can't find it, over the weekend?
A. That's true.
Q. What I'm trying to figure out is the last time you saw that file. You don't remember when you last saw that file, right?
A. I do not remember the last time I saw the file.
Q. Does it refresh your recollection that you saw the file when you were composing Exhibit 3?
A. No, it does not refresh my recollection.
Q. So you may have had the file available to you when you drafted 3, you may not have, you don't remember. Is that what you're saying?
A. I do not know.

Q. So you don't recall whether when you were drafting Exhibit 3 you had that file, the dash 01 file, to look at, do you?
A. No, I do not.
Q. How about when you were looking, drafting attachment A, or Exhibit A, to Exhibit 3, which is the declaration that you signed apparently in January of 2011, do you recall whether you had the dash 01 file available to you when you drafted that declaration?
A. I don't recall.
Q. Just so I'm clear, you don't recall whether you referred to the dash 01 file when you drafted either of the declarations which compose Exhibit 3?
A. I may have, but I do not recall.
Q. You don't recall, okay.
Do you recall, when you were drafting Exhibit 3, that you referred to the dash 05 file?
A. I referred to documents in the file.
Q. The 06 file, did you refer to that when you were drafting Exhibit 3?
A. I referred to documents in the file.
Q. And the G 181-01 file, did you refer to that when you were drafting Exhibit 3?
A. I would refer to documents in the file.
Q. Over the weekend you took a look for the dash

01 file and you couldn't find it, right?
A. That's true.
Q. Where did you look? In your office, or storage, or where?
A. I looked in my office and in storage.
Q. Is your storage offsite from your office?
A. Yes.
Q. Did you personally look in your office to find that file?
A. Yes.
Q. Did you ask anybody in your office to help you find that file?
A. Prior to that point, yes.
Q. When did you ask somebody to help you find that file, prior to that point?
A. Sometime within the last two months.
Q. Do you remember who it was that you asked to help you find that file?
A. I asked René Moore.
Q. Did you ask anybody else to help you find that file?
A. No.
Q. Would René Moore know as much as anybody on the planet as to where that file might be?
A. No.

Q. Okay. Who would know more?
A. No one.
Q. Now, did you ask René Moore this weekend to help you find that file again?
A. No.
Q. Several months ago when you asked René Moore to help you find the 01 file, she couldn't find it either. Is that what she reported to you?
A. When we last looked for it, she could not find it.
Q. And have you asked her recently to help you find that file?
A. Yes.
Q. When was the last time you asked her to help you find that file?
A. Within the last two months.
Q. How about over the weekend?
A. She doesn't work on the weekend. I did not ask her on the weekend.
Q. Did you ask her this morning to help you find that file, the 01 file?
A. No.
Q. Does she work today?
A. Yes.
Q. Is there a reason you didn't ask her to try and

help you find that file this morning, knowing you had a deposition this afternoon?
MR. LESSER: What's the point of this?
MR. WARE: I want to know how thoroughly he's looked for that file.
MR. LESSER: Well, I think he's told you what he did.
BY MR. WARE:
Q. Okay, the question stands.
A. I can't answer that question, because it has some predicates in it that are emotional and not factual.
Q. Let me ask you again.
Did you ask René Moore any time today to help you find the 01 file?
A. No.
Q. Why not?
MR. LESSER: Objection. Relevance.
THE WITNESS: It was not necessary that I ask her.
BY MR. WARE:
Q. Why not?
A. I had made a thorough search of three offsite locations. I had made a thorough search at the office in all possible locations. I have not found the file at

this moment.
Q. That's fine. Okay, I understand.
At some point back in, I think it was 2000, the year 2000, you represented the Bank of America as trustee in the San Francisco proceedings, BPR 99273030, correct?
A. I don't know anything about the numbers, but I did represent the Bank of America in a motion hearing.
Q. Right, the motion was brought by Michael Goodall to replace the Bank of America as the trustee. Do you remember that?
A. I remember the motion was brought by Michael Goodall, that's all I remember.
Q. Do you remember that you represented Bank of America in that proceeding?
A. Yes.
Q. Is there a file that you have with regard to your representation of the Bank of America in that proceeding?
A. Yes.
Q. Is it one of those four files that we talked about earlier?
A. Yes.
Q. In which file would records of that proceeding be contained?

A. I presume it was after the death of his mother, so it would be the 06 file.
Q. Thank you.
MR. WARE: Just, Mr. Lesser, for the record, you're objecting to producing the 05, 06, and that is the files G 080-05, correct?
MR. LESSER: Well, we've objected to the form of the requests, on the grounds that we've stated in the objections. I told you before that we have, in the interest of avoiding disputes, made an investigation for the existence of documents that would reflect the intentions of the settlors, so that's what Mr. Hastings has looked for. I think he's told you where he looked and what he found.
BY MR. WARE:
Q. My question is this. Earlier in this proceeding we identified that G 080-05 has to do with Kenneth Goodall, correct?
MR. LESSER: Objection. Vague and ambiguous.
BY MR. WARE:
Q. Does G 080-05 have to do with Kenneth Goodall?
MR. LESSER: Same objection.
BY MR. WARE:
Q. The question stands.
A. I don't remember the father's name at this

moment.
Q. You don't remember Michael Goodall's father's name?
A. Right at this moment, I don't, no.
Q. Would you refer to the declaration that I marked as Exhibit 3, and I ask whether that refreshes your recollection.
A. The dash 05 file concerns Kenneth Goodall.
Q. Then referring you to the deposition note, the deposition subpoena, Exhibit 1, you see attachment 3 asks for, "Any and all writings as defined by Evidence Code section 250, which include e-mails which is in any way related to the following: 1, Kenneth F. Goodall."
Do you see that?
A. Yes, I see that.
Q. Would you agree with me that G 080-05 relates to Kenneth Goodall?
MR. LESSER: Mr. Ware, one of our objections, as you know, is that a request for documents that relate to a particular individual is not just vague and ambiguous, but unintelligible, and so to ask him whether the file somehow relates to Mr. Goodall has the same problem and warrants the same objections.
MR. WARE: Okay.
(Record read as requested.)

MR. LESSER: Same objections.
BY MR. WARE:
Q. The question stands.
A. I don't understand the question.
Q. Why not? What's unintelligible about the question?
A. To me it's unintelligible.
Q. Why?
A. Because that's my understanding. It is unintelligible, in my understanding.
Q. So what you're saying is that you can't tell me as you sit here today whether G 080-05, which you've described as the trust administration file for Kenneth Goodall, relates to Kenneth Goodall, you can't tell me that?
MR. LESSER: Same objections.
THE WITNESS: Same response.
BY MR. WARE:
Q. Which is? You can't answer that question?
A. I can't answer that question.
Q. It's too vague and unintelligible?
A. Among the answers, yes.
Q. Let me ask you this. Can you tell me whether in your understanding G 080-06, which you've described as the trust administration file for Mrs. Goodall,

relates to Rachel Goodall, which is number 2 on attachment 3 to the subpoena that I served upon you.

MR. LESSER: Same objections.

THE WITNESS: Same answer.

BY MR. WARE:

Q. You can't tell me whether in your mind the trust administration file, the 06 file, relates to Rachel Goodall?

MR. LESSER: Well, look, Mr. Ware. I don't see the point of asking Mr. Hastings to give you his personal understanding of what the word relates to. The problem with the subpoena is that you have propounded one that does not comply with the Code of Civil Procedures requirement that the categories be specifically and reasonably specified, so whatever Mr. Hastings may or may not think is the relationship between the Goodalls and these files is really irrelevant. The problem is that the subpoena is procedurally invalid, and so I think we're just wasting everybody's time here to argue with Mr. Hastings about whether these relate or don't relate to the Goodalls.

MR. WARE: Okay. I'm not arguing with Mr. Hastings, I don't intend to argue with Mr. Hastings to obtain information from Mr. Hastings, one of which is his understanding as to the meaning of certain words and

certain names and files, and if he doesn't understand whether or not his dash 06 file, which he's described as Mrs. Goodall's trust administration file, relates to Mrs. Goodall, so be it, but I can ask the question to find out whether or not he is able to answer questions such as that. That's all.

MR. LESSER: If that's the way you want to use your time, that's your choice.

MR. WARE: Okay.

Q. So just back, do you understand that the G 080-06 file relates to the administration of the trust of Mrs. Rachel Goodall?

MR. LESSER: Objection. Vague, ambiguous, unintelligible, not likely to lead to discovery of relevant evidence.

(Record read as requested.)

MR. LESSER: Same objections.

Go ahead.

THE WITNESS: I don't know what to say, because I'm being harassed and harangued by a word that you want to put in something, and you want to argue about that as opposed to get on with the case. I'm here to help you find out that the Goodalls intended the Guide Dogs for the Blind to get the assets of their trust. And if you want to find that out, then ask me the questions that

relate to my affidavit. Don't play games with me.

No, I do not understand what you say when you say those things in this document.

MR. WARE: Okay. I'll move to strike as nonresponsive.

Can you just ask the question one more time, then we'll move on.

(Record read as requested.)

MR. LESSER: Same objections. Also asked and answered.

MR. WARE: The question stands.

MR. LESSER: You can answer one more.

THE WITNESS: No, I don't understand your question.

BY MR. WARE:

Q. Okay.

With regard to the G 181-01 file, which you described as Michael Goodall's file, do you understand that that file relates to Michael Goodall?

MR. LESSER: Objection. Same objections.

THE WITNESS: No, I do not understand.

BY MR. WARE:

Q. Well, is that the reason that you did not bring these files, the 05, 06, and 01 files, is that you didn't understand that the subpoena asked you to bring

such documents?

MR. LESSER: Mr. Hastings didn't bring the documents for the reasons that we have set forth in the objections.

MR. WARE: So it was you who decided not to bring the files, Mr. Lesser. I want to know who is going to pay the sanctions here.

MR. LESSER: I'm not testifying, Mr. Ware.

BY MR. WARE:

Q. I'll ask any one of you to answer the questions. Is the reason you didn't bring the 05, 06, and G 181-01 file is because you didn't understand that those files were requested in the subpoena?

MR. LESSER: The reasons that Mr. Hastings has or has not brought things to the deposition is set forth in the objections.

MR. WARE: Okay.

Let me just state here for the record. As the representative of the estate of Michael Goodall, we request that you provide to us, at the very least, a copy of the G 181-01 file, which is Michael Goodall's file, without further ado, and that request is made pursuant to Rules of Professional Conduct, Rule 3-00 D, open paren D, which says that subject to any protective order or non-disclosure agreement, a lawyer is to promptly release to the client, at the request of the client, all the client's papers and property, and that of course is Mr. Sloan. Mr. Goodall is dead now, so that's Mr. Sloan who is making that request. That's in addition to the subpoena. That's just another reason why we're entitled to at least documents. We'll table that request, just so you know it's out there.

MR. LESSER: All I'll say to that is this is the first time that we've heard that request. So we'll take that under advisement.

MR. WARE: Other than in the subpoena, that of course --

MR. LESSER: Well, the subpoena didn't ask anything to be produced pursuant to the rules of professional responsibility or --

MR. WARE: Professional Conduct, yeah.

MR. LESSER: Well, I'm adding that as a further request.

BY MR. WARE:

Q. Now, I guess I'd better get clear what we're going to be doing here.

G 080-01 is not being produced because it doesn't exist and because based upon the objections which are raised in Exhibit 2, right?

A. That's wrong.

MR. LESSER: Say that again.

BY MR. WARE:

Q. G 080-01, what would you call that, best description of that file? The estate planning file?

A. Yes.

Q. That the estate planning file is not being produced today because it doesn't exist. That's one reason?

MR. LESSER: That misstates his testimony. He didn't say it didn't exist. He said he can't find it, after a reasonable and diligent search.

BY MR. WARE:

Q. It doesn't exist in your possession, correct?

A. I don't believe that's correct.

Q. It does exist in your possession?

A. I don't believe that's a correct statement.

Q. Because the file is lost? How are we going to talk about this file?

MR. LESSER: You can talk about it in the way he testified, which is that he looked for it and he can't find it. We're just wasting everybody's time. You keep trying to put words in his mouth. He said he's looked for it, he told you how he looked for it, he told you where he looked for it, he told you who he asked to help, and he can't find it. That's what the witness has

testified to.

MR. WARE: Okay. Can we agree, Mr. Lesser, that a motion to compel production of these documents and to answer -- to compel production of these documents, can be served on you so that I don't have to personally serve Mr. Hastings with that motion?

MR. LESSER: Yeah. I mean, without conceding that you have done anything necessary to, as a predicate to bringing such a motion, including meeting and conferring, yeah, you can serve me rather than Mr. Hastings.

MR. WARE: Great. Thanks. Okay.

Q. Now, turning to Exhibit 3, I've got some questions about some statements that were made in that. Exhibit 3 is your declaration.

At page 1, at line 28, you say that "I was the family estate planning counsel for the son of Kenneth F. Goodall and Michael A. Goodall, K. Michael Goodall, from on or about 1999 until his death on October 5, 2010."

Do you see that?

A. Yes.

Q. What is the source of your recollection when you were drafting this declaration that you represented him from about July 1, 1999? Do you recall looking at any notes or anything then?

A. Well, I see in that statement, the word "for the son" should not be there. I was trying to say I was the family estate planning counsel for Kenneth and Rachel and Michael.

Q. Then you see on page -- sorry?

A. Let me look and understand what is the sentence taken out of the paragraph. I have to make sure what I'm looking at here.

Okay, "for the son" does belong there.

Q. When you refer to "from on or about July of 1999," do you recall what you were looking at when you drafted that statement?

MR. LESSER: If anything.

BY MR. WARE:

Q. If anything, correct.

A. The 1999 is incorrect. I was trying to build that I was with the parents -- well, I don't know if July of 1999 is correct, because I don't know when Michael first came to me to assist him. So I presume that's what the file would show.

Q. That's Michael Goodall's file?

A. Yes.

Q. Then the paragraph goes on and says, I'm paraphrasing, that you were the estate attorney for the Executors Ray Hoppe and Frank Thornally from October of

2010, until about January of 2011. Do you see that?
A. Yes.
Q. Do you have a file with regard to that representation?
A. Yes. It's within the Michael Goodall file.
Q. So that would be within the G 181-01 file?
A. Yes.
Q. Did they retain you to represent them?
A. Yes.
Q. Was it a written retention?
A. I don't recall.
Q. Would you expect that you got those dates from looking at Michael Goodall's file?
A. Yes.
Q. Do you recall what it was in your mind, if you do recall, why it was that it was October of 2010? Is there something that happened on that date that would make you write that date?
A. The previous sentence says -- one of the previous sentence says Michael died on October 5th of 2010.
Q. Do you recall that Ray Hoppe and Frank Thornally came to you after Michael died and asked you to represent them?
A. I don't recall that. But generally yes, that

would be true.
Q. Do you recall what it was that terminated that relationship in January of 2011?
A. Essentially all the work was done and they were not responsive any more.
Q. Moving down a little bit here on your declaration, if I can refer you to page 2.
MR. WARE: Do you have a copy of these things?
MS. ADORNATO: I don't.
MR. WARE: Do you want me to shoot you a copy so you can follow along here?
MS. ADORNATO: Yes.
MR. WARE: Off the record.
(Off the record.)
BY MR. WARE:
Q. Page 2, I'm still on page 2, about line 9, it says, "On their own volition, Kenneth Goodall and Rachel Goodall chose Guide Dogs for the Blind in San Rafael as the residual beneficiary of their estate."
Do you have any records which reflect that assertion?
A. I don't know.
Q. If you did, it would be in the misplaced file?
A. I presume so.
Q. Do you have a recollection as to why they chose

Guide Dogs for the Blind?
A. No, I do not.
Q. Did you ever discuss that with them?
A. Yes.
Q. Do you recall what they said to you with regard to choosing Guide Dogs for the Blind as the residual beneficiary?
A. I recall that we had a discussion. I don't recall the details of the discussion.
Q. Do you recall that they said anything to you about having a blind family member, or anything like that, which is of particular interest in -- strike that.
Do you recall any significant fact, such as having a family member who was blind, as part of their explanation, if any, as to why they chose Guide Dogs for the Blind?
A. No.
Q. It's my overall understanding of this declaration that you had nothing to do with suggesting to the Goodalls that Guide Dogs for the Blind be a beneficiary of their estate in any fashion, is that true?
A. That's my recollection.
Q. The next statement with regard to Michael Goodall's understanding. Your statement there with

regard to Michael Goodall's understanding is based upon what he told you?
MR. LESSER: Excuse me. Are we talking about the statement that starts on line 11, page 2?
MR. WARE: Yes.
THE WITNESS: The statement comes from the discussion I had with Michael Goodall.
BY MR. WARE:
Q. So that conclusion as to Michael Goodall's understanding is based upon your recollection of what he told you, is that true?
A. It's based upon the discussion that he and I had, yes.
Q. That was a communication that you had when you were representing him in the construction of his estate plan?
A. Yes.
Q. That was a conversation that he had with you in confidence, correct?
A. Yes.
Q. The cat is sort of out of the bag here throughout as to what Mr. Michael Goodall's understanding was with regard to his rights and whatnot. But I'm going to say that with regard to lawyer-client communications with Mr. Goodall, Michael Goodall,

Mr. Sloan intends to assert the privilege, the lawyer-client privilege, as to statements that Mr. Goodall, Michael Goodall, made to you. So just for the record, we want to assert that privilege, what's been said has been said, and I'll deal with that in the papers.

To be polite about this, but still clear, as Michael Goodall's attorney, it's Michael Goodall's privilege -- and we don't want you talking about it, okay? That's just for the record. We don't want you saying anything more to anybody. Counsel is another matter, but he'll be bound by the same. Those are privileged communications between you and Michael and we want to maintain that privilege until further notice. That's just a statement for the record.

MR. LESSER: In that case, do you anticipate asking Mr. Hastings anything further about his discussions with Mr. Michael Goodall, because if that's true, I'm wondering what you want to do with the transcript of this deposition.

MR. WARE: That's why I'm cutting it off right now, because we haven't talked about that so far. If we're going to talk about that, I just want it to be Mr. Sloan and Mr. Hastings and you and me. I don't want anybody else being privy to those things. That's

exactly where we're going here. I mean, with regard to communications from Mr. Goodall as to his understanding of things, those are privileged and we want to keep them between ourselves until further notice.

Q. So I'm going to skip over that part.

Now, just as a general proposition, there are statements which follow on page 2 with regard to agreements with Guide Dogs for the Blind for any remuneration. You just flatly deny that, right? Guide Dogs for the Blind didn't pay anything to get Guide Dogs for the Blind on this trust, right?

A. That is true.

Q. They didn't pay anybody on your staff?

A. That is true.

Q. They've never done that sort of thing, right, that is pay you to encourage clients to put them as beneficiaries, is that correct?

A. That's true.

Q. That's something you wouldn't do, right?

A. No, I would not do that.

Q. All right. Thanks.

Moving to page 3, please, at paragraph 5. I'm going to focus at about line 11 here, Mr. Hastings. It says, "Unfortunately, his parents found him subject to the undue influence of others, resulting in caution in

their ultimate estate plan."

Are there any notes that you recall looking at to remind you that that was his parents' finding with regard to their son at the time you drafted this declaration?

A. No, that is my clear memory.

Q. Is that memorialized anywhere, such as notes or letters or anything that might be in the file that has been misplaced?

A. I have no idea.

Q. But you have a clear understanding, you have a clear recollection of that?

A. Yes.

Q. Do you recall that that was expressed to you by the Goodalls?

A. Yes.

Q. And do you recall when that was expressed to you by the Goodalls?

A. Prior to amending their trust.

Q. Do you remember what they said in that regard?

A. No.

Q. What you're saying is as you sit here today, you just recall that impression from the words they said, you don't recall the exact words they used. Is that basically true?

A. I do not recall exact words they used.

Q. That's the impression, based upon what you recall them communicating to you. Is that true?

A. It's more than an impression. It was their communication.

Q. Again, with regard to asking you to recall for us here today what words they used to express that feeling or intention, can you tell us anything specifically that they said?

A. No.

Q. Do you recall whether or not they gave you any examples of instances where they had begun to mistrust his management of money?

A. I believe they always mistrusted that. Michael is concerned regarding the original will, where they talked about their concerns for him and decided to do what they did at that time and later changed their mind after watching his conduct.

Q. Do you recall what they later watched to make them change their mind?

A. No.

Q. Did they tell you what they had seen?

A. I do not recall what they told me.

Q. Do you recall whether or not you have notes in your file, the missing file, that might relate to that

subject?
A. I do not know.
Q. In 1990, the Goodalls engaged you to advise them and draw up an estate plan, correct?
A. Yes.
Q. And at that time you drew up a trust for them. That's the September 12, 1990 trust, correct?
A. Yes.
Q. And at that time did you sit down with them and review their assets, to know the universe of their estate?
A. Yes.
Q. And do you recall that at that point the Peach Stone house was part of their estate, correct?
A. Yes.
Q. What else was part of their estate at that time?
A. I don't recall.
Q. Do you recall that they had investments with USAA?
A. At some point in time that came to my attention.
Q. Do you recall that that was brought to your attention at the time that you were employed by them in 1990, to draw up the original trust?

A. Whatever their investments were was brought to my attention at that time.
Q. Okay. The 1990 trust includes, as in the list of the corpus of the trust, it includes the house, which is stated. Do you recall that?
A. Yes.
Q. And plus $1, right?
A. No.
Q. What else is there?
MR. SLOAN: $10.
THE WITNESS: $10.
BY MR. WARE:
Q. Thanks. There's nothing else listed there, right?
A. That's true.
Q. Now, at some point later the house was transferred or quitclaimed to the house, correct?
A. Probably the same day, yes.
Q. That's something you were instrumental in, as I recall the county records. Do you recall that?
A. Yes.
Q. Now, at that point did you assist them in moving any other property into the trust?
A. Yes.
Q. What else?

A. All of the other assets.
Q. Do you recall how that was accomplished in 1990?
A. I would make the exception all of the other aspects, as discussed with them. We made decisions about all the assets, and then the major assets we definitely transferred to the trust. It's possible that the bank accounts were not, because that was not the practice at the time. But any major asset was transferred to the trust, accomplished through paperwork, initiated and monitored by my office.
Q. That's your practice and procedure, correct?
A. Yes.
Q. Do you recall that that happened in this case, with regard to the Goodalls?
A. To my best of recollection, yes.
Q. Mr. Hastings, the distinction I'm trying to draw is this. Clearly that is your practice and procedure, and I respect that, but my question is very specific, and that is, do you recall transferring anything but the house to the Goodalls' trust in 1990? As you sit here today, do you recall specifically transferring anything else to the trust other than the house?
A. I can't answer the question the way it's posed.

Q. What's ambiguous about it? If it's unclear, let me fix it, but I don't know how to fix it.
A. I know those things were transferred. Whether I recall it right now is a different question.
Q. You know those things were transferred because that's the way you always do things. Is that basically it?
A. No.
Q. How do you know that they were done?
A. Because I know they were done.
Q. Okay. So why wasn't it listed on the schedule of assets?
A. It's not my practice. It's a waste of time.
Q. Because?
A. It's more important to change the title to the assets.
Q. Like the real property title was changed, right?
A. Yes.
Q. So the idea is that you don't include in the schedule of assets anything but real property in your practice?
A. That's true. In almost every case.
Q. Would the file, the missing file, contain a record of your office's activity in transferring assets

to the trust?
A. Yes.
Q. That's the sort of thing that file would contain, is that true?
A. Yes. The record may be elsewhere, as well.
Q. Such as in the coffers of the asset management company that had the assets, for example?
A. Yes.
Q. So, for example, in if the assets, if it did turn out that USAA had investment portfolios or annuities, that sort of thing, in the names of the Goodalls, USAA might have those records, correct?
A. That's true.
Q. But as far as your universe of records is concerned, the only place that those records would exist would be in the missing file, correct?
A. No.
Q. Where else would they be in your office?
A. There may be some reference to them in the other trust administration files.
Q. I see. That would be in the 05 or 06 files?
A. Yes.
Q. Just to close the loop on that, though. If your office participated in the transferring of assets to the trust in 1990, a record of that activity would

have been retained or made, kept, by your office in one of the files, correct?
MR. LESSER: You're asking as a matter of --
MR. WARE: Procedure.
MR. LESSER: Matter of procedure?
MR. WARE: Right.
THE WITNESS: There should be some record of what we did, yes.
BY MR. WARE:
Q. Okay, great. Thanks.
MR. LESSER: Going for an hour. Could we take a short break?
MR. WARE: You betcha.
(Short break taken.)
THE COURT REPORTER: Are you going to want a copy of this deposition?
MR. LESSER: Yes, please. Thank you.
(Off the record.)
(Record read as requested.)
BY MR. WARE:
Q. Continuing. Do you recall instructing or advising the Goodalls that they should execute, transfer, title documents with regard to assets that they wanted to put into the trust?
A. Yes.

Q. It's the practice and procedures to advise clients generally that if they want something in the trust, transfer the title into the trust, correct?
A. Yes.
Q. Just to ask. You've had a chance, a little break here. Is there anything you would like to add or change to anything you've said here today so far?
A. I want the opportunity to review the deposition after the fact.
Q. Just as you sit here today, you wouldn't change any answers to any answers you recall making so far?
MR. LESSER: He just wants to know as a result of our conversation on the break if you want to change your testimony.
BY MR. WARE:
Q. Right, that, or your own musings.
A. I'd have to review the whole deposition to know if there's anything. I would doubt it.
Q. That's fine. Thank you.
Then if I can direct your attention to 1994, you recall that there's another document that purports to be a restatement of the trust, and some changes were made to the 1990 trust or estate plan in 1994, correct?
A. Yes.
Q. And if I can direct your attention to page 4,

I'm beginning at paragraph 7, at page 3. It describes that in late July or early August of '94, you met again with the Goodalls.
Do you see that, generally speaking, there?
A. Where are you talking about?
Q. Page 4, paragraph 7.
A. Okay.
Q. Beginning at line 3, "On or about late July, early August 1994." Do you see that?
A. Yes.
Q. "Kenneth Goodall and Rachel Goodall again visited me for advice."
Do you recall what date specifically that was that they visited you?
A. No.
Q. Do you recall whether they visited you on more than one occasion, or one occasion when they were in the process of doing that activity?
A. They visited me at least once. I don't recall how many times.
Q. That was in 1994, correct?
A. Yes.
Q. And would the missing file contain notes with regard to what they wanted to change in their estate plan at that meeting?

A. Probably.
Q. Would the missing file also contain notes with regard to what their assets were at that time?
A. Probably.
Q. When it says they came to visit you, did they visit you at your office, is that your recollection?
A. That is my recollection.
Q. Do you recall your observations with regard to Mr. Goodall's health at that time?
A. No, I don't.
Q. Do you recall anything with regard to Mrs. Goodall's health?
A. No.
Q. Do you recall that Mrs. Goodall was in a wheelchair?
A. I don't recall on that date whether she was or was not.
Q. Do you recall ever seeing Mrs. Goodall in a wheelchair?
A. As you speak of it, it sounds familiar, but I don't have a visual of that in my mind.
Q. Do you recall ever seeing Mr. Goodall in a wheelchair?
A. I don't have a recollection, no.
Q. If I can direct your attention to page 5,

paragraph 10, which begins at line 3, you state there, "Kenneth F. Goodall died on September 10, 1994."
Does that refresh your recollection as to any observations you made about Kenneth Goodall's health when he met with you and Mrs. Goodall in July or early August 1994?
A. No.
Q. This page 4, paragraph 7, it goes on, "During the discussions," this is picking up at line 5, "During the discussion they told me of the changes they wished to make to their estate plan."
Do you recall what changes they described they wanted to make to their estate plan, as you sit here today?
A. The primary one is to revise the direct gift to their son, to a trust for their son.
Q. Anything else come to mind of any changes they had in mind?
A. No.
Q. Do you recall whether they made any provisions or expressed to you what they wanted to happen to their assets, should their son die after they were gone?
A. Yes.
Q. What did they say?
A. If they're both gone and when their son dies,

things are supposed to go to Guide Dogs for the Blind.
Q. Unless he had gotten married and had kids or something like that, is that right?
A. I'd have to read back. I presume that's in there, yes.
Q. Okay. At the time that they made that change in 1994, do you recall the size of their estate that they were going to be leaving to Guide Dogs for the Blind, when their son died?
A. I recall in general terms they had their house and investments equal, at least to the value of their house.
Q. Value of the house being in the neighborhood of 5 or $6,000, something like that, do you recall?
A. I don't recall the value of the house.
Q. Less than a million?
A. Less than a million.
Q. So you recall that their assets, other than their home, were in the neighborhood of about the same value of their house, correct?
A. That's generally what I recall, yes.
Q. When they, in the 1994 trust, appointed Bank of America as the trustee, did you have any influence on that appointment?
A. No.

Q. Do you know why they chose Bank of America as opposed to any other bank?
A. No.
Q. In 1994, was it necessary to obtain some input from Bank of America as to what size an estate they would be interested in administering, as a trustee?
A. Not that I recall.
Q. When you're going to describe an institution as a trustee, do you typically check with that institution to see whether or not they're willing to act as trustee?
A. No.
Q. That's something for your clients to figure out, is that basically right?
A. No.
Q. How do you figure that out, who to designate as the trustee in trusts that you draw up in, say, 1994?
A. The clients and I have a discussion and the clients select a trustee.
Q. Do you have any recollection, again, did any of that discussion refresh your recollection as to why Bank of America was described as the trustee in this 1994 trust?
A. No.
Q. Do you recall who the trustee was in the 1990 trust?

A. I don't recall the trust. I couldn't tell you.
Q. At the bottom of paragraph 7 there on page 4, it refers to Exhibit A, to your declaration. Oh, but before we get to that.
As a general proposition, when you were drafting this declaration, that is August 18, 2011, do you recall discussing the contents of that declaration when drafting it with any person, such as a secretary, did you have any discussions with Bank of America or anybody else, trying to put together this chronology?
A. Not that I recall.
Q. Have you ever had any discussions with the attorney in this proceeding, Mr. Rothstein?
A. Yes.
Q. Did you ever discuss with him the matters of the Goodall family's matters at any time prior to drafting this declaration?
A. I don't understand the question.
Q. Before you drafted this declaration, Exhibit 3, on August 18, 2011, had you had any discussions with Mr. Rothstein?
A. Yes.
Q. About what?
A. I don't recall.
Q. Do you recall making any notes of your

discussions with Mr. Rothstein, at any time, any discussions?
A. No.
Q. Now, digress, now we're on Exhibit A to Exhibit 3, it's Declaration in Support of Petition for Determination of the Beneficiaries, et cetera. Second page is of interest to me, paragraph 4, begins on line 2. I'm sorry, I think we've covered that.
Let me ask it, anyway. At page 4, line 4, it begins, "It was my understanding, based on that discussion," that is with Kenneth and Rachel Goodall, "that Rachel and Kenneth intend the balance of the trust established for the benefit of Michael remaining at Michael's death to be distributed," et cetera.
Do you see that?
A. Yes.
Q. Again, we don't have any notes of that discussion, correct?
A. I don't know.
Q. Would you expect to have notes of that discussion in the missing file, knowing what you know about your practice of discussing matters with clients, that sort of thing?
A. I would probably have a statement as to the direction as to what they wanted me to do.

Q. That's all for Exhibit A. Let me just review my notes here, please.
If you recall, Mr. Hastings, at the time of the 1994 amendment and restatement, did you have a discussion with the Goodalls as to what assets were in the trust at that time, in the 1990 trust at that time?
A. You asked that question already.
Q. I beg your pardon. If I did, I forgot the answer.
A. Probably.
Q. It would be your practice and procedure to find out what's in the 1990 trust, if we're going to amend that trust and restate it, let's find out what's in there, right?
A. Probably.
Q. Probably, as we discussed, you would have made notes of that, correct?
A. If it was discussed, I would have made notes.
Q. I'd like to ask you about the execution of those documents in 1994.
You recall that two documents were prepared. One was a trust -- three, actually. A trust and two pour-over wills, correct?
A. Yes.
Q. Those documents were signed by the Goodalls in

your presence?
A. Yes.
Q. The trust is not witnessed, correct?
A. That's true.
Q. But it is notarized, correct?
A. Yes.
Q. At that point you were a notary public, correct?
A. Correct, yes.
Q. And you notarized the trust, correct?
A. Yes.
Q. With regard to the pour-over wills, they were witnessed, as I recall?
A. Yes.
Q. They were witnessed by you and your secretary, was that it?
A. I believe so.
Q. That's the usual practice, as you recall your activities in 1994?
A. Yes.
Q. Was your secretary then still your secretary?
A. No.
Q. Your secretary then who witnessed that will, is she still around, as far as you know? She hasn't died or anything, I hope.

A. I don't recall who it was.
Q. Let me just pull that up, so I can ask that.
Let me ask you this. I have asked the clerk's office to pull those two wills for me. They're able to find Mrs. Goodall's will, they can't find Kenneth's will. Do you know why that might be?
A. Of course not.
Q. Other than just the clerk, yeah, who knows. Unless I ask the question, I can't be sure.
There's nothing that happened that you know of that would explain why the clerk seems to have misplaced Mr. Goodall's will?
A. I know of nothing.
Q. Thank you. That's what I need to know.
At page 5, paragraph 12, at line 24, it says, "During the administration of the estate of Rachel Goodall, all assets of the bypass trust and the survivor's trust were passed to Bank of America as trustee and placed into the trust for Michael, as directed by the declaration of trust dated August 24, 1994."
Do you see that statement?
A. Yes.
Q. Do you recall what assets were transferred to Bank of America at that time?

A. The house, USAA assets and all investment assets. I don't recall the specific assets beyond that.
Q. The house and the USAA assets and what else?
A. All other investment assets.
Q. Do you recall what those included?
A. I just said I do not.
Q. Thank you. In the files that you maintain, would there be a list of those assets which were transferred to Bank of America, as described in that paragraph?
A. Probably.
Q. Do you know probably what file they would be in?
A. In Mrs. Goodall's file.
Q. Mrs. Goodall's file that we still have. That's the 06 file, right?
A. Yes.
Q. Do you recall how long it took to get those assets transferred?
A. No.
Q. Do you recall whether there was any resistance by USAA to transferring those assets to Bank of America?
A. I don't recall that there was any resistance.
Q. Neither of the pour-over wills are probated, right?

A. That's true.
Q. What role did you have in transferring the assets to Bank of America, if you recall?
A. We ran the trust administration, and it was our job to get all the assets to Bank of America once it was determined that the trust administration was complete.
Q. Once the trust administration was complete, will you tell me what you mean by that.
A. The trust administration is a process.
Q. The trust administration process to which you refer is the process of transferring the assets to the new trustee, which was then Bank of America, correct?
A. That's the end result of the process, yes.
Q. At that point the trust administration process is concluded, correct?
A. Yes.
Q. Thank you. Was the trust administration process, the trust administration process of the estate of Rachel Goodall, complete before you met with Michael to draw up his will?
A. Yes.
MR. WARE: I would just like to take a brief recess, talk to Mr. Sloan and we'll come back. We're nearly done.
(Short break taken.)

BY MR. WARE:
Q. Mr. Hastings, I'm almost through.
When you met were the Goodalls to change the plan in 1994, it's your recollection that they came to your office to do that?
A. I don't believe they did. I thought about that since you asked the question.
Q. Thank you. Tell me what you recall about that meeting, or meetings.
A. I don't really recall anything about the meeting, but I refreshed my recollection as to where it might have been.
Q. Thank you.
A. And it apparently was at their house.
Q. Do you recall what it is that refreshed your recollection?
A. Looking at the trust document.
Q. The trust document. You looked at it here? Do you have a copy of the trust document?
A. This one right here.
Q. This one. What is it about the trust document that --
A. It says was executed in San Rafael, California.
Q. Your office at the time was not in San Rafael?
A. That's true.

Q. Where was your office at the time?
A. San Anselmo.
Q. Fair enough. Does that further refresh your recollection as to the physical condition of Mr. Goodall at the time?
A. At the moment it does not.
Q. But at this point, so we're clear, you recall probably you went to their office in San Rafael rather than met at your office in San Anselmo at the time?
A. I would say I went to their house in San Rafael, yes.
Q. That is a fine point, but let me just ask you this.
The document that you're looking at, the trust, the amendment and restatement of the trust, says what it says. It says San Rafael, fair enough. But what you're saying is that seeing that San Rafael refreshes your recollection, as you sit here today. So you're beginning to recall it was at their house that you met them?
A. Yes.
Q. I hate to belabor it. Thank you very much.
Do you recall that you met them together, that you were all together at the same time, you did not meet them separately?

A. The only time I met separately was with Mrs. Goodall, after his death.
Q. Thank you. Do you recall that your secretary came with you to their house to witness the signing of the will, as well?
A. I don't specifically recall that she did, but she would have, yes.
Q. It's something in your practices and procedures in 1994, at times you would need a witness, you would bring your secretary with you when you were calling on clients, doing house calls, so to speak?
A. Yes.
Q. It was not unheard of?
A. No.
Q. Now, with regard to your representation of Mr. Thornally and Hoppe, if there is a signed retention agreement between you and them, it would be in the Michael Goodall file, correct?
A. Yes.
Q. The dispositive provisions which make Guide Dogs for the Blind the beneficiary of this trust, now that Michael has died, is where in the trust? I put the trust here. I don't intend to defoliate the planet by attaching it, but if you would help me find those provisions.

MR. SLOAN: Page 18.
MR. LESSER: I'll object to the question on the grounds it calls for a legal conclusion.
MR. WARE: Yeah, I understand.
Q. If you would answer the question, I would be appreciative.
A. I have not reviewed all of this. I have not read the trust completely today.
Q. Yes.
A. But the gist of the whole thing is that after the Goodalls, everything goes to the trust for Michael. The trust for Michael then says what happens on the termination of the trust, which doesn't take into effect, doesn't take into account that Michael may die. Or it takes into account that he died, but it wasn't the intention of the clients that it go just by B.
What the intention was, was that instead, at that point in time, it would revert back to 6.3, as if Michael had predeceased them and will go through, without issue, and you would go through the line and then it gets to 6.3-D, which gives the $20,000 gifts to family members and then to Guide Dogs for the Blind.
Q. Okay. You were just pointing to page 19 and then back to 18?
A. That's true.

Q. I understand.
MR. SLOAN: My question, since he's an attorney, why doesn't the document that he drafted say what he says it says? Because it doesn't say that.
BY MR. WARE:
Q. Well, you have referred us to pages 18 and 19 of the trust, correct?
A. Yes.
MR. WARE: That's enough. The document says what the document says.
That's all I have.
MR. SLOAN: You're not going to ask him why he didn't do a better job of drafting the document?
MR. WARE: No, I'm not.
MR. SLOAN: To say what he claims it should have said?
MR. WARE: No, I'm not.
BY MR. WARE:
Q. The only thing I'd like to say, is that I don't know, you know -- not quite yet, not quite yet.
Because if that file turns up, I'd sure like to find out what it says. So is there any place that you might look for it, that file, that you haven't looked for it, Mr. Hastings?
A. I'll answer that question off record, so you

have an understanding.
Q. That's okay, for now at least. I don't want to embarrass anybody here, but you can understand how it's pretty important to me.
MR. WARE: We'll go off the record for a moment.
(Off the record.)
MR. WARE: So just for the record, we had a discussion off the record, and Mr. Hastings was describing what sounded like a diligent search of the file, and we've also been discussing that he will continue to look for the file and if it shows up, I will be notified promptly by Mr. Lesser that the file has been discovered and then we can figure out where to go from there with regard to reconvening the deposition.
Q. I'm not just throwing this twist at the end. I'm not asking you to come back when you find the file, but I'll do what I have to do to accomplish that. All I'm asking for is your continued good efforts to find the file, please.
A. Yes.
Q. And notification if it turns up.
MR. LESSER: The problem is I don't want some ambiguous commitment to continue to look for this forever. I think his testimony reflects what's already

been a diligent search. If Mr. Hastings wants to commit to looking in a few places that he hasn't already looked, that's fine with me, but I want the record to be clear that he has already made a diligent search and that we are not committing to anything that will support some additional motion or legal proceeding to try to force Mr. Hastings to do anything more than he's already done.
MR. WARE: Right. Now, with regard to getting other files, though, you, Mr. Lesser, will accept service of any motions with regard to compelling the production of those other files that I would file, so I need not trouble Mr. Hastings with serving him with that document, correct? We've covered this before, but I just want to cover it again.
MR. LESSER: Yes, I think you have some meeting and conferring to do before you do that, but as a matter of service, yes, I will self-service of whatever you choose is fine.
MR. SLOAN: May I ask you a question? I'll ask him.
Our understanding is that the original signed 1994 trust is in the missing file and he does not know where that trust is.
MR. WARE: That's a question, if we could, this

last one.
Q. Where is the original 1994 restatement of trust?
A. I don't know. I would presume I have it.
Q. You would think it would be in one of the files that you do have?
A. Yes.
Q. Not the missing file?
A. Yes.
MR. WARE: Okay.
MR. SLOAN: We want to see the signed original 1994 trust to see if he really signed it, because we don't believe he did sign it, we think it's a forgery. I'll go on record right now. We think it's a forgery. We do not think that Colonel Goodall signed the 1994 documents. We don't think he was capable of signing that 1994 document because he had a feeding tube inserted in his abdomen, he was hospitalized, in the hospital, he wasn't walking anywhere, he never saw Mr. Hastings. The whole thing is a fraud. I'm right on the record telling you exactly what's going on in this case.
BY MR. WARE:
Q. Where would you expect to find the original 1994 trust, among the files that we were discussing

earlier, in the Kenneth Goodall trust administration file?
A. I don't know which one.
Q. It would be in one of the two, either the Kenneth or the Rachel Goodall trust administration files?
A. Yes.
MR. WARE: Thanks. I'll take that up.
(Whereupon, the proceedings were concluded at 4:06 p.m.)
-oOo-

JAMES R. HASTINGS

STATE OF CALIFORNIA
SONOMA COUNTY

I, CINDY J. KAISER, duly authorized to administer oaths pursuant to Section 2093(b) of the California Code of Civil Procedure, do hereby certify that

JAMES R. HASTINGS,

the witness in the foregoing deposition, was duly sworn by me to testify to the truth in the within entitled cause; that said deposition was taken at the time and place set forth; that the testimony of said witness was reported by me, a Certified Shorthand Reporter and a disinterested person, and was thereafter transcribed by computer under my direction into booklet form; that the witness was given an opportunity to read and correct said deposition and to subscribe to the same.

I further certify that I am not of counsel or attorney for either or any of the parties in the foregoing deposition and caption named, nor in any way interested in the outcome of the cause named in said caption.

Executed November 28, 2011, at Rohnert Park California.

____
Deposition Officer

WEST COAST REPORTERS, INC.
117 Paul Drive, Suite A
San Rafael, CA 94903
(415) 472-2361 * 1-800-979-2361
FAX (415) 472-2371

November 28, 2011

To: JAMES R. HASTINGS
1003 Third Street
San Rafael, CA 94901

Re: In the Matter of the Goodall Trust

Dear Mr. Hastings:

Please be advised that the transcript of your deposition, taken on November 14, 2011 in the above-entitled matter, has been transcribed and is now ready for your review by calling for an appointment in our San Rafael Office.

In the alternative, you may choose to discuss this matter with your attorney to determine if counsel requires that you do read, make any corrections that you think are appropriate, and sign the transcript of your deposition before it is sealed.

Your rights regarding signature of this deposition are contained in the Code of Civil Procedure, and the original deposition transcript will be sealed after 30 days plus 5 days for mailing, from the date of this letter, and thereafter sent to the noticing attorney.

Yours very truly,
WEST COAST REPORTERS, INC.

CINDY J. KAISER, CSR 7647

cc: Original transcript
All Counsel

SAM WARE
ATTORNEY AT LAW

700 Larkspur Landing Circle, #199
Larkspur, CA 94939
415-461-4872 (tele) 415-532-2412 (fax)
sam@samware.us

November 11, 2011

Don Lesser
1010 B St. Suite 350
San Rafael, CA 94901
By facsimile to 415-295-4122

Re: Goodall Trust

Dear Don,

We are coming up on the deposition of Mr. Hastings on Monday at 2 PM and I have your objections to the document portion of the subpoena.

I do not see any legal requirement for a formal meet and confer letter here, but, to save a step, I thought I would address your objections at this time.

First, I frankly do not see anything incomprehensible about the requests. I want him to bring everything he has related to the Goodalls, Kenneth, Rachel, and Michael, and everything he has related to the actions in San Francisco, both past and present, and in Marin. Plainly he had all of this data to refer to in drafting the declarations he has filed, and I want to be able to cross-examine him on not only what he looked at but also what he might have looked at when he was preparing these declarations, which purport to tell the Courts the whole story.

With regard to the lawyer-client and attorney work-product objections, please take a look at Evidence Code §§957, 960 which relates to probate/trust litigation, and please also take a look at Section 912, which relates to the issue of waiver of such privileges, expressly as to the lawyer – client privilege and by extension under case law as to the work product privilege. *Wells Fargo Bank v Superior Court* (2000) 22 Cal 4th 201, 21[illegible].

In short, I want to cross-examine Mr. Hastings on every aspect of his involvement with the Goodalls, including, but not limited to, his collection of information, advise, and drafting of the estate plans of Kenneth,

E

E

Rachel, and Michael Goodall, his participation in collecting the Goodall assets and transferring them to Bank of America (including, but not limited to, the USAA accounts), his representation of the trust in earlier days when Michael Goodall tried to replace Bank of America as the trustee, his later representation of Michael Goodall in planning his estate, and, his communications with anybody in recent days in preparing his declarations.

That's where I'm going, and that's the way I see the law.

Sincerely,

Sam Ware

Cc Rothstein
and McDonnell by e-mail

SAM WARE
ATTORNEY AT LAW

700 Larkspur Landing Circle, #199
Larkspur, CA 94939
415.464.4872(tele) 415.532.2412(fax)
sam@samware.us

December 2, 2011

Don Lesser
1010 B St. Suite 350
San Rafael, CA 94901
By facsimile to 415-295-4122

Re: Goodall Trust

Dear Don,

I received a copy of Mr. Hastings deposition yesterday, and so I am ready to go to court and bring a motion to compel.

Please consider this my further and last meet and confer demand that he comply with the subpoena by producing the four Goodall files identified at the deposition and submit to a further deposition on the contents of those files.

Please give me your written reply by the close of business Monday next, December 5, 2011.

Sincerely,

Sam Ware

CC Rothstein and McDonnell (by e-mail)

EXHIBIT F

F

Sam Ware

From: Don A. Lesser [DLesser@LesserGroup.com]
Sent: Friday, December 02, 2011 10:59 AM
To: 'Sam Ware'
Subject: RE: motion to compel "meet and confer" letter

Mr. Ware:

I have your letter and will of course pass it on to my client for review and consideration. I will note, however, that neither your letter, nor any of your previous demands for full compliance with the subpoena, constitute any sort of good faith meet and confer. You have never addressed any of our objections to categories of documents demanded in the subpoena on the merits, or at all. Let me take a moment to be more specific so that the record will be clear that Mr. Hastings, at least, has meet and conferred in good faith.

1. The scope of the proceeding in which you have taken the deposition, that brought by Bank of America in the San Francisco Superior Court, is narrow: it is to determine, according to the wording of the *Restated* Goodall Trust of 1994, and perhaps any extrinsic evidence at that time or afterward, the Goodalls' intentions regarding trust assets other than the San Rafael home upon their son's death. Demands for "all writings which relate in any way" to each of the Goodalls, the San Francisco proceeding, the Marin County proceeding, and Mr. Hastings several declarations in those proceedings, plainly do not comply with the requirement of the Code of Civil Procedure that subpoena contain "specification with reasonable particularity of any materials or category of materials to be produced." C.C.P. s. 2025.220(a)(4). Nor is the scope of the subpoena consistent with the Court's order that defined the purpose for which the Court was authorizing Ms. Hastings' deposition before ruling on the Bank's petition.

   First, the term "relate" is so inherently subjective that no one can know with any certainty what documents Mr. Sloan is demanding.

   Second, a demand for *all* documents, regardless of when they were created, that merely "relate" to a person, or a lawsuit, or even a declaration, is such an overbroad categorization that it surely encompasses documents not within the permissible scope of discovery, particularly when the underlying claim is of such narrow scope.

   This overbreadth involves specific prejudice to a non-party witness such as Mr. Hastings, who to respond would have to undertake the substantial burden of reviewing every page of his voluminous files , created over an almost 25-year time period, for documents protected from disclosure by the attorney-client privilege and the attorney work product rule, among other grounds for non-disclosure. He would then have to speculate about whether each page of those files "relates," in the same sense that you intended it, to any of the vague and unparticularized categories you listed in the subpoena. Given that Mr. Hastings has acted as counsel not only for the Goodalls, but also for their trustee following their death, Ms. Hastings cannot assume that Evidence Code sections 957 or 960 would except all his attorney-client communications from the lawyer-client privilege. Also, those statutes do not provide any exceptions to Ms. Hastings' right of protection in his work product. Imposing such burden on a non-party witness is particularly inappropriate under applicable court decisions.

2. To the extent your letter of this morning constitutes an implied clarification that the subpoena is limited to the client files Mr. Hastings described at his deposition, it does not address the issues of overbreadth, burden or attorney-client privilege and work product with respect to a 25-year engagement.

3. As Ms. Hastings has explained, the documents in his possession, custody or control that are likely to contain evidence potentially relevant to the Goodalls' intentions, and which would be excepted from the attorney-client privilege for that reason, are contained in a single file, the "01" file, which he agreed to produce if it can be located. Before the deposition he conducted a good faith and diligent search, the scope of which you explored

EXHIBIT 6

at the deposition. Apparently you are declining Mr. Hastings' offer of compromise regarding his objections to your subpoena. Thus the burden of engaging in a good faith meet and confer process is now on you to propose a reasonable narrowing of the subpoena to address Ms. Hastings' objections. He remains open to a reasonable compromise of this dispute that does not require him, as a non-party witness, to spend inordinate amounts of time searching through voluminous files he assembled over a 25-year series of engagements related to the Goodalls' estate plan.

Regards,

Don A. Lesser
THE LESSER LAW GROUP
1010 B Street, Suite 350
San Rafael, California 94901
Ph: 415.453.7600
Fx: 415.295.4122
Web: www.lessergroup.com

This email communication may contain CONFIDENTIAL INFORMATION, WHICH ALSO MAY BE LEGALLY PRIVILEGED, and is intended only for the use of the intended recipients identified above. If you are not the intended recipient of this communication, you are hereby notified that any unauthorized review, use, dissemination, distribution, downloading, or copying of this communication is strictly prohibited. If you are not the intended recipient and have received this communication in error, please immediately notify us by reply email, delete the communication and destroy all copies.

From: Sam Ware [mailto:sam@samware.us]
Sent: Friday, December 02, 2011 9:22 AM
To: 'Don A. Lesser'; 'Rothstein, Gary'; 'McDonnell, John'; 'Adornato, Alicia A.'
Subject: motion to compel "meet and confer" letter

PROOF OF SERVICE

I certify and declare as follows:

I am over the age of 18 years, not a party to this action. My business address is 700 Larkspur Landing Circle #199, Larkspur, CA 94939. I am readily familiar with the business practices of my firm for the collection, processing and service of items with the United States Postal Service, express service providers (same day messenger and overnight) and facsimile transmission.

On the date set forth below, I served the foregoing documents described as a motion to compel and separate statement on the parties who have appeared in this action as follows:

__X__: BY FIRST CLASS MAIL — By placing [ ] the original [X] a true and correct copy thereof in each sealed envelope addressed as indicated below. Said sealed envelopes, with postage fully prepaid, were deposited with the United States Postal Service in San Francisco, California this same day in the ordinary course of business.

____: BY FEDERAL EXPRESS — By placing [ ] the original [ ] a true and correct copy thereof in each sealed envelope addressed as indicated below. Said envelopes were deposited for collection and processing by Federal Express, Priority Overnight Service, in San Francisco, California.

____: BY PERSONAL SERVICE: By placing [ ] the original [x] a true and correct copy thereof in each sealed envelope addressed as indicated below and causing said envelopes to be delivered by hand, by our firm's messenger, to the offices of the addressees indicated below.

____: BY FACSIMILE TRANSMISSION — The foregoing document was transmitted between 9:00 a.m. and 5:00 p.m. to the fax number indicated below each address.

____: BY EMAIL TRANSMISSION — The foregoing document was transmitted between 9:00 a.m. and 5:00 p.m. to the e-mail address indicated below.

Gary D. Rothstein
Manatt, Phelps & Phillips, LLP
One Embarcadero Center, 30th Floor
San Francisco CA 94111

John L McDonnell
Reed Smith
1999 Harrison St. # 2400
Oakland, CA 94612

Don Lesser
1010 B St. Suite 350
San Rafael, CA 94901

I declare under penalty of perjury under the laws of the State of California that the foregoing statements are true and correct.

Executed December 14, 2011

Don A. Lesser, SBN #112887
THE LESSER LAW GROUP
1010 B Street, Suite 350
San Rafael, California 94901
Telephone: (415) 453-7600
Facsimile: (415) 295-4122
E-mail: DLesser@LesserGroup.com

Attorney for Subpoenaed Witness
JAMES R. HASTINGS

FILED
Superior Court of California
County of San Francisco
DEC 29 2011
CLERK OF THE COURT
BY: [signature]
Deputy Clerk

CALIFORNIA SUPERIOR COURT

SAN FRANCISCO COUNTY

In the Matter of the Trust for Michael created under the Goodall Trust dated January 19, 1999	Case No. PTR-99-273030 **DEPONENT JAMES R. HASTINGS' OPPOSITION TO RESPONDENT SAM SLOAN'S MOTION TO COMPEL PRODUCTION OF DOCUMENTS AND FURTHER DEPOSITION** **Hearing: January 12, 2012** **Time: 2:15 p.m.** **Department: 204**

BY FAX

I. INTRODUCTION AND FACTUAL BACKGROUND

Non-party witness James R. Hastings was the estate planning attorney for Kenneth and Rachel Goodall, whose intentions in preparing a 1994 amendment of their testamentary trust are the subject of this action brought by the Goodalls' appointed trustee, Bank of America. In a single cause of action, the Bank seeks a judicial declaration as to the Goodalls' intended residual beneficiary under the 1994 trust amendment. Mr. Hastings has stated in a declaration filed in this proceeding that his clients' intended residual beneficiary was Guide Dogs for the Blind. Respondent Estate of Michael Goodall (the Goodalls' deceased son) disputes Mr. Hastings' testimony. In its opposition to the Bank's petition, the Estate of Michael asked this Court to allow limited discovery regarding Kenneth Goodall's intent in changing the trust, questioning his competency to do so a few weeks before his death in 1994. At a hearing on August 23, 2011, the Court postponed its ruling on the Bank's petition to allow discovery on that limited issue only.

The Estate of Michael, though its representative Sam Sloan, then issued a subpoena for Mr. Hastings's deposition. The Estate appended a demand that Ms. Hastings produce documents at the deposition. Instead of seeking documents reflecting the Goodalls' testamentary intentions, consistent with the Court's order, Mr. Sloan propounded demands for "Any and all writings . . . which in any way relate to the following:

1. Kenneth F. Goodall
2. Rachel A. Goodall
3. K. Michael Goodall
4. San Francisco action number PTR-99-273030
5. Marin probate action number PR 1100596
6. The declarations you filed in the actions described in #4 and #5 above."

Mr. Hastings served objections to the scope of the document requests prior to the deposition, a copy of which is attached as Exhibit B to the Declaration of Sam Ware supporting Respondent's Motion to Compel Production ("Ware Decl."). Nevertheless, Mr. Hastings searched for, and was prepared to produce, his Goodall file containing his notes and other documents generated while preparing the Goodalls' estate plan and drafting the trust and its amendment. (Deposition of Hastings ("Hastings Depo.") at 10:18-11:5, 22:7-14, attached as Exh. A to Declaration of Don A. Lesser Opposing Motion to Compel Production of Documents ("Lesser Decl.").) He performed what the Estate of Michael's counsel, Mr. Ware, has acknowledged was a diligent search (Hastings Depo. at 65:8-20, Lesser Decl., Exh. A), but was unable to find the file.

Sloan's motion to compel Hastings to produce every shred of paper that "relates to" his former clients should be denied because the subpoena *duces tecum* Sloan seeks to enforce: (1) exceeds the scope of discovery this Court has allowed, (2) is legally defective, and (3) is grossly overbroad. Sloan's motion should be denied for the further reason that he eschewed any good faith effort to resolve this dispute in meet and confer discussions prior to filing, as the applicable statute requires. Having failed to prove any right to further production of documents, Sloan is not entitled to reconvene Mr. Hastings' deposition either.

II. SLOAN'S DOCUMENT DEMANDS EXTEND FAR BEYOND PERMISSIBLE DISCOVERY AND ABUSE THIS COURT'S DISCOVERY ORDER

The narrow issue presented by the pleadings in this action is whether the Goodalls intended to amend their trust to name Guide Dogs for the Blind as their residual beneficiary, or whether their son Michael remained their intended residual beneficiary following the trust amendment. (Sloan's Memorandum of Points & Authorities ("Supp. Memo.") at 2:22-3:15.) At the August 25, 2011 hearing in this matter, the Court allowed Sloan to take discovery solely regarding the Goodalls' "intent" in furtherance of his contention that the Estate of Michael is the Goodalls' intended residual beneficiary.[1] Sloan's document demands, to the extent they are understandable, reach far beyond any file materials Mr. Hastings has that could shed light on the Goodalls' testamentary intentions. Mr. Ware's November 11, 2011 letter responding to Mr. Hastings' objections (Ware Declaration, Exh. E) baldly admits Mr. Sloan's intent to ignore the Court's parameters on his discovery. Mr. Ware states: "In short, ***I want to cross-examine Mr. Hastings on every aspect of his involvement with the Goodalls***, including, but not limited to, his collection of information, advise [sic], and drafting of the estate plans of Kenneth, Rachel and Michael Goodall, ,his participation in collecting the Goodall assets and transferring them to Bank fo America (including, but not limited to, the USAA accounts), his representation of the trust in earlier days when Michael Goodall tried to replace Bank of America as the trustee, his later representation fo Michael Goodall in planning his estate, and, his communications with anybody in recentn days in preparing his declarations. That's where I'm going, and that's the way I see the law." [Emphasis added.]

Perhaps even more troubling than Mr. Sloan's eagerness to ignore the scope of the Court's order is his obvious intent to abuse it. The ulterior purpose in his document demands is

---

[1] Counsel has initiated a request for the transcript of the hearing and will submit it to the Court as soon as it is obtained from the court reporter.

blindingly clear: to further Mr. Sloan's claims of wrongdoing against Mr. Hastings, which he asserts *not in this action* but in another action the Estate of Michael has filed against Mr. Hastings in Marin County. (Lesser Decl., ¶ 3, Exh. B.) For that purpose, Mr. Sloan wants every piece of paper Mr. Hastings generated or received in the course of performing legal services for the Goodalls, for their trustee, Bank of America, and, for a brief period, for Michael Goodall. But if Sloan wants discovery to support his claims against Mr. Hastings in the Marin County action, he must pursue discovery in that action. He cannot burden this Court, these parties, and Mr. Hastings, as a non-party witness in this action, with grossly overbroad and burdensome discovery requests having nothing to do with the narrow issue before the Court here.[2]

III. THE DOCUMENT DEMANDS ARE LEGALLY DEFECTIVE, GROSSLY OVERBROAD, AND UNDULY BURDENSOME FOR HASTINGS

A deposition subpoena that includes a demand for documents must provide a "specification with reasonable particularity of any material or category of materials to be produced." Code Civ. Proc. § 2025.220(a)(4). Defining the requested categories merely as "all writings which relate in any way" to the Goodalls, the San Francisco and Marin proceedings and Mr. Hastings' declarations plainly does not provide "reasonable particularity" of the materials being sought. First, the term "relate" is so inherently subjective that no one can know with any certainty what documents Mr. Sloan is demanding, or what documents must be produced to comply with the requirements of the Discovery Act. Second, a demand for *all* documents that "relate" to an individual, regardless of when they were created or received, or what may be their subject matter, is so overbroad that it surely encompasses documents not within the scope of discovery as defined by the parties' pleadings, particularly when the Bank's petition here is of such narrow scope. *See, e.g., Calcor Space Facility, Inc. v. Superior Court,* 53 Cal.App.4th 216,

[2] Sloan's argument that he must have all Mr. Hastings' files to cross-examine him on his declarations in this action misleads the Court about the scope of those declarations. They address only the issue on which the Court has allowed Sloan to take discovery: the Goodalls' intentions with respect to their trust. Thus he does not need, and the Court has not authorized him to seek, documents having nothing to do with the Goodalls' intentions, even to cross-examine Mr. Hastings regarding his declarations, which speak only to that issue.

222 (1997).

Further, the overbreadth of Sloan's document demands involves specific prejudice to a non-party witness such as Mr. Hastings, who to comply with the demands would have to undertake the substantial burden of reviewing every page of his files, created over the 25 years that have elapsed since he first consulted with the Goodalls regarding their estate plan in 1990. Since then he continued to represent the Goodalls, and then after Ms. Goodall's death in 1999 he represented the trustee, Bank of America, in handling trust administration matters. Thereafter he represented Michael Goodall, and then his executors, until about January 2011. (Declaration of James R. Hastings, Family and Estate Planning Attorney for the Goodalls, dated August 18, 2011, at ¶ 2, Ware Decl., Exh. C.) He would have to review all those documents for those that might be protected from disclosure by the attorney-cleint privilege and the attorney work product rule, among other grounds for non-disclosure. He would then have to speculate about whether each page of those files "relates," in the same sense that Mr. Sloan intended the term, to any of the overbroad categories in the subpoena. As a non-party witness, Mr. Hastings should not be put to this burden when Sloan refuses to particularize his demands to correspond with the narrow scope of discovery the Court authorized.

Sloans' arguments, in his Separate Statement, that neither the attorney-client privilege nor the work product rule apply to Mr. Hastings documents are wrong, and miss the point of Mr. Hastings objections. Evidence Code Sections 960 and 975 provide that there is no privilege as to communications relevant to "an issue between parties all of whom claim through a deceased client" (§ 975) or "an issue concerning the intention" of a deceased client with respect to a writing the client signed. Sloan overlooks the fact that Mr. Hastings' files include documents generated in his capacity as a lawyer for Bank of America, the Goodalls' trustee, Michael Goodall, and his executors, none of whose communications with him are subject to these statutory exceptions to the privilege. Sloan is also wrong in his argument that Mr. Hastings has "waived" the privilege by his statements in his declarations in this action. Only the "holder" of the privilege can waive it, and the client, not the attorney, holds the attorney-client privilege. Ev. C. § 912; *Rittenhouse v. Superior Court,* 235 Cal.App.3d 1584, 1588 (1991). In the trust context, the holder of the privilege is the "current trustee," who can assert the privilege against beneficiaries of the trust in matters of trust administration. *Moeller v. Superior Court,* 16 cal.4th 1124, 1129-1131 (1997); *Wells Fargo Bank, N.A. v. Superior Court,* 22 Cal.4th 201, 213 (2000).

Sloan's arguments about the merits of any privilege claim are also largely beside the point. As the former counsel for Bank of America, Mr. Hastings is *required* to assert the privilege as to any communications with the Bank in his capacity as their counsel. Thus, in responding to Sloan's wide-ranging document demands, Mr. Hastings must review all the requested documents for potential privileges – a daunting task from which he could easily be relieved if Sloan had complied with this Court's order limiting his discovery to that relevant to the Goodalls' intentions in amending their trust in 1994.

IV. HASTINGS PERFORMED A DILIGENT SEARCH FOR DISCOVERABLE DOCUMENTS

There is no basis for Sloan's demand that the Court order Mr. Hastings "go back and conduct an exhaustive search in order to find" his "Goodall Estate Planning File," i.e., the file Mr. Hastings has acknowledged is within the scope of the Court's ordered discovery, but which he was unable to locate. (Supp. Memo. at 5:21-28.) Sloan's lawyer examined Mr. Hastings at length at his deposition concerning the scope of his search for the file, which included all parts of his office and off-site storage locations where the file might be. (Hastings Depo. at 17:22-22:1, Lesser Decl., Exh. A.) Apparently satisfied with Mr. Hastings' efforts, Mr. Ware admitted on the record that Ms. Hastings had conducted a diligent search. (*Id.* at 65:8-15.) There is nothing further for the Court to order Mr. Hastings to do.

V. SLOAN HAS NOT MEET AND CONFERRED IN GOOD FAITH.

Code Civ. Proc. § 2025.480(b) requires the moving party to file a "meet and confer declaration" compliant with § 2016.040. Sloan has failed to file a compliant declaration because his declaration and "meet and confer" letters make clear he did not meet and confer in good faith. The only substantive discussion of Sloan's position appears in his November 11, 2011 letter attached as Exhibit E to Mr. Ware's supporting declaration. Nowhere does he address the objections that the scope of the document demands exceeded the Court's order and the bounds of the parties' pleadings. Nowhere does he explain why Sloan is entitled legally to demand such a broad scope of documents. His only explanation of his position, which does not address these issues, is his statement simply reiterating the demands themselves, i.e., "I want him [Hastings] to bring everything he has related to the Goodalls . . . [and] the actions in San Francisco . . . and Marin." His only attempt at justifying the scope of these demands is his statement that Mr. Hastings "had all this data to refer to in drafting the declarations he has filed, and I want to be able to cross-examine him" on the that material.

Central to the "meet and confer" process is an explanation of why the disputed demands were proper, and a willingness to engage in "give and take" in order to reach a reasonable compromise that will avoid a discovery motions. Brown & Weil, *California Practice Guide: Civil Procedure Before Trial* (The Rutter Group) at §§ 8:1161 – 8:1163, pp. 8F-67-8F-70. (Supp. 2011). The moving party fails to meet and confer in good faith when it makes no effort to explain how its requests were proper, and insists on full compliance with grossly overbroad requests. *Obregon v. Superior Court,* 67 Cal.App.4th 424, 431 (1998).

Sloan's meet and confer letters dated November 11 and December 2, 1011 (Ware Decl., Exhs. E and F) reveal no meaningful explanation of why Sloan's document demands were proper, and no compromise proposal, even after Mr. Hastings offered to produce the Goodall Estate Planning File. The *only* proposed compromise in this matter has been Mr. Hastings'. Throughout, Sloan has insisted on full compliance with his overbroad demands, which clearly exceed what this Court authorized as discovery in aid of his opposition to Bank of America's petition. Sloan has not demonstrated, and cannot prove, that he engaged in a good faith meet and confer effort to avoid this motion. Had he done so, it could have been avoided. Because he has failed to comply with a condition to prevailing on his motion, the motion should be denied on that ground as well.

VI. CONCLUSION

Sloan's motion should be denied because his document demands exceed the scope of discovery this Court allowed him to oppose the Bank's petition; fail to particularize the documents requested; and are grossly overbroad and unduly burdensome to Mr. Hastings, who is a non-party witness in this matter. The motion should also be denied for Sloan's failure to engage in a good faith meet and confer process, including his failure to offer *any* compromise proposal.

DATED: December 29, 2011 LESSER LAW GROUP

By: ______________________
Don A. Lesser
Attorneys for Subpoenaed Witness
James R. Hastings

FILED
Superior Court of California
County of San Francisco
DEC 29 2011
CLERK OF THE COURT
BY: [signature]
Deputy Clerk

Don A. Lesser, SBN #112887
LESSER LAW GROUP
1010 B Street, Suite 350
San Rafael, California 94901
Telephone: (415) 453-7600
Facsimile: (415) 295-4122
E-mail: DLesser@LesserGroup.com

Attorney for Subpoenaed Witness
JAMES R. HASTINGS

CALIFORNIA SUPERIOR COURT

SAN FRANCISCO COUNTY

In the Matter of the Trust for Michael created under the Goodall Trust dated January 19, 1999.]	Case No.: PTR-99-273030 **PROOF OF SERVICE**

BY FAX

PROOF OF SERVICE

I, the undersigned, declare: I am over the age of 18 years at the time of service, and am not a party to the within action. I am employed in the County of Marin. My business address is 1010 B Street, Suite 350, San Rafael, California 94901.

On this date, December 29, 2011, the following document(s) were served:

DECLARATION OF DON A. LESSER OPPOSING RESPONDENT SAM SLOAN'S MOTION TO COMPEL PRODUCTION OF DOCUMENTS AND FURTHER DEPOSITION

DEPONENT JAMES R. HASTINGS' OPPOSITION TO RESPONDENT SAM SLOAN'S MOTION TO COMPEL PRODUCTION OF DOCUMENTS AND FURTHER DEPOSITION

PROOF OF SERVICE

on the parties, through their attorneys of record, by means of service designated below:

Samuel G. Ware 700 Larkspur Landing Circle Suite 199 Larkspur, CA 94939	**(By Federal Express) I caused** each such envelope with shipping charges fully prepaid, to be delivered to a Federal Express pick-up box at San Rafael, California, for next business day delivery.
John L. McDonnell, Jr. Reed Smith LLP 1999 Harrison Street, 24th Floor Oakland, CA 94612	**(By First Class Mail)** I caused each such envelope, with first-class postage thereon fully prepaid, to be deposited in the United States mail at San Rafael, California.
Gary D. Rothstein Manat Phelps Phillips One Embarcadero Center, 30th Fl. San Francisco, CA 94111	**(By First Class Mail)** I caused each such envelope, with first-class postage thereon fully prepaid, to be deposited in the United States mail at San Rafael, California.

I declare under penalty of perjury that the foregoing is true and correct and that this Declaration was executed on December 29, 2011, at San Rafael, California.

GINA ANTHONY

Don A. Lesser, SBN #112887
THE LESSER LAW GROUP
1010 B Street, Suite 350
San Rafael, California 94901
Telephone: (415) 453-7600
Facsimile: (415) 295-4122
E-mail: DLesser@LesserGroup.com

Attorney for Subpoenaed Witness
JAMES R. HASTINGS

FILED
Superior Court of California
County of San Francisco
DEC 29 2011
CLERK OF THE COURT
BY: [signature]
Deputy Clerk

CALIFORNIA SUPERIOR COURT

SAN FRANCISCO COUNTY

In the Matter of the Trust for Michael created under the Goodall Trust dated January 19, 1999	Case No. PTR-99-273030 **DECLARATION OF DON A. LESSER OPPOSING RESPONDENT SAM SLOAN'S MOTION TO COMPEL PRODUCTION OF DOCUMENTS AND FURTHER DEPOSITION** **Hearing: January 12, 2012** **Time: 2:15 p.m.** **Department: 204**

BY FAX

I, Don A. Lesser, declare as follows;

1. I am an attorney at law licensed to practice before all courts of this State. I am counsel James R. Hastings, subpoenaed to appear for a deposition as a non-party witness in this action. I represented Mr. Hastings at his deposition, and continue to represent him in connection with proceedings associated with the deposition. The following facts are personally known to me. If called upon to do so, I could and would testify competently to them.

2. Exhibit A hereto consists of excerpted pages from the transcript of Mr. Hastings' deposition, taken November 14, 2011. They are true and correct copies of those pages. The

transcript is an accurate record of the questions posed, the answers given and the colloquy among counsel.

3. Mr. Hastings is a named defendant in an action filed by Mr. Sloan in Marin Superior Court, Case No. 1100596. Exhibit B hereto is a true and correct copy of the caption page of Mr. Sloan's petition filed in that action.

I declare under penalty of perjury under the laws of the State of California that the foregoing is true and correct and that this declaration was executed this 29th day of December 2011 at San Rafael, California.

Don A. Lesser

EXHIBIT A

EXHIBIT A

SUPERIOR COURT OF THE STATE OF CALIFORNIA

FOR THE COUNTY OF SAN FRANCISCO

In the Matter of the NO. PTR-99-273030

CERTIFIED COPY

Trust for Michael created under the Goodall Trust dated January 19, 1999

)

Deposition of

JAMES R. HASTINGS

NOVEMBER 14, 2011

DEPOSING ATTORNEY: SAM WARE, ESQ.

REPORTED BY: CINDY J. KAISER, CSR #7647

WEST COAST REPORTERS INC

117 Paul Drive, Suite A, San Rafael, CA 94903

415-472-2361 · 800-979-2361 · Fax 415-472-2371 · depos@westcoastreporters.com

Pursuant to Notice of Deposition, and on Monday, November 14, 2011, commencing at the hour of 2:03 p.m., at the Law Offices of Sam Ware, 700 Larkspur Landing Circle, #199, Larkspur, California, before me, CINDY J. KAISER, a Certified Shorthand Reporter and Deposition Officer of the State of California, there personally appeared

JAMES R. HASTINGS,

called as a witness by the Respondent, who having been duly sworn, was examined and testified as hereinafter set forth.

--oOo--

A P P E A R A N C E S

SAM WARE, Attorney at Law, LAW OFFICES OF SAM WARE, 700 Larkspur Landing Circle, #199, Larkspur, California 94939, appeared as counsel on behalf of the Respondent. (415) 464-4872.

DON A. LESSER, Attorney at Law, LESSER LAW GROUP, 101 B Street, Suite 350, San Rafael, California 94901, appeared as counsel on behalf of the Subpoenaed Witness, James R. Hastings. (415) 453-7600.

ALSO PRESENT: Sam Sloan.

--oOo--

EXAMINATION

(Respondent's Exhibit 1 was were marked for
identification.)

BY MR. WARE:

Q. Mr. Hastings, would you state your name for the record, please.

A. James Hastings.

Q. My name is Sam Ware. I represent Sam Sloan, who is the administrator of the estate of Michael Goodall. Do you understand that?

A. I understand it, yes.

Q. Have you had your deposition taken before on any occasion?

A. Yes.

Q. How many times?

A. Once.

Q. How long ago was that?

A. Approximately nine years ago.

Q. Have you ever taken a deposition as an attorney?

A. Yes.

Q. How many times, would you say?

A. I don't know.

Q. More than 100?

A. I don't believe so.

that that's --

MR. LESSER: They are.

BY MR. WARE:

Q. Let me ask you something.

When you looked for documents which reflected the intentions of Kenneth Goodall, where did you look?

A. In all of the locations in my office where documents would be and in the particular files that would be related.

Q. That is related to the Goodall matter?

A. Yes.

Q. And how voluminous are those documents? Bankers box? Two bankers boxes? A couple files? What's the universe of documents with regard to the Goodalls that you looked at?

A. Less than a bankers box.

Q. Are they categorized by file, that is, Goodall trust 1990? Goodall trust 1994? How are those kept in your office?

A. Which is the question? You asked two questions.

Q. Can you give me a description of how those documents related to the Goodalls are kept in your office.

A. Some were in manila folders, some were in

expandable folders, some were marked with file numbers and some aren't.

Q. How recently did you review those documents?

A. This weekend.

Q. Are they all kept in one place in your office?

A. Yes.

Q. In one box?

A. Well, apparently not.

Q. What does that mean to you?

A. There were some documents I could not locate.

Q. Documents which you thought existed, which you just couldn't find, is that what you're saying to me?

A. Yes.

Q. What documents did you expect to find that you did not find?

A. A file marked G 080-01.

Q. What does that number mean to you, in your record keeping practices?

A. It means it's the initial estate planning file for Mr. and Mrs. Goodall.

Q. G 080-01?

A. That's right.

Q. What files did you find there, in your office, when you were reviewing your files to see whether you had documents which reflected the intentions of the

Goodalls?

A. G 080-05 and G 080-86 and G 181-01.

Q. Now, what sorts of documents are included within the dash 05 file?

A. Mr. Goodall's trust administration.

Q. The 06 number.

A. Mrs. Goodall's trust administration.

Q. And the G 181-01 file.

A. That's Michael Goodall's will.

Q. Then I'll focus, if I may, on the G 080-01. Does the G stand for Goodall?

A. Yes.

Q. I notice that the numbers jump from dash 01 to dash 05. Would you expect to find a 02, 3, 4 someplace?

A. No.

Q. The reason for that gap is what?

A. That's not the way I identify files.

Q. Now, the G 080-01 file, what would you expect that file to contain?

A. The initial paperwork concerning the estate plan of Mr. and Mrs. Goodall.

Q. Initial paperwork would include your notes regarding your discussions with them?

A. It may.

Q. And in your record keeping practices, would you

expect that file to contain such notes?

A. Yes.

Q. Typically during the estate planning process, do you keep notes --

A. Yes.

Q. -- with regard to the client?

MR. LESSER: Let him finish the question before you answer.

MR. WARE: I paused, and I should have nodded. So there you have it. Thank you.

Q. Do you recall when it was you last saw that file?

A. No.

Q. Let's turn to the dash 05 file, which is Mr. Goodall's trust administration file.

A. Yes.

Q. What sorts of things would be contained within such a file, the trust administration file?

MR. LESSER: Well, you're asking him generally as a matter of custom and practice, or this particular client?

BY MR. WARE:

Q. Fine. This particular file, let's go for that. What sorts of documents did you find in there when you looked at it?

A. The trust, the will.
Q. Anything else?
A. Any other estate planning documents which had become obsolete.
Q. Such as? Would you give me an example.
A. Power of attorney is obsolete at the death, any paperwork relating to the trust administration.
Q. And when you say "trust administration" in this instance, what did the trust administration of Kenneth Goodall's trust administration include?
A. That pieces of the process that are necessary to make the distributions required by the trust.
Q. Okay. With regard to the dash 06 file, that's Mrs. Goodall's trust administration file, what sorts of documents are in there?
A. The same sorts of documents as in Mr. Goodall's file.
Q. That is a copy of the trust, right?
A. Yes.
Q. Would there be a copy of the 1990 trust in there? Was there a copy of the 1990 trust in there?
A. I don't know.
Q. You don't recall?
A. I don't recall.
Q. Do you recall seeing a copy of the 1994 trust

A. That's not a valid statement.

Q. When did you first start looking for the G 080-01 file?

A. Several weeks before I hired Mr. Lesser. I don't know when that was. Someplace within the last three months.

Q. Within the last three months you discovered that it did not exist, when you looked for it at that time?

A. I can't answer that question, because it has a predicate in it that's not true.

Q. What's untrue about that question? What's the predicate that's not true there?

A. You're saying something does not exist.

Q. Where is it? Where's the file?

A. I do not know.

Q. Why not?

A. Because I can't find it.

Q. When was the last time you saw it?

A. I don't know.

Q. Was it that several weeks ago when you first started looking for the file, before you hired Mr. Lesser?

A. No.

Q. You couldn't find it then either?

Q. So you don't recall whether when you were drafting Exhibit 3 you had that file, the dash 01 file, to look at, do you?
A. No, I do not.
Q. How about when you were looking, drafting attachment A, or Exhibit A, to Exhibit 3, which is the declaration that you signed apparently in January of 2011, do you recall whether you had the dash 01 file available to you when you drafted that declaration?
A. I don't recall.
Q. Just so I'm clear, you don't recall whether you referred to the dash 01 file when you drafted either of the declarations which compose Exhibit 3?
A. I may have, but I do not recall.
Q. You don't recall, okay.
Do you recall, when you were drafting Exhibit 3, that you referred to the dash 05 file?
A. I referred to documents in the file.
Q. The 06 file, did you refer to that when you were drafting Exhibit 3?
A. I referred to documents in the file.
Q. And the G 181-01 file, did you refer to that when you were drafting Exhibit 3?
A. I would refer to documents in the file.
Q. Over the weekend you took a look for the dash

01 file and you couldn't find it, right?
A. That's true.
Q. Where did you look? In your office, or storage, or where?
A. I looked in my office and in storage.
Q. Is your storage offsite from your office?
A. Yes.
Q. Did you personally look in your office to find that file?
A. Yes.
Q. Did you ask anybody in your office to help you find that file?
A. Prior to that point, yes.
Q. When did you ask somebody to help you find that file, prior to that point?
A. Sometime within the last two months.
Q. Do you remember who it was that you asked to help you find that file?
A. I asked René Moore.
Q. Did you ask anybody else to help you find that file?
A. No.
Q. Would René Moore know as much as anybody on the planet as to where that file might be?
A. No.

Q. Okay. Who would know more?
A. No one.
Q. Now, did you ask René Moore this weekend to help you find that file again?
A. No.
Q. Several months ago when you asked René Moore to help you find the 01 file, she couldn't find it either. Is that what she reported to you?
A. When we last looked for it, she could not find it.
Q. And have you asked her recently to help you find that file?
A. Yes.
Q. When was the last time you asked her to help you find that file?
A. Within the last two months.
Q. How about over the weekend?
A. She doesn't work on the weekend. I did not ask her on the weekend.
Q. Did you ask her this morning to help you find that file, the 01 file?
A. No.
Q. Does she work today?
A. Yes.
Q. Is there a reason you didn't ask her to try and

help you find that file this morning, knowing you had a deposition this afternoon?

MR. LESSER: What's the point of this?

MR. WARE: I want to know how thoroughly he's looked for that file.

MR. LESSER: Well, I think he's told you what he did.

BY MR. WARE:

Q. Okay, the question stands.

A. I can't answer that question, because it has some predicates in it that are emotional and not factual.

Q. Let me ask you again.

Did you ask René Moore any time today to help you find the 01 file?

A. No.

Q. Why not?

MR. LESSER: Objection. Relevance.

THE WITNESS: It was not necessary that I ask her.

BY MR. WARE:

Q. Why not?

A. I had made a thorough search of three offsite locations. I had made a thorough search at the office in all possible locations. I have not found the file at

this moment.

Q. That's fine. Okay, I understand.

At some point back in, I think it was 2000, the year 2000, you represented the Bank of America as trustee in the San Francisco proceedings, BPR 99273030, correct?

A. I don't know anything about the numbers, but I did represent the Bank of America in a motion hearing.

Q. Right, the motion was brought by Michael Goodall to replace the Bank of America as the trustee. Do you remember that?

A. I remember the motion was brought by Michael Goodall, that's all I remember.

Q. Do you remember that you represented Bank of America in that proceeding?

A. Yes.

Q. Is there a file that you have with regard to your representation of the Bank of America in that proceeding?

A. Yes.

Q. Is it one of those four files that we talked about earlier?

A. Yes.

Q. In which file would records of that proceeding be contained?

Q. I understand.
MR. SLOAN: My question, since he's an attorney, why doesn't the document that he drafted say what he says it says? Because it doesn't say that.
BY MR. WARE:
Q. Well, you have referred us to pages 18 and 19 of the trust, correct?
A. Yes.
MR. WARE: That's enough. The document says what the document says.
That's all I have.
MR. SLOAN: You're not going to ask him why he didn't do a better job of drafting the document?
MR. WARE: No, I'm not.
MR. SLOAN: To say what he claims it should have said?
MR. WARE: No, I'm not.
BY MR. WARE:
Q. The only thing I'd like to say, is that I don't know, you know -- not quite yet, not quite yet.
Because if that file turns up, I'd sure like to find out what it says. So is there any place that you might look for it, that file, that you haven't looked for it, Mr. Hastings?
A. I'll answer that question off record, so you

have an understanding.

Q. That's okay, for now at least. I don't want to embarrass anybody here, but you can understand how it's pretty important to me.

MR. WARE: We'll go off the record for a moment.

(Off the record.)

MR. WARE: So just for the record, we had a discussion off the record, and Mr. Hastings was describing what sounded like a diligent search of the file, and we've also been discussing that he will continue to look for the file and if it shows up, I will be notified promptly by Mr. Lesser that the file has been discovered and then we can figure out where to go from there with regard to reconvening the deposition.

Q. I'm not just throwing this twist at the end. I'm not asking you to come back when you find the file, but I'll do what I have to do to accomolish that. All I'm asking for is your continued good efforts to find the file, please.

A. Yes.

Q. And notification if it turns up.

MR. LESSER: The problem is I don't want some ambiguous commitment to continue to look for this forever. I think his testimony reflects what's already been a diligent search. If Mr. Hastings wants to commit to looking in a few places that he hasn't already looked, that's fine with me, but I want the record to be clear that he has already made a diligent search and that we are not committing to anything that will support some additional motion or legal proceeding to try to force Mr. Hastings to do anything more than he's already done.

MR. WARE: Right. Now, with regard to getting other files, though, you, Mr. Lesser, will accept service of any motions with regard to compelling the production of those other files that I would file, so I need not trouble Mr. Hastings with serving him with that document, correct? We've covered this before, but I just want to cover it again.

MR. LESSER: Yes, I think you have some meeting and conferring to do before you do that, but as a matter of service, yes, I will self-service of whatever you choose is fine.

MR. SLOAN: May I ask you a question? I'll ask him.

Our understanding is that the original signed 1994 trust is in the missing file and he does not know where that trust is.

MR. WARE: That's a question, if we could, this

STATE OF CALIFORNIA
SONOMA COUNTY

I, CINDY J. KAISER, duly authorized to administer oaths pursuant to Section 2093(b) of the California Code of Civil Procedure, do hereby certify that

JAMES R. HASTINGS,

the witness in the foregoing deposition, was duly sworn by me to testify to the truth in the within entitled cause; that said deposition was taken at the time and place set forth; that the testimony of said witness was reported by me, a Certified Shorthand Reporter and a disinterested person, and was thereafter transcribed by computer under my direction into booklet form; that the witness was given an opportunity to read and correct said deposition and to subscribe to the same.

I further certify that I am not of counsel or attorney for either or any of the parties in the foregoing deposition and caption named, nor in any way interested in the outcome of the cause named in said caption.

Executed November 28, 2011, at Rohnert Park California.

Cindy J. Kaiser
Deposition Officer

EXHIBIT B

EXHIBIT B

Samuel H. Sloan
Administrator with Will Attached of
Estate of K. Michael Goodall
461 Peachstone Terrace
San Rafael CA 94903
415-491-1269
415-894-7201
samhsloan@gmail.com

SUPERIOR COURT OF THE STATE OF CALIFORNIA

FOR THE COUNTY OF MARIN

Estate of K. Michael Goodall, Petitioner, vs. James Raymond Hastings and Bank of America, N.A., Defendants	Case No.: PR 1100596 Petition under California Probate Code Section 850 to Recover Estate Property

Samuel H. Sloan, being duly sworn, states:

1. I am the administrator of the Estate of K. Michael Goodall. This is a proceeding to recover property of the estate. Specifically, this proceeding seeks to recover $1.6 million that was left to K. Michael Goodall by his mother, Rachel A. Goodall, when she died in June, 1999. At the time her death, substantially all of her liquid funds were held by USAA Investment Management in Texas in a securities trading account established by her late husband, Col. Kenneth F. Goodall. By improper means, Bank of America through its attorney, James R. Hastings, was able to obtain this $1.6 million. Mike Goodall then filed a petition to recover the funds from Bank of America or to have the funds

John McDonnell, Jr. (SBN 34729)
Email: jmcdonnell@reedsmith.com
Alicia A. Adornato (SBN 254228)
Email: aadornato@reedsmith.com
REED SMITH LLP
101 Second Street, Suite 1800
San Francisco, CA 94105-3659
Telephone: +1 415 543 8700
Facsimile: +1 415 391 8269

Attorneys for
Guide Dogs for the Blind, Inc.

SUPERIOR COURT OF THE STATE OF CALIFORNIA

FOR THE COUNTY OF SAN FRANCISCO

In the Matter of the

Trust for Michael created under the Goodall Trust dated September 12, 1900,

Case No. PTR-99-273030

GUIDE DOGS FOR THE BLIND, INC.'S JOINDER IN DEPONENT JAMES R. HASTINGS' OPPOSITION TO RESPOND SAM SLOAN'S MOTION TO COMPEL DOCUMENTS AND FURTHER DEPOSITION

Date: January 12, 2012
Time: 2:15 p.m.
Place: Department 201

Honorable Peter J. Busch

Guide Dogs for the Blind, Inc. ("Guide Dogs") hereby joins in the arguments raised in Deponent James R. Hastings' Opposition to Respondent Sam Sloan's Motion to Compel Production of Documents and Further Deposition.

First, Guide Dogs agrees that the Court allowed limited discovery regarding the Goodalls' intent in changing their Trust. The documents and further deposition testimony requested Respondent Sam Sloan ("Sloan") are outside the scope of discovery permitted by Judge Wiss at the August 23, 2011 hearing. Consequently, Sloan is not entitled to this discovery and his Motion to Compel should be denied.

Second, Guide Dogs agrees that the document demands are overbroad and unduly burdensome since they request all of deponent James R. Hastings' ("Hastings") documents related to the Goodalls, including files concerning the administration of their Trust. *Calcor Space Facility, Inc. v. Superior Court*, 53 Cal. App. 4th 216, 222 ("'reasonably' in the statute implies a requirement such categories be reasonably particularized from the standpoint of the party who is subjected to the burden of producing the materials"). As Hastings points out, Sloan asks him to review over 25 years of documents which include documents that are subject to review for attorney-client privilege.

Third, from the correspondence submitted it is apparent that there was no adequate "meet and confer".[1] The parties did not engage in a give and take discussion about the requested discovery, especially since it does not appear that Sloan's counsel responded to Hastings' counsel's detailed position regarding the deficiency of the discovery requests.

Consequently, Guide Dogs submits that Sloan's Motion to Compel should be denied.

DATED: January 4, 2012. REED SMITH LLP

By [signature]
Alicia A. Adornato
Attorneys for Guide Dogs for the Blind, Inc.

[1] With regard to the prerequisites for a meaningful "meet and confer" effort, the California Court of Appeal has set forth the following standard: "***The parties must present to each other the merits of their respective positions with the same candor, specificity, and support during informal negotiations as during the briefing of discovery motions***. Only after all the cards have been laid on the table, and a party has meaningfully assessed the relative strengths and weaknesses of its position in light of all available information, can there be a sincere effort to resolve the matter. [...] The law requires that counsel attempt to talk the matter over, compare their views, consult, and deliberate." *Townsend v. Super. Ct.*, 61 Cal. App. 4th 1431, 1435, 1439 (1998) (emphasis added).

PROOF OF SERVICE

I am a resident of the State of California, over the age of eighteen years, and not a party to the within action. My business address is REED SMITH LLP, 1999 Harrison Street, Oakland, CA 94612. On January 4, 2012, I served the following document(s) by the method indicated below:

GUIDE DOGS FOR THE BLIND, INC.'S JOINDER IN DEPONENT JAMES R. HASTINGS' OPPOSITION TO RESPOND SAN SLOAN'S MOTION TO COMPEL DOCUMENTS AND FURTHER DEPOSITION

☐ by transmitting via facsimile on this date from fax number 510.273.8832 the document(s) listed above to the fax number(s) set forth below. The transmission was completed before 5:00 PM and was reported complete and without error. The transmission report was properly issued by the transmitting fax machine. Service by fax was made by agreement of the parties, confirmed in writing. The transmitting fax machine complies with Cal.R.Ct 2003(3).

☒ by placing the document(s) listed above in a sealed envelope with postage thereon fully prepaid, in the United States mail at Oakland, California addressed as set forth below. I am readily familiar with the firm's practice of collection and processing of correspondence for mailing. Under that practice, it would be deposited with the U.S. Postal Service on that same day with postage thereon fully prepaid in the ordinary course of business. I am aware that on motion of the party served, service is presumed invalid if the postal cancellation date or postage meter date is more than one day after the date of deposit for mailing in this Declaration.

☒ by transmitting via email to the parties at the email addresses listed below.

Sam Ware
700 Larkspur Landing Circle
Suite 199
Larkspur, CA 94939
Email: sam@samware.us

Don Lesser
1010 B Street
Suite 350
San Rafael, CA 94901
Email: DLesser@LesserGroup.com

Gary D. Rothstein
Manatt, Phelps & Phillips, LLP
One Embarcadero Center,
30th Floor
San Francisco, CA 94111
Email: GRothstein@manatt.com

I declare under penalty of perjury under the laws of the State of California that the above is true and correct. Executed on January 4, 2012, at Oakland, California.

Karen Ellis
Karen Ellis

0604

SAM WARE (State Bar No. 105005)
700 Larkspur Landing Circle, #199
Larkspur, CA 94939

Telephone 415-464-4872

E-mail sam@samware.us

Attorney for Sam Sloan, administrator of Estate of Michael Goodall

FILED
SUPERIOR COURT
COUNTY OF SAN FRANCISCO

2012 JAN -5 PM 9:36

CLERK OF THE COURT
BY: [signature]
DEPUTY CLERK

SUPERIOR COURT OF THE STATE OF CALIFORNIA

COUNTY OF SAN FRANCISCO

In the Matter of the Trust for Michael created under the Goodall Trust dated September 12, 1990	Case No. PTR-99-273030 Reply to Opposition to Motion to Compel Hearing Date: January 12, 2012 Time: 2:15 PM Department: 204

BY FAX

The Estate of Michael Goodall replies to the opposition of James Hastings and to the Joinder of Guide Dogs for the Blind (a curious thing in a discovery motion) as follows:

The best evidence of the Goodalls' intent is in the files of James Hastings and what he has to say about it.

Hastings has composed a lengthy and detailed declaration with regard to many matters, including the intent the Goodalls in creating the trust in 1990 and in amending it in 1994, upon which petitioner Bank of America relies in support of its motion that Guide Dogs for the Blind be declared the residual beneficiary of the Goodalls' trust.

What the Goodalls told Hastings and what he told them in 1990 when the trust was originally composed and then again in 1994 would certainly be the subject of copious notes and correspondence of any competent attorney, and would have been referred to by Hastings in composing the declaration he has filed in this action. It is the best evidence of those subjects with out question and the Estate of Michael ought to have the opportunity to see those documents and cross examine Hastings on the contents.

Otherwise, the declaration of Hastings ought to be ignored by this Court when declaring the intent of the Goodalls beyond the ambiguities of the 1994 amendment.

There is no Court Order prohibiting the Estate of Michael Goodall access to those file.

Hastings says in his opposition that he is obtaining a copy of the Court's transcript to support his otherwise unsupportable proposition that the scope of his deposition was limited by the Court at a prior hearing. So be it. The Estate of Michael welcomes such a presentation.

The fact will remain that there was never any motion to limit discovery and that the Court did not to prohibit the Estate of Michael access to files which would contain notes and correspondence relevant to the subject matter of the intent of the Goodalls and Hasting's advise in drafting their trust in 1990 and the amendment in 1994.

It is not unduly burdensome or overbroad to ask James Hastings to produce his *four files*.

All we are talking about here is four files, and yes the Estate of Michael has the right to see the contents of all four files as any one of them could reasonably be expected to include notes and correspondence which reflect the intent of the Goodalls and Hastings advice to implement their intent in drafting the 1990 trust and/or the 1994 amendment.

The Estate of Michael Goodall has done all it can to "meet and confer" in an effort to persuade James Hastings to produce those files.

The clearest evidence that Estate of Michael has done all it can in an effort to avoid this motion is a review of the record, which shows that Hastings is simply not cooperating, is not willing to produce any files, is not willing to be cross examined as to the contents of those files and that this Court has got to get involved.

James Hastings has done nothing to continue to try locate and produce those files and he should be ordered to do so.

Conspicuously absent from Hastings opposition papers is any declaration that he or anyone from his office as done anything more look for the "missing file", as he agreed at his deposition (Hastings deposition 65:16-21).

Nor has Hastings done anything to produce the other files that he clearly does have. (One of which files as noted in the moving papers are Michael Goodall's files in the first place!) Rather, he had simply continued to refuse to produce them.

//

These files are within the scope of discovery and should be ordered located and produced.

The Estate of Michael Goodall ought to have the opportunity to cross examine James Hastings on the contents of those files.

A further deposition of Hastings is going to be required once those files are produced so as to make sense of them and so as to cross examine Hastings on some of the conclusions he has made in his declaration with regard to the intent of the Goodalls.

Finally, the hearing on Bank of America's motion presently scheduled for February 8, 2012 should be ordered continued until after the production of these files and Hastings further deposition.

Date: January 5, 2012

Attorneys for Estate of Michael

PROOF OF SERVICE

I certify and declare as follows:

I am over the age of 18 years, not a party to this action. My business address is 700 Larkspur Landing Circle #199, Larkspur, CA 94939. I am readily familiar with the business practices of my firm for the collection, processing and service of items with the United States Postal Service, express service providers (same day messenger and overnight) and facsimile transmission.

On the date set forth below, I served the foregoing documents described as a motion to compel and separate statement on the parties who have appeared in this action as follows:

X : BY FIRST CLASS MAIL — By placing [ ] the original [X] a true and correct copy thereof in each sealed envelope addressed as indicated below. Said sealed envelopes, with postage fully prepaid, were deposited with the United States Postal Service in San Francisco, California this same day in the ordinary course of business.

____: BY FEDERAL EXPRESS — By placing [ ] the original [ ] a true and correct copy thereof in each sealed envelope addressed as indicated below. Said envelopes were deposited for collection and processing by Federal Express, Priority Overnight Service, in San Francisco, California.

____: BY PERSONAL SERVICE: By placing [ ] the original [x] a true and correct copy thereof in each sealed envelope addressed as indicated below and causing said envelopes to be delivered by hand, by our firm's messenger, to the offices of the addressees indicated below.

____: BY FACSIMILE TRANSMISSION — The foregoing document was transmitted between 9:00 a.m. and 5:00 p.m. to the fax number indicated below each address.

X : BY EMAIL TRANSMISSION — The foregoing document was transmitted between 9:00 a.m. and 5:00 p.m. to the e-mail address indicated below.

Gary D. Rothstein
Manatt, Phelps & Phillips, LLP
One Embarcadero Center, 30th Floor
San Francisco CA 94111

Don Lesser
1010 B St. Suite 350
San Rafael, CA 94901

John L McDonnell
Alicia Adornato
Reed Smith
1999 Harrison St. # 2400
Oakland, CA 94612

I declare under penalty of perjury under the laws of the State of California that the foregoing statements are true and correct.

Executed January 5, 2012

PTR-99-273030

IN RE: THE GOODALL TRUST

609

MINI MINUTES FOR JAN-12-2012 02:15 PM FO

Appearances: Sam Ware for and with Sam Sloan. Gary Rothstein for Bank of America (Trustee). Don Lesser for James Hastings

Counsel presented oral argument to support their positions. The Motion to Compel Production of Documents, etc. is denied subject to Mr. Hastings providing a further declaration within 10-days expressing that either he has made a further good faith effort to locate the file but has not found it or if he finds the file, that it is produced. Mr. Lesser is to prepare the order.

Judge: Peter Busch. Clerk: Rosie Noguera.

FILED
San Francisco County Superior Court

0610 JAN 20 2012

CLERK OF THE COURT
By: [signature]
Deputy Clerk

Don A. Lesser, SBN #112887
THE LESSER LAW GROUP
1010 B Street, Suite 350
San Rafael, California 94901
Telephone: (415) 453-7600
Facsimile: (415) 295-4122
E-mail: DLesser@LesserGroup.com

Attorney for Deponent
JAMES R. HASTINGS

CALIFORNIA SUPERIOR COURT

SAN FRANCISCO COUNTY

In the Matter of the Trust for Michael created under the Goodall Trust dated January 19, 1999	Case No. PTR-99-273030 **~~[PROPOSED]~~** **ORDER DENYING MOTION TO COMPEL PRODUCTION OF DOCUMENTS AND FURTHER DEPOSITION** Hearing Date: 1/12/12 Time: 2:15 p.m. Dept.: 204

BY FAX

On January 12, 2012, the Motion to Compel Production of Documents and Further Deposition, brought by the Estate of Michael Goodall (the "Motion"), came on regularly hearing in Department 204 of this Court. Deponent James R. Hastings and the parties to this action appeared through their counsel of record as reflected in the minutes.

The Court, having considered the moving and opposing papers and the argument of counsel, affirms the tentative ruling as follows:

Except as set forth below, the Motion is denied. The Court cannot order production of a file the responding party has diligently looked for but cannot find. Except as to the estate planning file, the other files fall outside the scope of discovery previously delineated in this limited proceeding. In any event, the categories as requested in the subpoena are overbroad.

///

Within ten days of this Order, Mr. Hastings shall either: (1) make the estate planning file available to the parties for inspection and copying; or (2) file and serve a declaration stating what additional search he has made for the file.

Dated: January 20, 2012

Hon. Peter Busch
JUDGE OF THE SUPERIOR COURT

APPROVED AS TO FORM

DATED: January 17, 2012
THE LESSER LAW GROUP

By: DON A. LESSER
Attorney for Deponent James R. Hastings

DATED: January 19, 2012
SAM WARE

SAM WARE
Attorney for Sam Sloan, Administrator of Estate of Michael Goodall

0612

FILED
SUPERIOR COURT
COUNTY OF SAN FRANCISCO

2012 FEB -2 PM 3:26

CLERK OF THE COURT
BY: [signature]
DEPUTY CLERK

Don A. Lesser (SBN #112887)
THE LESSER LAW GROUP
1010 B Street, Suite 300
San Rafael, California 94901
Telephone: (415) 453-7600
Facsimile: (415) 295-4122
E-mail: DLesser@LesserGroup.com

Attorney for Subpoenaed Witness
JAMES R. HASTINGS

CALIFORNIA SUPERIOR COURT

SAN FRANCISCO COUNTY

In the Matter of the

Trust for Michael created under the Goodall Trust dated January 19, 1999

Case No. PTR-99-273030

DECLARATION OF JAMES R. HASTINGS PURSUANT TO COURT ORDER ON RESPONDENT'S MOTION TO COMPEL PRODUCTION OF DOCUMENTS AND FURTHER DEPOSITION

Hearing: January 12, 2012
Time: 2:15 p.m.
Department: 204

BY FAX

I, James R. Hastings, declare as follows:

1. I am an attorney at law licensed to practice in the State of California. I provide this declaration in response to this Court's order on Respondent's Motion to Compel Production of Documents and Further Deposition. The following facts are personally known to me. If called upon to do so, I could and would testify competently to them.

2. This declaration describes my further search for my Estate Planning file relating to Kenneth and Rachel Goodall, following my November 14, 2011 deposition in this matter. Since then, I have re-examined the two groups of files I have at my home. As the number of the file I

am looking for begins with the letter "G," I looked at every "G" file in those files at my home and did not find the Goodalls' file. I also looked in both storage areas at my office, active and inactive, again looking at every "G" file, and again found nothing. I also looked at all of the Goodall files retained in an armoire near my assistant's work area, which contains "active" files. I then looked at *all* of the files in that armoire, and still found nothing. I have searched my entire office, where I prepared the declarations I have submitted in this matter. Previously I inquired of all the staff people who work in my office when and where they last saw the file, and no one could recall.

3. I have not knowingly discarded or destroyed the file, or instructed anyone else to do so, nor have I knowingly given it to anyone else. At this point, I have searched everywhere I can think of where the file might be found.

I declare under penalty of perjury under the laws of the State of California that the foregoing is true and correct and that this declaration was executed this 1 day of February, 2012 at San Rafael, California.

James R. Hastings

PROOF OF SERVICE

I, the undersigned, declare: I am over the age of 18 years at the time of service, and am not a party to the within action. I am employed in the County of Marin. My business address is 1010 B Street, Suite 350, San Rafael, California 94901.

On this date, February 2, 2012, the following document(s) were served:

DECLARATION OF JAMES R. HASTINGS PURSUANT TO COURT ORDER ON RESPONDENT'S MOTION TO COMPEL PRODUCTION OF DOCUMENTS AND FURTHER DEPOSITION

on the parties, through their attorneys of record, by means of service designated below:

Samuel G. Ware 700 Larkspur Landing Circle Suite 199 Larkspur, CA 94939	**(By First Class Mail)** I caused each such envelope, with first-class postage thereon fully prepaid, to be deposited in the United States mail at San Rafael, California.
John L. McDonnell, Jr. Reed Smith LLP 1999 Harrison Street, 24th Floor Oakland, CA 94612	**(By First Class Mail)** I caused each such envelope, with first-class postage thereon fully prepaid, to be deposited in the United States mail at San Rafael, California.
Gary D. Rothstein Manat Phelps Phillips One Embarcadero Center, 30th Fl. San Francisco, CA 94111	**(By First Class Mail)** I caused each such envelope, with first-class postage thereon fully prepaid, to be deposited in the United States mail at San Rafael, California.

I declare under penalty of perjury that the foregoing is true and correct and that this Declaration was executed on February 2, 2012, at San Rafael, California.

Gina Anthony

GINA ANTHONY

SAM WARE (State Bar No. 105005)
700 Larkspur Landing Circle, #199
Larkspur, CA 94939
Telephone 415-464-4872
E-mail sam@samware.us
Attorney for Respondent Sam Sloan,
administrator of Estate
of Michael Goodall

FILED
San Francisco County Superior Court
FEB 06 2012
CLERK OF THE COURT
By: ________ Deputy Clerk

SUPERIOR COURT OF THE STATE OF CALIFORNIA

COUNTY OF SAN FRANCISCO

In the Matter of the Trust for Michael created under the Goodall Trust dated September 12, 1990	Case No. PTR-99-273030 *FURTHER* SUPPLEMENTAL OBJECTIONS TO PETITION FOR DETERMINATION OF BENEFICIARIES Hearing Date: February 8, 2012 Time: 9 AM Department: 204

BY FAX

The Estate of K. Michael Goodall and Samuel Sloan, as the duly appointed administrator of the Estate of K. Michael Goodall, a beneficiary under the 1990 Goodall Trust (hereinafter the Estate of Michael), hereby further objects to the Petition filed by Bank of America in this matter. The Petition should be denied, and the Estate of Michael Goodall be declared the residual beneficiary of the assets of the Goodall Trust dated

September 12, 1990 for the following reasons:

1. By necessity the Estate of Michael has delayed in the filing of this Further Supplemental Opposition while it awaited the response of James R Hastings to the Discovery Order filed January 20, 2012. Only yesterday did Mr. Hastings file that declaration, and in it he states that he still cannot find the estate planning file for Kenneth Goodall and Rachel Goodall.

2. In its Petition the Bank of America relies heavily upon Hastings declaration in urging the Court to follow and interpret the provisions of the 1994 Amendment to the 1990 Goodall Trust and to exclude consideration of the Estate of Michael as the residual beneficiary.

3. **The Estate of Michael objects to the Court considering the declarations of James R Hastings:**

First, because Hastings' recollection cannot be trusted without his file. In his declarations Hastings purports to recount his recollection of what the Goodalls intended 20 years ago. Yet, when he was subpoenaed to testify about that recollection by the Estate of Michael he did not bring his file which would have included his notes and correspondence with the Goodalls as to what they intended to accomplish by their estate plan. In this way, the Estate of Michael has been deprived of the opportunity of any meaningful cross-examination of Hastings as to his conclusory statements with regard to the intent of Kenneth and Rachel Goodall and as to the events he as described in his declarations. It is respectfully submitted that the Court should disregard any consideration of those declarations as evidence in deciding the matters raised by Bank of America's petition.

4. Further, the Estate of Michael specifically objects to the declaration of Hastings filed on August 19, 2011 on the grounds that Mr. Hastings had and continues to have no standing to file such a declaration, as he is not a petitioner, a respondent, nor is he an attorney of any party to this action. For that reason, the Estate of Michael hereby moves to strike that declaration. Evidence Code §353. The only Hastings declaration which was properly filed in this matter is that filed by Bank of America on or about June 8, 2011 and upon which it relies in its Petition. As to that Hastings declaration, the Estate of Michael contends that it is unreliable without his file, as described above, and should be disregarded.

5. The Estate of Michael further objects and moves to strike those portions of the declaration of Hastings filed August 19, 2011 which reveal confidential communications made by Michael Goodall to Mr. Hastings while he represented Michael. (See Objections to Evidence filed herewith). The Estate of Michael hereby objects to the admissibility of any statements by Hastings as to the state of mind of Michael Goodall, specifically those appearing in Hastings' August 19, 2011 Declaration at ¶ 2 (2:11 - 14), ¶ 13 (6:7-11, 14-18) and ¶ 14 (7:2-6). In short, the Court should exclude from evidence in strike from the record any references to what Michael Goodall told Hastings about what Michael knew at any time.

6. The Estate of Michael also objects to the Court considering the 1994 Amendment to the 1990 Goodall Trust unless and until the original of that amendment can be produced.

Authentication of a writing is required before it may be received into evidence. Evidence Code §1401(a). The Court shall exclude secondary evidence of the content of the writing if the Court determines that a genuine dispute exists concerning material terms of the writing and justice requires the exclusion. Evidence Code §1521(a). The Estate of Michael contends that there is a genuine dispute as to the authenticity of the 1994 Amendment to the 1990 Goodall Trust, purportedly executed August 24, 1994, because other writings purportedly executed by Kenneth Goodall Rachel Goodall that same day (i.e. their pour over wills) are seemingly not genuine. As set forth in the Declaration of Sam Sloan filed herewith, it is apparent that these purported "original" wills on file at the Marin County Superior Court are not in fact original wills at all.

Furthermore, one of the purported witnesses to those wills, Nancy Rogers, has no recollection of ever signing any such documents. See declaration Nancy Rogers filed herewith.

The Estate of Michael submits that there is good cause to question the authenticity of all documents purportedly signed by Kenneth Goodall and Rachel Goodall on August 24, 1994, including the purported 1994 Amendment to the 1990 Goodall Trust. Accordingly, pursuant to the Evidence Code, the original of that purported 1994 Amendment should be ordered produced.

7. The Estate of Michael further contends that the provisions of the 1994 Amendment are so fatally defective, uncertain, and circular that they cannot be followed as an expression of the true intent of the Goodalls.

The Petition of Bank of America unabashedly admits that the

dispositive provisions of the 1994 amendment can not be given effect as written, which, of course, is why the Petition was brought in the first place. (See paragraphs 4 and 5 of the Petition). This is why Bank of America relies so heavily upon the declaration of James Hastings (see paragraph 6 of the Petition). Without the declaration of Hastings, to which the Estate of Michael has voiced its objections above, the intent of the Goodalls cannot be determined from the language of purported 1994 Amendment, and so it must be disregarded.

8. The Estate of Michael contends that the provisions of the original 1990 Goodall Trust control the disposition of the trust assets.

It follows therefore that among the documents before the Court the only clear statement of the intent of the Kenneth Goodall and Rachel Goodall is that found in the original 1990 Goodall Trust, which clearly bequeaths the assets of the 1990 Goodall Trust to Michael Goodall.

PRAYER FOR RELIEF

WHEREFORE Sam Sloan is the duly appointed administrator of the Estate of K Michael Goodall prays for the following relief:

1. That the Petition filed by Bank of America be dismissed;

2. For a declaration that the assets of the 1990 Goodall Trust be distributed according to the 1990 Goodall Trust to the Estate of K. Michael Goodall;

3. For such other and further relief as the Court deems just and proper.

Date: February 3, 2011

Attorneys for Respondent

I declare under penalty of perjury under the laws of the state of California that the foregoing is true and correct and that this declaration was executed on February 3, 2011.

Sam Sloan

PROOF OF SERVICE

I certify and declare as follows:

I am over the age of 18 years, not a party to this action. My business address is 700 Larkspur Landing Circle #199, Larkspur, CA 94939. I am readily familiar with the business practices of my firm for the collection, processing and service of items with the United States Postal Service, express service providers (same day messenger and overnight) and facsimile transmission.

On the date set forth below, I served the foregoing documents described as Further Supplemental Opposition, Declaration of Samuel Sloan, Declaration of Nancy Rogers, Objections to Evidence on the parties in this action as follows:

__X__: BY FIRST CLASS MAIL — By placing [ ] the original [X] a true and correct copy thereof in each sealed envelope addressed as indicated below. Said sealed envelopes, with postage fully prepaid, were deposited with the United States Postal Service in San Francisco, California this same day in the ordinary course of business.

____: BY FEDERAL EXPRESS — By placing [ ] the original [ ] a true and correct copy thereof in each sealed envelope addressed as indicated below. Said envelopes were deposited for collection and processing by Federal Express, Priority Overnight Service, in San Francisco, California.

____: BY PERSONAL SERVICE: By placing [ ] the original [x] a true and correct copy thereof in each sealed envelope addressed as indicated below and causing said envelopes to be delivered by hand, by our firm's messenger, to the offices of the addressees indicated below.

____: BY FACSIMILE TRANSMISSION — The foregoing document was transmitted between 9:00 a.m. and 5:00 p.m. to the fax number indicated below each address.

____: BY EMAIL TRANSMISSION — The foregoing document was transmitted between 9:00 a.m. and 5:00 p.m. to the e-mail address indicated below.

See attached service list

I declare under penalty of perjury under the laws of the State of California that the foregoing statements are true and correct.

Executed February 3, 2011

Service List

Gary D. Rothstein
Manatt, Phelps & Phillips, LLP
One Embarcadero Center, 30th Floor
San Francisco CA 94111

John L McDonnell
Reed Smith
1999 Harrison St. # 2400
Oakland, CA 94612

Julia Bentley Lemons
Apt. 308
12800 Marion Lane W
Minnetonka, MN 55305-1368

Robert Bentley
Bradford Village #504
906 N Boulevard Street
Edmond, OK 73030

Helen Beth Bentley Perry
7926 Praver Drive W
Jacksonville, FL 32217

Clenda Fern Bentley Zinar
4536 Chatman Street
The Colony, TX 75056

Beverly Gale Bentley Young
2316 Trenton
McKinney, TX 75070

Vickie Bentley Hankins
14580 NE 6th
Choctaw, OK 73020

Jeffrey Bentley
4701 N Douglas Boulevard
Spencer, OK 73084

Chad Everett Bentley
1609 Teepee Trail
Kingsland, TX 78639

Jeanette Goodall Phillips
152 S 11th Street
Salina, Kansas 67401

Kristin Kane
University of California
Berkeley College of Engineering
College Relations
208 Mclaughlin Hall #1722
Berkeley, CA 9472A-1722

Mr. Thomas Horton
Guide Dogs for the Blind, Inc.
350 Los Ranchitos Road
San Rafael, CA 94903

0623

SAM WARE (State Bar No. 105005)
700 Larkspur Landing Circle, #199
Larkspur, CA 94939

Telephone 415-464-4872

E-mail sam@samware.us

Attorney for Sam Sloan,
administrator of Estate
of K. Michael Goodall

FILED
San Francisco County Superior Court
FEB 06 2012
CLERK OF THE COURT
By: [signature] Deputy Clerk

SUPERIOR COURT OF THE STATE OF CALIFORNIA

FOR THE COUNTY OF SAN FRANCISCO

In the Matter of the Goodall Family Trust dated September 12, 1990	Case No. PTR-99-273030 Declaration of Sam Sloan Hearing Date: February 8, 2012 Time: Department: 204

BY FAX

Sam Sloan declares:

1. I make this declaration based upon my own personal knowledge unless otherwise stated.

2. I have examined at the Marin County Superior Court the recently discovered purported originals of the purported Last Will of Kenneth F. Goodall, a copy of which is attached hereto as Exhibit A, and the purported Last Will of Rachel A Goodall, copy of which is attached hereto as Exhibit B.

3. The originals of these documents are on file at the Marin County Superior Court, Kenneth Goodall's will is number W001916 and Rachel Goodall's will is number W001919.

4. What is remarkable about these documents on file with the Court is that they do not appear to be original documents; that is, that the three signatures and the two dates which appear on each of these documents at page 7 of each of these documents are not in blue ink, and I can feel no depression on the back or front of these pages to indicate that a pen was pressed on the paper to otherwise indicate an original signature. The total of six signatures do not show any variation in pressure or indentation in the paper. Thus, the documents appear to be copies and are not originals.

I declare under penalty of perjury under the laws of the State of California that the foregoing is true and correct.

DATED: February 2, 2012

Sam Sloan

EXHIBIT A

LAST WILL OF
KENNETH F. GOODALL

I, KENNETH F. GOODALL, a resident of Marin County, California, declare that this is my will. I hereby revoke all my previous wills and codicils.

ARTICLE ONE
INTRODUCTORY PROVISIONS

1.1. Marital Status. I am married to RACHEL A. GOODALL, and all references in this will to "my wife" are to her.

1.2. Identification of Living Child. I have one living child, KENNETH MICHAEL GOODALL.

1.3. No Deceased Children. I have no deceased children.

ARTICLE TWO
RESIDUARY PROVISIONS

2.1. Disposition of Residue. I give the residue of my estate to the trustee of the GOODALL TRUST, created under the declaration of trust executed on September 12, 1990, by KENNETH F. GOODALL and RACHEL A. GOODALL, as Settlors and Trustees. The trustee of that trust shall add the residue of my estate to the trust principal and hold, administer, and distribute the property in accordance with the provisions of that declaration of trust, including any amendments of that declaration of trust that have been made before or after execution of this will.

2.2. Alternate Disposition of Residue. If the GOODALL TRUST has been revoked, terminated, or declared invalid for any reason, I give the portion of the residue of my estate not taken to the executor of this will, as trustee, who shall hold, administer, and distribute the property under a testamentary trust, the terms of which shall be identical to the terms of the GOODALL TRUST that are in effect on the date of execution of this will.

ARTICLE THREE

EXECUTOR

3.1. Nomination of Executors. I nominate my wife as executor of this will. If, for any reason, my wife fails to qualify or ceases to act as executor, I nominate BANK OF AMERICA, NT & SA, San Francisco, California, or any corporation that is a successor thereto by merger, consolidation, transfer of assets, or other manner provided by law, as executor of this will.

3.2. Waiver of Bond. No bond or undertaking shall be required of any executor nominated in this will.

3.3. General Powers of Executor. The executor shall have full authority to administer my estate under the California Independent Administration of Estates Act. The executor shall have all powers now or hereafter conferred on executors by law, except as otherwise specifically provided in this will, including any powers enumerated in this will.

3.4. Power to Invest. The executor shall have the power to

invest estate funds in any kind of real or personal property, as the executor deems advisable.

3.5. Division or Distribution in Cash or in Kind. In order to satisfy a pecuniary gift or to distribute or divide estate assets into shares or partial shares, the executor may distribute or divide those assets in kind, or divide undivided interests in those assets, or sell all or any part of those assets and distribute or divide the property in cash, in kind, or partly in cash and partly in kind. Property distributed to satisfy a pecuniary gift under this will shall be valued at its fair market value at the time of distribution.

3.6. Power to Sell, Lease, and Grant Options to Purchase Property. The executor shall have the power to sell, at either public or private sale and with or without notice, lease, and grant options to purchase any real or personal property belonging to my estate, on such terms and conditions as the executor determines to be in the best interest of my estate.

3.7. Power to Purchase Estate Property. The executor shall have the power to sell any property of my estate to, or exchange any property of my estate with the property of, my wife, even though she is also an executor at the time of the sale or exchange, provided that any such sale or exchange shall be for adequate consideration.

3.8. Payments to Legally Incapacitated Persons. If at any time any beneficiary under this will is a minor or it appears to the executor that any beneficiary is incapacitated, incompetent,

or for any other reason not able to receive payments or make intelligent or responsible use of the payments, then the executor, in lieu of making direct payments to the beneficiary, may make payments to the beneficiary's conservator or guardian; to the beneficiary's custodian under the Uniform Gifts to Minors Act or Uniform Transfers to Minors Act of any state; to one or more suitable persons, as the executor deems proper, such as a relative or a person residing with the beneficiary, to be used for the benefit of the beneficiary; to any other person, firm, or agency for services rendered or to be rendered for the beneficiary's assistance or benefit; or to accounts in the beneficiary's name with financial institutions. The receipt of payments by any of the foregoing shall constitute a sufficient acquittance of the executor for all purposes.

ARTICLE FOUR

CONCLUDING PROVISIONS

4.1. Nonprobate Transfers of Community Property. If I predecease my wife, I revoke any consent I have given during my lifetime to any nonprobate transfer on the death of any person, to anyone other than my wife, of all or part of my community property interest in any asset described in California Probate Code Section 5000 (or any successor section), and instead I give to my wife my community property interest in any assets affected by this revocation of consent. Notwithstanding the preceding sentence, this revocation of consent shall be inapplicable to any community property included in any express trust of which I am the settlor or a cosettlor, which shall continue to be governed by the terms of the applicable trust instrument. It is my intention that my wife shall have full power to dispose of all community property assets to which this section of the will applies. If my wife and I die simultaneously or if it cannot be established by clear and convincing evidence whether my wife or I died first, this section shall not apply.

4.2. Definition of Death Taxes. The term "death taxes," as used in this will, shall mean all inheritance, estate, succession, and other similar taxes that are payable by any person on account of that person's interest in my estate or by reason of my death, including penalties and interest, but excluding the following:

(a) Any addition to the federal estate tax for any "excess retirement accumulation" under Internal Revenue Code Section 4980A.

(b) Any additional tax that may be assessed under Internal Revenue Code Section 2032A.

(c) Any federal or state tax imposed on a "generation-skipping transfer," as that term is defined in the federal tax laws, unless the applicable tax statutes provide that the generation-skipping transfer tax on that transfer is payable directly out of the assets of my gross estate.

4.3. Payment of Death Taxes. Pursuant to the declaration of trust executed on September 12, 1990, by KENNETH F. GOODALL and RACHEL A. GOODALL, as Settlors and Trustees, all death taxes, whether or not attributable to property inventoried in my probate estate, shall be paid by the trustee from that trust. However, if that trust does not exist at the time of my death, or if the assets of that trust are insufficient to pay the death taxes in full, I direct the executor to pay any death taxes that cannot be paid by the trustee from the assets of my probate estate by prorating and apportioning those taxes among the beneficiaries of this will, as provided in the California Probate Code.

4.4. Period of Survivorship. For the purposes of this will, a beneficiary shall not be deemed to have survived me if that beneficiary dies within forty (40) days after my death.

4.5. No-Contest Clause. If any person, directly or indirectly, contests the validity of this will in whole or in part, or opposes, objects to, or seeks to invalidate any of its provisions, or seeks to succeed to any part of my estate otherwise than in the manner specified in this will, any gift or other interest given to that person under this will shall be revoked and shall be disposed of as if he or she had predeceased me without issue.

4.6. Captions. The captions appearing in this will are for convenience of reference only, and shall be disregarded in determining the meaning and effect of the provisions of this will.

4.7. Severability Clause. If any provision of this will is invalid, that provision shall be disregarded, and the remainder of this will shall be construed as if the invalid provision had not been included.

4.8. California Law to Apply. All questions concerning the

validity and interpretation of this will, including any trusts created by this will, shall be governed by the laws of the State of California in effect at the time this will is executed.

Executed on 8/24/94, at San Rafael, California.

Kenneth F Goodall
KENNETH F. GOODALL

On the date written above, we, the undersigned, each being present at the same time, witnessed the signing of this instrument by KENNETH F. GOODALL. At that time, KENNETH F. GOODALL appeared to us to be of sound mind and memory and, to the best of our knowledge, was not acting under fraud, duress, menace, or undue influence. Understanding this instrument, which consists of seven (7) pages, including the pages on which the signature of KENNETH F. GOODALL and our signatures appear, to be the will of KENNETH F. GOODALL, we subscribe our names as witnesses thereto.

We declare under penalty of perjury under the laws of the State of California that the foregoing is true and correct. Executed on 8/24/94, at San Rafael, California.

James R. Hastings — residing at 18 San Rafael Avenue
San Anselmo, California

Nancy Rodgers — residing at 470 Peachstone Terrace
San Rafael, California 94903

0633

Will

RECEIVED FOR
SAFE KEEPING

NOV 17 1994

FROM J.R. Hastings

HOWARD HANSON
MARIN COUNTY CLERK

BY D. ROSS

LAW OFFICE OF
J. R. HASTINGS
18 SAN RAFAEL AVENUE
SAN ANSELMO, CALIFORNIA 94960
(415) 459-6635

SAM WARE (State Bar No. 105005)
700 Larkspur Landing Circle, #199
Larkspur, CA 94939

Telephone 415-464-4872

E-mail sam@samware.us

Attorney for Sam Sloan,
administrator of Estate
of K. Michael Goodall

SUPERIOR COURT OF THE STATE OF CALIFORNIA

FOR THE COUNTY OF SAN FRANCISCO

In the Matter of the Goodall Family Trust dated September 12, 1990	Case No. PTR-99-273030 Declaration of Sam Sloan Hearing Date: February 8, 2012 Time: Department: 204

Sam Sloan declares:

1. I make this declaration based upon my own personal knowledge unless otherwise stated.

2. I have examined at the Marin County Superior Court the recently discovered purported originals of the purported Last Will of Kenneth F. Goodall, a copy of which is attached hereto as Exhibit A, and the purported Last Will of Rachel A Goodall, copy of which is attached hereto as Exhibit B.

EXHIBIT B

LAST WILL OF
RACHEL A. GOODALL

I, RACHEL A. GOODALL, a resident of Marin County, California, declare that this is my will. I hereby revoke all my previous wills and codicils.

ARTICLE ONE
INTRODUCTORY PROVISIONS

1.1. Marital Status. I am married to KENNETH F. GOODALL, and all references in this will to "my husband" are to him.

1.2. Identification of Living Child. I have one living child, KENNETH MICHAEL GOODALL.

1.3. No Deceased Children. I have no deceased children.

ARTICLE TWO
RESIDUARY PROVISIONS

2.1. Disposition of Residue. I give the residue of my estate to the trustee of the GOODALL TRUST, created under the declaration of trust executed on September 12, 1990, by KENNETH F. GOODALL and RACHEL A. GOODALL, as Settlors and Trustees. The trustee of that trust shall add the residue of my estate to the trust principal and hold, administer, and distribute the property in accordance with the provisions of that declaration of trust, including any amendments of that declaration of trust that have been made before or after execution of this will.

2.2. Alternate Disposition of Residue. If the GOODALL TRUST has been revoked, terminated, or declared invalid for any reason, I give the portion of the residue of my estate not taken to the executor of this will, as trustee, who shall hold, administer, and distribute the property under a testamentary trust, the terms of which shall be identical to the terms of the GOODALL TRUST that are in effect on the date of execution of this will.

ARTICLE THREE

EXECUTOR

3.1. Nomination of Executors. I nominate my husband as executor of this will. If, for any reason, my husband fails to qualify or ceases to act as executor, I nominate BANK OF AMERICA, NT & SA, San Francisco, California, or any corporation that is a successor thereto by merger, consolidation, transfer of assets, or other manner provided by law, as executor of this will.

3.2. Waiver of Bond. No bond or undertaking shall be required of any executor nominated in this will.

3.3. General Powers of Executor. The executor shall have full authority to administer my estate under the California Independent Administration of Estates Act. The executor shall have all powers now or hereafter conferred on executors by law, except as otherwise specifically provided in this will, including any powers enumerated in this will.

3.4. Power to Invest. The executor shall have the power to

invest estate funds in any kind of real or personal property, as the executor deems advisable.

3.5. Division or Distribution in Cash or in Kind. In order to satisfy a pecuniary gift or to distribute or divide estate assets into shares or partial shares, the executor may distribute or divide those assets in kind, or divide undivided interests in those assets, or sell all or any part of those assets and distribute or divide the property in cash, in kind, or partly in cash and partly in kind. Property distributed to satisfy a pecuniary gift under this will shall be valued at its fair market value at the time of distribution.

3.6. Power to Sell, Lease, and Grant Options to Purchase Property. The executor shall have the power to sell, at either public or private sale and with or without notice, lease, and grant options to purchase any real or personal property belonging to my estate, on such terms and conditions as the executor determines to be in the best interest of my estate.

3.7. Power to Purchase Estate Property. The executor shall have the power to sell any property of my estate to, or exchange any property of my estate with the property of, my husband, even though he is also an executor at the time of the sale or exchange, provided that any such sale or exchange shall be for adequate consideration.

3.8. Payments to Legally Incapacitated Persons. If at any time any beneficiary under this will is a minor or it appears to the executor that any beneficiary is incapacitated, incompetent,

or for any other reason not able to receive payments or make intelligent or responsible use of the payments, then the executor, in lieu of making direct payments to the beneficiary, may make payments to the beneficiary's conservator or guardian; to the beneficiary's custodian under the Uniform Gifts to Minors Act or Uniform Transfers to Minors Act of any state; to one or more suitable persons, as the executor deems proper, such as a relative or a person residing with the beneficiary, to be used for the benefit of the beneficiary; to any other person, firm, or agency for services rendered or to be rendered for the beneficiary's assistance or benefit; or to accounts in the beneficiary's name with financial institutions. The receipt of payments by any of the foregoing shall constitute a sufficient acquittance of the executor for all purposes.

ARTICLE FOUR
CONCLUDING PROVISIONS

4.1. Nonprobate Transfers of Community Property. If I predecease my husband, I revoke any consent I have given during my lifetime to any nonprobate transfer on the death of any person, to anyone other than my husband, of all or part of my community property interest in any asset described in California Probate Code Section 5000 (or any successor section), and instead I give to my husband my community property interest in any assets affected by this revocation of consent. Notwithstanding the preceding sentence, this revocation of consent shall be

inapplicable to any community property included in any express trust of which I am the settlor or a cosettlor, which shall continue to be governed by the terms of the applicable trust instrument. It is my intention that my husband shall have full power to dispose of all community property assets to which this section of the will applies. If my husband and I die simultaneously or if it cannot be established by clear and convincing evidence whether my husband or I died first, this section shall not apply.

4.2. Definition of Death Taxes. The term "death taxes," as used in this will, shall mean all inheritance, estate, succession, and other similar taxes that are payable by any person on account of that person's interest in my estate or by reason of my death, including penalties and interest, but excluding the following:

(a) Any addition to the federal estate tax for any "excess retirement accumulation" under Internal Revenue Code Section 4980A.

(b) Any additional tax that may be assessed under Internal Revenue Code Section 2032A.

(c) Any federal or state tax imposed on a "generation-skipping transfer," as that term is defined in the federal tax laws, unless the applicable tax statutes provide that the generation-skipping transfer tax on that transfer is payable directly out of the assets of my gross estate.

4.3. Payment of Death Taxes. Pursuant to the declaration of trust executed on September 12, 1990, by KENNETH F. GOODALL and RACHEL A. GOODALL, as Settlors and Trustees, all death taxes, whether or not attributable to property inventoried in my probate

estate, shall be paid by the trustee from that trust. However, if that trust does not exist at the time of my death, or if the assets of that trust are insufficient to pay the death taxes in full, I direct the executor to pay any death taxes that cannot be paid by the trustee from the assets of my probate estate by prorating and apportioning those taxes among the beneficiaries of this will, as provided in the California Probate Code.

4.4. Period of Survivorship. For the purposes of this will, a beneficiary shall not be deemed to have survived me if that beneficiary dies within forty (40) days after my death.

4.5. No-Contest Clause. If any person, directly or indirectly, contests the validity of this will in whole or in part, or opposes, objects to, or seeks to invalidate any of its provisions, or seeks to succeed to any part of my estate otherwise than in the manner specified in this will, any gift or other interest given to that person under this will shall be revoked and shall be disposed of as if he or she had predeceased me without issue.

4.6. Captions. The captions appearing in this will are for convenience of reference only, and shall be disregarded in determining the meaning and effect of the provisions of this will.

4.7. Severability Clause. If any provision of this will is invalid, that provision shall be disregarded, and the remainder of this will shall be construed as if the invalid provision had not been included.

4.8. <u>California Law to Apply</u>. All questions concerning the validity and interpretation of this will, including any trusts created by this will, shall be governed by the laws of the State of California in effect at the time this will is executed.

Executed on 8/24/94, at San Rafael, California.

Rachel A. Goodall
RACHEL A. GOODALL

On the date written above, we, the undersigned, each being present at the same time, witnessed the signing of this instrument by RACHEL A. GOODALL. At that time, RACHEL A. GOODALL appeared to us to be of sound mind and memory and, to the best of our knowledge, was not acting under fraud, duress, menace, or undue influence. Understanding this instrument, which consists of seven (7) pages, including the pages on which the signature of RACHEL A. GOODALL and our signatures appear, to be the will of RACHEL A. GOODALL, we subscribe our names as witnesses thereto.

We declare under penalty of perjury under the laws of the State of California that the foregoing is true and correct. Executed on 8/24/94, at San Rafael, California.

James R. Hastings residing at 18 San Rafael Avenue
San Anselmo, California

Nancy Rodgers residing at 470 Peachstone Terrace
San Rafael, California 94903

PROOF OF SERVICE

I certify and declare as follows:

I am over the age of 18 years, not a party to this action. My business address is 700 Larkspur Landing Circle #199, Larkspur, CA 94939. I am readily familiar with the business practices of my firm for the collection, processing and service of items with the United States Postal Service, express service providers (same day messenger and overnight) and facsimile transmission.

On the date set forth below, I served the foregoing documents described as Further Supplemental Opposition, Declaration of Samuel Sloan, Declaration of Nancy Rogers, Objections to Evidence on the parties in this action as follows:

__X__: BY FIRST CLASS MAIL -- By placing [ ] the original [X] a true and correct copy thereof in each sealed envelope addressed as indicated below. Said sealed envelopes, with postage fully prepaid, were deposited with the United States Postal Service in San Francisco, California this same day in the ordinary course of business.

____: BY FEDERAL EXPRESS — By placing [ ] the original [ ] a true and correct copy thereof in each sealed envelope addressed as indicated below. Said envelopes were deposited for collection and processing by Federal Express, Priority Overnight Service, in San Francisco, California.

____: BY PERSONAL SERVICE: By placing [ ] the original [x] a true and correct copy thereof in each sealed envelope addressed as indicated below and causing said envelopes to be delivered by hand, by our firm's messenger, to the offices of the addressees indicated below.

____: BY FACSIMILE TRANSMISSION -- The foregoing document was transmitted between 9:00 a.m. and 5:00 p.m. to the fax number indicated below each address.

____: BY EMAIL TRANSMISSION -- The foregoing document was transmitted between 9:00 a.m. and 5:00 p.m. to the e-mail address indicated below.

See attached service list

I declare under penalty of perjury under the laws of the State of California that the foregoing statements are true and correct.

Executed February 3, 2011

Service List

Gary D. Rothstein
Manatt, Phelps & Phillips, LLP
One Embarcadero Center, 30th Floor
San Francisco CA 94111

John L McDonnell
Reed Smith
1999 Harrison St. # 2400
Oakland, CA 94612

Julia Bentley Lemons
Apt. 308
12800 Marion Lane W
Minnetonka, MN 55305-1368

Robert Bentley
Bradford Village #504
906 N Boulevard Street
Edmond, OK 73030

Helen Beth Bentley Perry
7926 Praver Drive W
Jacksonville, FL 32217

Glenda Fern Bentley Zinar
4536 Chatman Street
The Colony, TX 75056

Beverly Gale Bentley Young
2316 Trenton
McKinney, TX 75070

Vickie Bentley Hankins
14580 NE 6th
Choctaw, OK 73020

Jeffrey Bentley
4701 N Douglas Boulevard
Spencer, OK 73084

Chad Everett Bentley
1609 Teepee Trail
Kingsland, TX 78639

Jeanette Goodall Phillips
152 S 11th Street
Salina, Kansas 67401

Kristin Kane
University of California
Berkeley College of Engineering
College Relations
208 Mclaughlin Hall #1722
Berkeley, CA 9472A-1722

Mr. Thomas Horton
Guide Dogs for the Blind, Inc.
350 Los Ranchitos Road
San Rafael, CA 94903

0646

SAM WARE (State Bar No. 105005)
700 Larkspur Landing Circle, #199
Larkspur, CA 94939

Telephone 415-464-4872

E-mail sam@samware.us

Attorney for Respondent Sam Sloan, administrator of Estate of Michael Goodall

ENDORSED FILED
San Francisco County Superior Court
FEB 06 2012
CLERK OF THE COURT
By: LESLIE GOMEZ Deputy Clerk
LESLIE GOMEZ

SUPERIOR COURT OF THE STATE OF CALIFORNIA

COUNTY OF SAN FRANCISCO

In the Matter of the Trust for Michael created under the Goodall Trust dated September 12, 1990	Case No. PTR-99-273030 OBJECTIONS TO EVIDENCE Hearing Date: February 8, 2012 Time: 9 AM Department: 204

BY FAX

The Estate of K. Michael Goodall and Samuel Sloan, as the duly appointed administrator of the Estate of K. Michael Goodall, a beneficiary under the 1990 Goodall Trust (hereinafter the Estate of Michael), hereby objects to admitting the following into evidence and moves to strike them from the record:

//

1. The Estate of Michael objects to admitting any part of the Declaration of James R Hastings filed August 19, 2011 on the grounds that he is not a party to this action, nor does he represent any party to this action. Said declaration was purportedly filed as an attorney for Roy Hoppe and Frank Thornally (who are also not parties to this action incidentally), and, moreover, at the hearing last August 22, 2011, Hastings was challenged in court as to his representation of Mr. Hoppe and Mr. Thornally, and he quickly acknowledged that he was not their lawyer and all.

2. The Estate of Michael further objects to admitting those portions of the declaration of Hastings filed August 19, 2011 which reveal confidential communications made to him by Michael Goodall.

Confidential communications between lawyer and client are privileged. Evidence Code §952. The holder of that privilege after the client is died is the personal representative of the client (i.e. Sam Sloan). Evidence Code §953(c). A the holder of the privilege has the right to prevent another (i.e. a lawyer such as Hastings) from disclosing a confidential communication. Evidence Code §954. Therefore, the Estate of Michael hereby objects to admitting, and moves to strike (Evidence Code §353), those statements made by Hastings in his August 19, 2011 Declaration; namely, at ¶ 2 (2:11 - 14) ["K Michael Goodall understood he had no right to the residuary estate of Kenneth F Goodall and Rachel A Goodall, and he understood that he had no power to direct the residuary benefits of their estate"], ¶ 13 (6:7-11) ["During that visit K Michael Goodall inform me that he had no children, had not had any previous marriages and that his assets included personal property, his automobile and a bank account"] , ¶ 13 (15 - 18) ["A will was completed, though K. Michael Goodall understood he did not have any assets which would ever require a probate, to insure personal property and his minimal bank account would be properly handled that his passing"] and ¶ 14 (7:2-6) ["During our discussions and at the signing of his Last Wills, I clearly understood that K Michael Goodall understood he had no residuary interest or power of appointment in the estate of his parents as comprised of the Trust for Michael of the Goodall Trust, the trust managed by the Bank of America following the death of his mother"].

3. The Estate of Michael also objects to admitting into evidence the 1994 Amendment to the 1990 Goodall Trust unless and until the original of that amendment can be produced.

Authentication of a writing is required before it may be received into evidence. Evidence Code §1401(a). The Court shall exclude secondary evidence of the content of the writing if the Court determines that a genuine dispute exists concerning material terms of the writing and justice requires the exclusion. Evidence Code §1521(a). The Estate of Michael contends that there is a genuine dispute as to the authenticity of the 1994 Amendment to the trust, purportedly executed August 24, 1994, because there is evidence that other writings purportedly executed by Kenneth Goodall Rachel Goodall that same day (i.e. their pour over wills) are not genuine. As set forth in the declaration of Sam Sloan filed herewith, it is apparent that these purported "original" wills on file at the Marin

County Superior Court are not in fact original wills at all but in fact are photocopies.

Furthermore, one of the purported witnesses to those wills, Nancy Rogers, has no recollection of ever signing any such documents. See declaration Nancy Rogers filed herewith.

There is a genuine issue as to the authenticity of the documents reportedly signed on August 24, 1994, including the purported 1994 Amendment to the 1990 Goodall Trust. Therefore, pursuant to the Evidence Code Sections quoted above, secondary evidence of that document should be excluded.

Date: February 3, 2011

Attorneys for Respondent

PROOF OF SERVICE

I certify and declare as follows:

I am over the age of 18 years, not a party to this action. My business address is 700 Larkspur Landing Circle #199, Larkspur, CA 94939. I am readily familiar with the business practices of my firm for the collection, processing and service of items with the United States Postal Service, express service providers (same day messenger and overnight) and facsimile transmission.

On the date set forth below, I served the foregoing documents described as Further Supplemental Opposition, Declaration of Samuel Sloan, Declaration of Nancy Rogers, Objections to Evidence on the parties in this action as follows:

__X__: BY FIRST CLASS MAIL — By placing [ ] the original [X] a true and correct copy thereof in each sealed envelope addressed as indicated below. Said sealed envelopes, with postage fully prepaid, were deposited with the United States Postal Service in San Francisco, California this same day in the ordinary course of business.

____: BY FEDERAL EXPRESS — By placing [ ] the original [ ] a true and correct copy thereof in each sealed envelope addressed as indicated below. Said envelopes were deposited for collection and processing by Federal Express, Priority Overnight Service, in San Francisco, California.

____: BY PERSONAL SERVICE: By placing [ ] the original [x] a true and correct copy thereof in each sealed envelope addressed as indicated below and causing said envelopes to be delivered by hand, by our firm's messenger, to the offices of the addressees indicated below.

____: BY FACSIMILE TRANSMISSION — The foregoing document was transmitted between 9:00 a.m. and 5:00 p.m. to the fax number indicated below each address.

____: BY EMAIL TRANSMISSION — The foregoing document was transmitted between 9:00 a.m. and 5:00 p.m. to the e-mail address indicated below.

See attached service list

I declare under penalty of perjury under the laws of the State of California that the foregoing statements are true and correct.

Executed February 3, 2011

Service List

Gary D. Rothstein
Manatt, Phelps & Phillips, LLP
One Embarcadero Center, 30th Floor
San Francisco CA 94111

John L McDonnell
Reed Smith
1999 Harrison St. # 2400
Oakland, CA 94612

Julia Bentley Lemons
Apt. 308
12800 Marion Lane W
Minnetonka, MN 55305-1368

Robert Bentley
Bradford Village #504
906 N Boulevard Street
Edmond, OK 73030

Helen Beth Bentley Perry
7926 Praver Drive W
Jacksonville, FL 32217

Clenda Fern Bentley Zinar
4536 Chatman Street
The Colony, TX 75056

Beverly Gale Bentley Young
2316 Trenton
McKinney, TX 75070

Vickie Bentley Hankins
14580 NE 6th
Choctaw, OK 73020

Jeffrey Bentley
4701 N Douglas Boulevard
Spencer, OK 73084

Chad Everett Bentley
1609 Teepee Trail
Kingsland, TX 78639

Jeanette Goodall Phillips
152 S 11th Street
Salina, Kansas 67401

Kristin Kane
University of California
Berkeley College of Engineering
College Relations
208 Mclaughlin Hall #1722
Berkeley, CA 9472A-1722

Mr. Thomas Horton
Guide Dogs for the Blind, Inc.
350 Los Ranchitos Road
San Rafael, CA 94903

SAM WARE (State Bar No. 105005)
700 Larkspur Landing Circle, #199
Larkspur, CA 94939

Telephone 415-464-4872

E-mail sam@samware.us

Attorney for Sam Sloan,
administrator of Estate
of K. Michael Goodall

FILED
Superior Court of California
County of San Francisco
FEB 06 2012
CLERK OF THE COURT
BY: Deputy Clerk

SUPERIOR COURT OF THE STATE OF CALIFORNIA

FOR THE COUNTY OF SAN FRANCISCO

In the Matter of the Goodall Family Trust dated September 12, 1990	Case No. PTR-99-273030 Declaration of Nancy Rodgers Hearing Date: February 8, 2012 Time: Department: 204

BY FAX

Nancy Rodgers declares:

1. I make this declaration based upon my own personal knowledge unless otherwise stated.

2. I reside at 470 Peachstone Terrace, San Rafael, CA 94903 and have resided there since before 1970.

3. I have examined the signature page of the purported Will of Kenneth F. Goodall, attached hereto in Exhibit A, and the signature page of the purported Last Will of Rachel A Goodall, attached hereto in Exhibit B.

4. At page 7 of each of these Exhibits, I see what purports to be my signature as a witness to those wills, along with James R Hastings as the other witness, purportedly executed on August 24, 1994 in San Rafael California.

5. Although the signatures there looks like mine, I do not recall ever acting as a witness to any will for either Kenneth Goodall or Rachel Goodall at any time, and I am sure that I would remember having done so, so these are not my signatures.

6. I do recall that at some time after Kenneth Goodall died that Rachel Goodall asked me and Barbara Dagitz, another of our neighbors, to be the two witnesses to a legal document pertaining to Rachel Goodall, which I recall being a health care directive or similar document, but never any will at any time.

7. I do not recall ever witnessing any signing of any document by Kenneth Goodall at any time, though I do remember quite clearly my husband and I visiting him in his home shortly before his death.

I declare under penalty of perjury under the laws of the state of California that the foregoing is true and correct.

Date: February 3, 2012 Nancy Rodgers

EXHIBIT B

LAST WILL OF

RACHEL A. GOODALL

I, RACHEL A. GOODALL, a resident of Marin County, California, declare that this is my will. I hereby revoke all my previous wills and codicils.

ARTICLE ONE

INTRODUCTORY PROVISIONS

1.1. Marital Status. I am married to KENNETH F. GOODALL, and all references in this will to "my husband" are to him.

1.2. Identification of Living Child. I have one living child, KENNETH MICHAEL GOODALL.

1.3. No Deceased Children. I have no deceased children.

ARTICLE TWO

RESIDUARY PROVISIONS

2.1. Disposition of Residue. I give the residue of my estate to the trustee of the GOODALL TRUST, created under the declaration of trust executed on September 12, 1990, by KENNETH F. GOODALL and RACHEL A. GOODALL, as Settlors and Trustees. The trustee of that trust shall add the residue of my estate to the trust principal and hold, administer, and distribute the property in accordance with the provisions of that declaration of trust, including any amendments of that declaration of trust that have been made before or after execution of this will.

2.2. Alternate Disposition of Residue. If the GOODALL TRUST has been revoked, terminated, or declared invalid for any reason, I give the portion of the residue of my estate not taken to the executor of this will, as trustee, who shall hold, administer, and distribute the property under a testamentary trust, the terms of which shall be identical to the terms of the GOODALL TRUST that are in effect on the date of execution of this will.

ARTICLE THREE

EXECUTOR

3.1. Nomination of Executors. I nominate my husband as executor of this will. If, for any reason, my husband fails to qualify or ceases to act as executor, I nominate BANK OF AMERICA, NT & SA, San Francisco, California, or any corporation that is a successor thereto by merger, consolidation, transfer of assets, or other manner provided by law, as executor of this will.

3.2. Waiver of Bond. No bond or undertaking shall be required of any executor nominated in this will.

3.3. General Powers of Executor. The executor shall have full authority to administer my estate under the California Independent Administration of Estates Act. The executor shall have all powers now or hereafter conferred on executors by law, except as otherwise specifically provided in this will, including any powers enumerated in this will.

3.4. Power to Invest. The executor shall have the power to

invest estate funds in any kind of real or personal property, as the executor deems advisable.

3.5. Division or Distribution in Cash or in Kind. In order to satisfy a pecuniary gift or to distribute or divide estate assets into shares or partial shares, the executor may distribute or divide those assets in kind, or divide undivided interests in those assets, or sell all or any part of those assets and distribute or divide the property in cash, in kind, or partly in cash and partly in kind. Property distributed to satisfy a pecuniary gift under this will shall be valued at its fair market value at the time of distribution.

3.6. Power to Sell, Lease, and Grant Options to Purchase Property. The executor shall have the power to sell, at either public or private sale and with or without notice, lease, and grant options to purchase any real or personal property belonging to my estate, on such terms and conditions as the executor determines to be in the best interest of my estate.

3.7. Power to Purchase Estate Property. The executor shall have the power to sell any property of my estate to, or exchange any property of my estate with the property of, my husband, even though he is also an executor at the time of the sale or exchange, provided that any such sale or exchange shall be for adequate consideration.

3.8. Payments to Legally Incapacitated Persons. If at any time any beneficiary under this will is a minor or it appears to the executor that any beneficiary is incapacitated, incompetent,

or for any other reason not able to receive payments or make intelligent or responsible use of the payments, then the executor, in lieu of making direct payments to the beneficiary, may make payments to the beneficiary's conservator or guardian; to the beneficiary's custodian under the Uniform Gifts to Minors Act or Uniform Transfers to Minors Act of any state; to one or more suitable persons, as the executor deems proper, such as a relative or a person residing with the beneficiary, to be used for the benefit of the beneficiary; to any other person, firm, or agency for services rendered or to be rendered for the beneficiary's assistance or benefit; or to accounts in the beneficiary's name with financial institutions. The receipt of payments by any of the foregoing shall constitute a sufficient acquittance of the executor for all purposes.

ARTICLE FOUR

CONCLUDING PROVISIONS

4.1. Nonprobate Transfers of Community Property. If I predecease my husband, I revoke any consent I have given during my lifetime to any nonprobate transfer on the death of any person, to anyone other than my husband, of all or part of my community property interest in any asset described in California Probate Code Section 5000 (or any successor section), and instead I give to my husband my community property interest in any assets affected by this revocation of consent. Notwithstanding the preceding sentence, this revocation of consent shall be

inapplicable to any community property included in any express trust of which I am the settlor or a cosettlor, which shall continue to be governed by the terms of the applicable trust instrument. It is my intention that my husband shall have full power to dispose of all community property assets to which this section of the will applies. If my husband and I die simultaneously or if it cannot be established by clear and convincing evidence whether my husband or I died first, this section shall not apply.

4.2. Definition of Death Taxes. The term "death taxes," as used in this will, shall mean all inheritance, estate, succession, and other similar taxes that are payable by any person on account of that person's interest in my estate or by reason of my death, including penalties and interest, but excluding the following:

(a) Any addition to the federal estate tax for any "excess retirement accumulation" under Internal Revenue Code Section 4980A.

(b) Any additional tax that may be assessed under Internal Revenue Code Section 2032A.

(c) Any federal or state tax imposed on a "generation-skipping transfer," as that term is defined in the federal tax laws, unless the applicable tax statutes provide that the generation-skipping transfer tax on that transfer is payable directly out of the assets of my gross estate.

4.3. Payment of Death Taxes. Pursuant to the declaration of trust executed on September 12, 1990, by KENNETH F. GOODALL and RACHEL A. GOODALL, as Settlors and Trustees, all death taxes, whether or not attributable to property inventoried in my probate

estate, shall be paid by the trustee from that trust. However, if that trust does not exist at the time of my death, or if the assets of that trust are insufficient to pay the death taxes in full, I direct the executor to pay any death taxes that cannot be paid by the trustee from the assets of my probate estate by prorating and apportioning those taxes among the beneficiaries of this will, as provided in the California Probate Code.

4.4. Period of Survivorship. For the purposes of this will, a beneficiary shall not be deemed to have survived me if that beneficiary dies within forty (40) days after my death.

4.5. No-Contest Clause. If any person, directly or indirectly, contests the validity of this will in whole or in part, or opposes, objects to, or seeks to invalidate any of its provisions, or seeks to succeed to any part of my estate otherwise than in the manner specified in this will, any gift or other interest given to that person under this will shall be revoked and shall be disposed of as if he or she had predeceased me without issue.

4.6. Captions. The captions appearing in this will are for convenience of reference only, and shall be disregarded in determining the meaning and effect of the provisions of this will.

4.7. Severability Clause. If any provision of this will is invalid, that provision shall be disregarded, and the remainder of this will shall be construed as if the invalid provision had not been included.

4.8. California Law to Apply. All questions concerning the validity and interpretation of this will, including any trusts created by this will, shall be governed by the laws of the State of California in effect at the time this will is executed.

Executed on 8/24/94, at San Rafael, California.

Rachel A. Goodall
RACHEL A. GOODALL

On the date written above, we, the undersigned, each being present at the same time, witnessed the signing of this instrument by RACHEL A. GOODALL. At that time, RACHEL A. GOODALL appeared to us to be of sound mind and memory and, to the best of our knowledge, was not acting under fraud, duress, menace, or undue influence. Understanding this instrument, which consists of seven (7) pages, including the pages on which the signature of RACHEL A. GOODALL and our signatures appear, to be the will of RACHEL A. GOODALL, we subscribe our names as witnesses thereto.

We declare under penalty of perjury under the laws of the State of California that the foregoing is true and correct. Executed on 8/24/94, at San Rafael, California.

James R. Hastings residing at 18 San Rafael Avenue
San Anselmo, California

Nancy Rodgers residing at 470 Peachstone Terrace
San Rafael, California 94903

PROOF OF SERVICE

I certify and declare as follows:

I am over the age of 18 years, not a party to this action. My business address is 700 Larkspur Landing Circle #199, Larkspur, CA 94939. I am readily familiar with the business practices of my firm for the collection, processing and service of items with the United States Postal Service, express service providers (same day messenger and overnight) and facsimile transmission.

On the date set forth below, I served the foregoing documents described as Further Supplemental Opposition, Declaration of Samuel Sloan, Declaration of Nancy Rogers, Objections to Evidence on the parties in this action as follows:

__X__: BY FIRST CLASS MAIL – By placing [ ] the original [X] a true and correct copy thereof in each sealed envelope addressed as indicated below. Said sealed envelopes, with postage fully prepaid, were deposited with the United States Postal Service in San Francisco, California this same day in the ordinary course of business.

____: BY FEDERAL EXPRESS — By placing [ ] the original [ ] a true and correct copy thereof in each sealed envelope addressed as indicated below. Said envelopes were deposited for collection and processing by Federal Express, Priority Overnight Service, in San Francisco, California.

____: BY PERSONAL SERVICE: By placing [ ] the original [x] a true and correct copy thereof in each sealed envelope addressed as indicated below and causing said envelopes to be delivered by hand, by our firm's messenger, to the offices of the addressees indicated below.

____: BY FACSIMILE TRANSMISSION – The foregoing document was transmitted between 9:00 a.m. and 5:00 p.m. to the fax number indicated below each address.

____: BY EMAIL TRANSMISSION – The foregoing document was transmitted between 9:00 a.m. and 5:00 p.m. to the e-mail address indicated below.

See attached service list

I declare under penalty of perjury under the laws of the State of California that the foregoing statements are true and correct.

Executed February 3, 2011

Service List

Gary D. Rothstein
Manatt, Phelps & Phillips, LLP
One Embarcadero Center, 30th Floor
San Francisco CA 94111

John L McDonnell
Reed Smith
1999 Harrison St. # 2400
Oakland, CA 94612

Julia Bentley Lemons
Apt. 308
12800 Marion Lane W
Minnetonka, MN 55305-1368

Robert Bentley
Bradford Village #504
906 N Boulevard Street
Edmond, OK 73030

Helen Beth Bentley Perry
7926 Praver Drive W
Jacksonville, FL 32217

Clenda Fern Bentley Zinar
4536 Chatman Street
The Colony, TX 75056

Beverly Gale Bentley Young
2316 Trenton
McKinney, TX 75070

Vickie Bentley Hankins
14580 NE 6th
Choctaw, OK 73020

Jeffrey Bentley
4701 N Douglas Boulevard
Spencer, OK 73084

Chad Everett Bentley
1609 Teepee Trail
Kingsland, TX 78639

Jeanette Goodall Phillips
152 S 11th Street
Salina, Kansas 67401

Kristin Kane
University of California
Berkeley College of Engineering
College Relations
208 Mclaughlin Hall #1722
Berkeley, CA 9472A-1722

Mr. Thomas Horton
Guide Dogs for the Blind, Inc.
350 Los Ranchitos Road
San Rafael, CA 94903

SAM WARE (State Bar No. 105005)
700 Larkspur Landing Circle, #199
Larkspur, CA 94939

Telephone 415-464-4872

E-mail sam@samware.us

Attorney for Sam Sloan,
administrator of Estate
of K. Michael Goodall

FILED
SUPERIOR COURT
COUNTY OF SAN FRANCISCO
2012 MAR -1 AM 8:06
CLERK OF THE COURT
BY: [signature]
DEPUTY CLERK

SUPERIOR COURT OF THE STATE OF CALIFORNIA

FOR THE COUNTY OF SAN FRANCISCO

In the Matter of the Goodall Family Trust dated September 12, 1990	Case No. PTR-99-273030 Petition of Sam Sloan for Forensic Document Examination of Documents Purported to be Trust Documents of the Goodall Family Trust Hearing Date: MAY 0 7 2012 Time: Department: 204

PROBATE DEPARTMENT
9:00 A.M. RM. 204

Sam Sloan declares:

1. I am the Administrator with Will Annexed of the Estate of K. Michael Goodall. I have personal knowledge of the matters set forth herein and, if called upon to testify, could and would competently testify thereto. I make this declaration based upon my own personal knowledge unless otherwise stated.

2. I reside at 461 Peachstone Terrace, San Rafael, CA 94903 and have resided there since 1998.

3. This estate is concerned with the authenticity of three documents all purportedly signed on the same date of August 24, 1994. These three documents consist of "Pour Over" wills purportedly signed by Kenneth and Rachel Goodall on August 24, 1994 and a trust document purportedly signed by both of them also bearing the same date.

4. I believe that these documents are all forgeries or are otherwise not authentic. The basis of my belief is that it was virtually impossible for Kenneth F. Goodall to have signed these documents on that date of August 24, 1994, just 17 days before his death on September 10, 1994. He was extremely ill. He had been ill for at least two years but his condition had gotten much worse. He had just survived an operation for esophageal cancer. He had a feeding tube inserted in his abdomen. A witness who visited him in the hospital with his son Mike and wife Rachel is prepared to testify that he was on life support, was unconscious and it was recommended that he not be awaken. The forger has changed his testimony several times as to where these documents were signed, first starting that it was in his office, then in his home, then in San Anselmo. We are prepared to prove that he was in none of those places. Most importantly, the witness to both of these wills states vehemently that she never signed these documents and would never have signed these documents. Her husband and daughter agree with her that they would have been involved and that she absolutely

would not have signed these documents. Finally, it is just inconceivable that Col. Kenneth Goodall would have written his only son out of his will just 17 days before he died, considering how devoted the father was to his son and how devoted his son was to his father. There is a handwritten statement in the ring binder left by Kenneth F. Goodall that states, "I have never encountered a lawyer who did not leave me feeling poluted afterwards. I despise them as a class and as individuals". It is thus inconceivable that on his death bed he would knowingly sign a document that virtually took all rights away from his only child and gave them to a lawyer.

5. As to the motivation of the forger, he was at that time an employee of Bank of America. These documents took the role of back-up trustee away from Security Pacific Bank and gave it to Bank of America, of which he was the manager. This has enabled him to earn administration and legal fees in the amount of several hundred thousand dollars since that time. Needless to say, all of these funds will have to be paid back if these documents are determined to be forged.

6. The wills are on file at the Marin County Superior Court. Kenneth Goodall's will is number W001916 and Rachel Goodall's will is number W001919. I have filed a motion in that court for a Forensic Document Examination of those two wills. I am confident that a forensic document examination will show that both of those wills are forged or are otherwise not authentic.

7. I am also seeking forensic examination of the trust documents. There are three known trust documents. They are:

A document entitled "The Goodall Trust" and dated September 12, 1990.

A document entitled "Declaration of the Goodall Trust" and dated August 24, 1994.

A document entitled "Second Amendment to Goodall Trust" and dated January 19, 1999.

8. All three of these documents bear the signature and notary seal of James R. Hastings. I have checked with the California Department of State in Sacramento and Mr. Hastings is still registered as a Notary Public in the State of California and has been so continuously since at least the 1970s. I have demanded of Mr. Hastings pursuant to California Government Code Section 8206 (c) a photostatic copy of the line item representing each of the transactions in which he acted as a Notary Public and notarized the signatures of Kenneth F. Goodall, Rachel A. Goodall and/or Kenneth Michael Goodall. A copy of my letter demanding a copy of these line items is annexed hereto and Marked Exhibit A. Sufficient time has passed and Mr. Hastings has not responded to my demand.

9. I believe that the documents dated September 12, 1990 and January 19, 1999 are genuine but that the document dated August 24, 1994 is a forgery. Michael certainly was not going to object to the trust dated September 12, 1990, because that Trust gives everything

to Michael. Attached hereto as Exhibit B is the relevant page of the September 12, 1990 trust. As can plainly be seen, that trust gives the entire Goodall Estate to Michael.

10. Mr. Hastings claims to have lost the Trust Documents. Even if he has lost the trust documents he cannot legally claim to have lost the notary public journal because California Government Code Section 8206 (a)(1) requires, "The journal shall be kept in a locked and secured area, under the direct and exclusive control of the notary."

11. I want all of these documents examined by a Forensic Document Examiner. The problem is that these documents are not in the files of the court. They are in the possession of James R. Hastings and/or Bank of America and/or Guide Dogs for the Blind, Inc. who refuse to let us see them. I want this court to order these documents to be turned over to the same Forensic Document Examiner.

12. In order to determine whether these documents are forged or altered or that they are mere copies, I have agreed to retain a Forensic Document Examiner who is vastly and eminently qualified in this field, having worked with the FBI and other governmental agencies to determine forgeries. He is David S. Moore. He has a laboratory located at 9010 Barrhill Way, Fair Oaks, California 95628. This laboratory contains highly sophisticated devices such as microscopes that easily enable him to determine if a document is

forged or not. These devices cannot be effectively transported out of the laboratory environment. Therefore, I am asking this court to order the release of these documents directly to him as the Forensic Document Examiner. I will of course not handle the documents myself.

13. I am specifically objecting to the validity of the August 24, 1994 Trust document. I am certain that this document is a forgery and that the perpetrator of this crime is none other than James R. Hastings. Facts that recently came to my attention demonstrate that this is a forgery.

14. The first fact is the declarations by James Hastings filed in San Francisco Probate Court. They state among other things that Kenneth Goodall had come to him in 1997 and said that he wanted to change his will because he was unhappy that Michael had quit his job and moved back into the family home. It is remarkable that Kenneth Goodall said this in 1997, since he died in 1994. Next, Hastings says that in August 1994, Kenneth and Rachel Goodall came to his office and asked him to prepare new trust documents for them to sign taking all powers out of the hands of their only son, Michael, and giving them to Bank of America, of which Hastings was the manager of the Trust Department. However, it is impossible for this to have happened because Kenneth Goodall was on his death bed at the time and his wife Rachel had always had difficulty walking and could not climb stairs and was not capable of going anywhere

without her husband's assistance. The Death Certificate of Kenneth Goodall which is annexed hereto and marked Exhibit C states on line 113.

"Was Operation performed for any condition in item 107 or 112? If yes, list type of operation and date.
"Feeding Jejunostomy 07/25/1994"

15. Kenneth Goodall died on September 10, 1994. During the time between the operation on July 25, 1994 in which a feeding tube was inserted into his abdomen and his death on September 10, 1994, he was entirely bedridden. He was either in the hospital or in his home in a hospital bed. He never went to the office of James R. Hastings or anywhere else for that matter. Thus, the claim by Hastings that he came to the office of James R. Hastings and asked for his will and his trust documents to be changed only 17 days before his death is simply a lie.

16. In addition to the purported Trust document dated August 24, 1994, there are two other documents bearing the same date. These are new wills signed by Kenneth and his wife Rachel Goodall. These are "pour over wills". They provide that the assets of Kenneth and Rachel be poured into the Trust. Without these wills, the trust has no money. However, both wills bear the purported signature of Nancy Rodgers, who was a close friend of Rachel Goodall and lived across the street at 470 Peachstone Terrace. Nancy Rodgers states that although the signatures look like hers, they are not hers and she never signed these documents. She says

that she never witnessed any wills signed by either Kenneth or Rachel Goodall. She is certain of this. However, she does remember signing quite a different document after Kenneth had died. She states that after the death of Kenneth, Rachel, who was her best friend, called her and another neighbor, Barbara Dagitz, who lived next door at 455 Peachstone Terrace, to come over and sign a health directive. She states that when she and Barbara Dagitz arrived in the house of Rachel Goodall, only a lawyer plus Rachel were present. Michael was not there and Kenneth had already died. She says that she was surprised that she was being asked to witness a health directive as she did not see any need for a witness to sign such a document. Nevertheless, she signed it. Attached hereto as Exhibit D is a declaration by Nancy Rodgers stating these facts.

17. Nancy Rodgers and her husband William Rodgers state that shortly before the death of Kenneth Goodall, they received a call from Rachel Goodall, asking them to come over, stating that if they wanted to see Kenneth they should come over now as Kenneth would not be with us much longer. At first, her husband, William Rodgers, did not want to go, but finally he agreed to go, as they had not seen Kenneth in a long time. They found Kenneth Goodall sitting up in bed with his arms folded trying to look as normal as possible. He was being fed through a feeding tube. The Rodgers expressed surprise that Rachel Goodall was able to handle this situation.

18. That was the last time they ever saw Kenneth. Both Nancy Rodgers and her husband William Rodgers are certain that neither of them signed any documents as witnesses for Kenneth Goodall on that date or at any other time.

19. Compare their statements with the statements made by James Hastings at a deposition we took of him on November 14, 2011. The transcript of the Deposition is annexed as Exhibit E. On page 49, he is asked if he can recall anything with regard to Mr. Goodall's health at the time. He answers "No". He is asked several other questions about the health or physical condition of Mr. or Mrs. Goodall at that time. In each case, Hastings says he can recall nothing about their health condition or what they specifically said to him at this or at any other time.

20. Surely any lawyer when asking a client to sign a will and other documents drastically changing and revoking his prior estate plans would inquire and would notice that the man signing the will was in a hospital bed and was being fed through a feeding tube, especially when he died only 17 days later.

21. From this we can infer what really happened: James Hastings never really saw Kenneth or Rachel Goodall in the months before the death of Kenneth Goodall in September 1994. However, after Kenneth Goodall had died and been buried, Hastings had Rachel Goodall ask her two best friends, Nancy Rodgers and Barbara Dagitz, witness a Health Care Directive. In the Goodall Estate Planning

binder, there is a document entitled "Durable Power of Attorney for Health Care" signed by Kenneth and a space for a similar document signed by Rachel, except that the document signed by Rachel is missing. This document signed by Kenneth checks the box for "I have obtained the signatures of two witnesses who personally know me". This explains why Nancy Rodgers and Barbara Dagitz were called.

22. What clearly happened is that this missing document is the document signed by Rachel Goodall and witnessed by Nancy Rodgers and Barbara Dagitz after Kenneth had died. James R. Hastings then took this document and, by using Adobe Photoshop or similar means, transposed the signatures of Rachel Goodall and Nancy Rodgers onto other documents including the two wills and the 1994 Trust. Thus, the Health Care Directive gave him all the signatures he needed to create the other documents, except for the signature of Kenneth Goodall, and that was readily available on numerous documents in the possession of Mr. Hastings. Hastings had plenty of signatures of Kenneth Goodall on other documents, so the fact that Kenneth was dead created no barrier to his creating a document signed by Kenneth.

23. Until January 2012, the Will of Kenneth Goodall was reported to be lost or missing by the Clerk's Office. The Marin County Clerk's Office including Stacy in the record room spent months in a frantic search for this missing will. Finally, a few days ago, the will was "found". It is highly irregular and unusual

for any document and especially for a will to go missing in the court files like that. Hastings of course knew that the Clerk's Office was searching for the will and that the entire case depended on that will, so he most likely slipped it back in, which is an easy thing to do for someone such as Mr. Hastings who has been working for years with documents in this Clerk's Office.

24. James R. Hastings has failed and refused to provide any documents from his files, although these files are the subject of a subpoena and court order. Hastings states that he has lost the entire Estate Planning File for the Goodalls and his other files pertaining to the Goodalls are not relevant and therefore he refuses to produce them. Among the files that Mr. Hastings claims are not relevant are presumably the Health Care Directive witnessed by Nancy Rodgers and Barbara Dagitz. If we had that document we could see if the signatures on that document are identical to the signatures on the wills.

25. I have examined at the Marin County Superior Court the recently discovered purported original of the purported Last Will of Kenneth F. Goodall, a copy of which is attached hereto as Exhibit F, and the purported Last Will of Rachel A Goodall, copy of which is attached hereto as Exhibit G. These documents are on file at the Marin County Superior Court. Kenneth Goodall's will is number W001916 and Rachel Goodall's will is number W001919.

26. What is remarkable about these documents on file with the Court is that they do not appear to be original documents; that is, that the three signatures and the two dates which appear on each of these documents at page 7 of each of these documents are not in blue ink, and I can feel no depression on the back or front of these pages to indicate that a pen was pressed on the paper to otherwise indicate an original signature. The total of six signatures do not show any variation in pressure or indentation in the paper. Thus, the documents appear to be copies and are not originals. As to how they were created I do not know but if I were creating them I would use Adobe Photoshop.

27. Attached hereto as Exhibit H is the Declaration filed by James R. Hastings in San Francisco Probate Court after he was ordered by that court to search for the files and produce them if he could find them. As you can see from his declaration, he is not able to find any of the Goodall files. It is at a minimum professional misconduct for a lawyer to lose or misplace files vitally important to such an important case involving millions of dollars.

28. Another document Hastings is unable or unwilling to produce is the original power of attorney that Rachel Goodall gave to her son Michael Goodall. We have been able to obtain a copy of this power of attorney from USAA Management, where the Goodalls kept substantially all of their money up until the death of Rachel

Goodall in 1999. However, their copy is not signed. Michael Goodall tried to obtain the original signed document from Mr. Hastings but Hastings refused to give it to him, just as Hastings is now refusing to give me any documents from the Michael Goodall Files, although I am legally entitled to them as I am the personal representative of K. Michael Goodall and thus am entitled to my own files back.

29. As can be seen, this Power of Attorney gave Michael Goodall the power to modify or vacate the Goodall Family Trust. Michael Goodall tried to do exactly that and wrote numerous letters to USAA Investment Management demanding changes in the accounts. These letters were ineffective because Michael did not have the original signed power of attorney. James Hastings had the original power of attorney presumably in the same files that he now refuses to give us. A copy of the unsigned Power of Attorney as provided to us by USAA Investment Management is annexed hereto and marked Exhibit I.

30. It could be argued and no doubt will be argued that Michael could have taken other and further steps to obtain that Power of Attorney, but it is clear that his efforts would have been futile especially since we have been trying to obtain these same documents from Hastings and have gotten nowhere.

31. Kenneth Goodall left two notebooks in Round Ring Binders. One has a green cover. The other has a blue cover. When

Bank of America broke into the Goodall Mansion on or about February 28, 2011 and took all the contents, they took these two binders. However, they were returned by the bank on June 10, 2011 under threat of court order. I do not know if any changes were made during the period when Bank of America had them.

32. One page found in the green covered binder is marked Exhibit J. It includes hand written notes regarding Kenneth's plans for his estate. It says the following:

"General Terms of the wills leave all property to the survivor of Ken or Rachel, and then to Mike, our son."

Below that, it says:

"It is best that you have some time to think about the subjects discussed at the first meeting, so try to defer any commitments until the next meeting. I have never encountered a lawyer who did not leave me feeling poluted afterwards. I despise them as a class and as individuals."

33. In view of the above statement by Kenneth Goodall, "I have never encountered a lawyer who did not leave me feeling poluted afterwards. I despise them as a class and as individuals", it is inconceivable that on his death bed he would knowingly sign a document that virtually took all rights away from his only child and gave them to a lawyer, James R. Hastings.

34. The major differences between the 1990 Trust and the 1994 Trust is that the 1994 Trust names Bank of America as the back up trustee whereas the 1990 Trust names Security Pacific Bank as the backup trustee. James R. Hastings was the manager of the Trust Department of Bank of America and this establishes his motivation for this change. Secondly, and most importantly, the 1990 Trust gives the estate directly to Michael Goodall and his heirs whereas Section 6.3 on Page 18 of the 1994 Trust consists of a convoluted and circular paragraph which makes no sense at all but basically gives the estate to the by-pass trust that in turn gives it to Michael. Thus, read logically, Michael still gets the estate. That is the reason why Hastings has filed statements that the intent of the trust was to give the estate to Guide Dogs to the Blind regardless of whether Michael died before or after his parents did. Hastings has not offered any explanation as to why he did not draft the trust so as to do exactly what he says was the intent of the trust. The standard Nolo Press book on Living Trusts, available at almost any bookstore, provides a fill-in-the-blanks form to do exactly what Hastings says was the intent of the convoluted trust he drew up. Why did he not use the Nolo Press form? Why does he have the right to say that the intent of the Trust he drew up was different from what the trust actually says? Even assuming that in Kenneth's weakened condition after just having undergone surgery and having a feeding tube inserted in his abdomen and awaiting his

death that he knew would come soon, and even assuming that Kenneth Goodall read and signed the documents, how does Hastings and the Courts have the right to decide that the intent of the trust is different from what is actually says, which is Guide Dogs for the Blind gets the money if and only if Michael dies before his parents do.

35. A third difference between the 1990 Trust and the 1994 purported Trust is that the 1994 Trust contains a no-contest clause. This is in section 8.3 on page 33 of the 1994 document. There is no "no-contest clause" in the 1990 document. James Hastings used this no contest clause to frighten Mike into believing that he would lose everything. In a pleading or paper filed in San Francisco Probate Court in 2000, Hastings stated that the objection by Michael Goodall to having Bank of America serve as Trustee constituted a challenge to the trust and therefore Michael should lose everything including the house and the money. However, now in this court Hastings reverses himself saying that Goodall did not challenge the Trust and therefore is time barred from doing so.

36. A fourth difference between the 1990 document and the 1994 document is the 1990 Trust shows only the house as being in the trust. There was no money in the trust. This is in accordance to the statement in Exhibit J that says "No Trust Fund is Established". However, the 1994 purported trust says there is $10

plus the house in this trust. While the ten dollars seems a trivial matter, it does establish a trust fund.

37. Everything about this case tells us that Hastings is a fraud, a liar and a scammer. He starts off by saying that Kenneth Goodall told him something in 1997 when Kenneth Goodall actually died in 1994. He has changed his story many times. He says that the Goodalls came to his office in August 1994 when in reality Kenneth Goodall was in bed being fed by a feeding tube and could not walk or go anywhere at that time. James Hastings refuses to produce any files on this matter including the original trust documents and says that he lost or misplaced them. He cannot remember anything that either Kenneth or Rachel Goodall said, yet he provides a declaration saying what their intent was. On December 27, 2011, he stated to Commissioner Randolph E. Heubach, in open court, "This matter has nothing to do with me. I am not involved in it at all". This was a lie. Hastings completely stonewalls at every step of the way.

38. At the time of the death of Rachel Goodall in 1999 there was no Goodall money in Bank of America. They did not even have a regular checking account there. Substantially all their money was with USAA Investment Management in Texas. Right after Rachel Goodall died, Hastings started writing letters to the USAA Investment Management demanding that the funds be transferred to Bank of America. As far as we can determine, there was at least

$610,000 in the USAA Investment Management account at that time. There was no right and no legal basis to this request by Hastings to transfer this money to Bank of America. If the Goodalls wanted the money transferred, they would have done it while they were alive. Hastings states on pages 58-59 of the transcript that it is normal not to transfer the cash assets from one financial institution to another until after the person has died. This is obviously nonsense. I have been informed by the Probate Examiner that the transfer of such a large amount of money as over $600,000 should have been done under the supervision of the Probate Court. Instead, no probate proceeding was filed. As a result, we still do not know how much money was transferred or where it came from. The estate documents show other Goodall accounts including a trading account with Charles Schwab, a stock brokerage firm. We do not know what happened to that money. We only know that it disappeared and that Hastings was aggressively writing to everybody who had had dealings with the Goodalls demanding that all Goodall funds be handed over to Bank of America. Examples of some of the letters Hastings wrote is annexed as Exhibit K.

39. We have received about 500 pages of documents from USAA Investment Management. They have been co-operating fully as opposed to Bank of America which has been completely stonewalling. Although some of these USAA documents do refer to a Trust account, none of the documents show how that account was set up. Neither the 1990

Trust nor the 1994 Trust is included in the documents provided by USAA Investment Management. We know that before Mr. Hastings arrived on the scene, the Goodalls had an attorney named Robert W. Pendergrass. He practiced law in Marin County for more than 50 years and died on March 24, 2009 at age 91 years. It is possible and indeed likely that he too set up a trust account for the Goodalls that preceded the 1990 and 1994 documents. With both Bank of America and James R. Hastings completely stonewalling and refusing to provide any documents or information and with Hastings saying that he has lost or misplaced all the files, there is no way for us to determine the truth of the matter. I am calling for the arrest and criminal prosecution of Mr. Hastings, not to mention disbarment.

40. For these reasons I want all of these documents examined by David S. Moore, forensic document examiner, at his laboratory located at 9010 Barrhill Way, Fair Oaks, California 95628. He has more than thirty years of document and investigative experience, including assignments with the Crime Laboratories of the United States Army, the United States Postal Inspection Service, the Las Vegas Metropolitan Police, and the California Department of Justice. He has received extensive training regarding handwriting identification, ink and document analysis, and examination, reflected in courses from the United States Army, the United States Secret Service, the Federal Bureau of Investigation, the American

Academy of Forensic Sciences, and the California Criminalistics Institute. He has been certified as a "Diplomate" of the American Board of Forensic Document Examiners since 1978. From 1999 to 2002, He served as one of the Directors on that Board. He has published numerous articles in the field of forensic document examination in the Journal of Forensic Sciences, including "lie Electrostatic Detection Apparatus (ESDA) and its Effect on Latent Prints on Paper", March 1988; "The Importance of Shading Habits in Handwriting Identification: A Case Study", January 1983; the "Evaluation of a Method to Detect the Site of Rubber Erasures by Powder", October 1981. In addition, he has presented numerous papers at meetings and conferences of the American Academy of Forensic Sciences, the American Society of Questioned Document Examiners, the International Association of Identification, the Southwestern Association of Forensic Document Examiners, and the Southeastern Association of Forensic Scientists.

41. He has presented numerous classes on questioned document subjects to federal, state and local law enforcement officials, both government and private attorneys, as well as to bank and insurance personnel.

42. He has testified as an expert in the field of questioned documents in justice, municipal, and superior, federal and military courts and administrative hearings in excess of 700 times in more than 20 states throughout the United States, including California.

43. In order to conduct a proper forensic document examination of the original questioned wills and trusts in this instant case, it is his professional opinion that the following tests may be necessary.

a. Visual examination;

b. Microscopic examination;

c. Photographic examination;

d. Ink examination;

e. Handwriting examination;

f. Indentation examination; and

g. Any other non-destructive examination necessary to determine the authenticity of the questioned documents.

44. All proposed examination will be entirely non-destructive to the document and will be conducted in a manner so as not to compromise future additional or confirmatory examinations or testing. Additionally, the original document will not be altered or changed by any of the proposed examinations.

45. These types of examinations are necessary to evaluate the genuineness of questioned documents. An ink examination allows him to analyze the inks used in the documents and draw conclusions about the use of different inks and to detect whether alternations and/or interlineations have been made. Indentation examination permits him to draw conclusions about whether certain documents

were together when they were originally created and also to ascertain whether there is other information contained on the documents in the form of indentations that may provide insight into when the document was created and under what conditions. The other examinations requested may enable him to draw conclusions about the time frame in which the document was created and about the genuineness of the document.

46. It is important that he conduct the examination of the questioned documents at his laboratory using specialized equipment. The indentation examination, the ink examination, the fluorescence and luminescence examinations require the use of laboratory equipment. For example, the microscope that he uses is a stereoscopic trinocular microscope that is not readily portable. The video spectral comparator (VSC) that he uses for ink evaluation is also not readily portable. Furthermore, it is often imperative to strictly control lighting conditions during an examination; this can be done in a laboratory setting, but often cannot be done elsewhere.

47. The various examinations that I have listed and the equipment that he proposes to employ during the examination of the questioned documents are routine in cases of this nature. Failure to examine the questioned document in a laboratory setting, with proper instrumentation, may result in loss of valuable evidence

that would directly address the issue of the document's authenticity.

WHEREFORE, for all of the reasons set forth above, this court should order that the trust documents of Kenneth and Rachel Goodall and the Goodall Family Trust be turned over to David S. Moore, Forensic Document examiner and including the originals of Goodall Family Trust Documents dated September 12, 1990, August 24, 1994 and January 19, 1999 be handed over to David S. Moore for Forensic Examination.

I declare under penalty of perjury under the laws of the State of California and the contents thereof are true and correct to the best of my knowledge and belief.

DATED: March 1, 2012

Sam Sloan

Verification:

Sam Sloan declares:

I have read the Petition and Declaration for an order to turn over documents to a Forensic Document Examiner filed in this matter, and I declare under penalty of perjury under the laws of the State of California and the contents thereof are true and correct to the best of my knowledge and belief.

DATED: March 1, 2012

Sam Sloan

Exhibit A

Letter demanding pursuant to California Government Code Section 8206 (c) that Mr. James Hastings provide a photostatic copy of the line item representing each of the transactions in which he acted as a Notary Public and notarized the signatures of Kenneth F. Goodall, Rachel A. Goodall and/or Kenneth Michael Goodall.

Sam Sloan
461 Peachstone Terrace
San Rafael CA 94903

Tel. 415-419-5980
415-349-6116
917-507-7226

samhsloan@gmail.com

February 22, 2012

James R. Hastings
1003 3rd Street
San Rafael, CA 94901

Re: Notary Public Law and Estate of Goodall
Demand pursuant to Section 8206(c)

Dear Mr. James Hastings,

Pursuant to California Government Code Section 8206 (c), I hereby demand that you provide to me a photostatic copy of the line item representing each of the transactions in which you acted as a Notary Public and notarized the signatures of Kenneth F. Goodall, Rachel A. Goodall and/or Kenneth Michael Goodall.

You acted as a Notary Public in at least the following purported transactions:

Your signature and seal appears as a notary public notarizing the signatures of both Kenneth F. Goodall and Rachel A. Goodall in a document entitled "Declaration of the Goodall Trust" and dated August 24, 1994 .

Your signature and seal as a notary public notarizing the signatures of both Kenneth Michael Goodall and Rachel A. Goodall in a document entitled "Second Amendment to Goodall Trust" and dated January 19, 1999.

Your signature as a notary public notarizing the signatures of both Kenneth F. Goodall and Rachel A. Goodall in a document entitled "The Goodall Trust" and dated September 12, 1990.

In addition, we have a copy of a Power of Attorney given by Rachel Goodall to Kenneth Michael Goodall but with no date. We demand that you provide a photostatic copy of the line item representing that transactions.

California Government Code Section 8206 (c) provides:

(c) Upon written request of any member of the public, which request shall include the name of the parties, the type of document, and the month and year in which notarized, the notary shall supply a photostatic copy of the line item representing the requested transaction at a cost of not more than thirty cents ($0.30) per page.

Enclosed please find $5.00, which more than covers the cost of this transaction at $0.30 per page.

Very Truly Yours,

Sam Sloan

Exhibit B

Relevant page of the Trust dated September 12, 1990

for the benefit of the surviving spouse so much of the net income and principal of the trust as the trustee deems proper for the health, education, support, and maintenance of the surviving spouse. In exercising discretion, the trustee shall give the consideration that the trustee deems proper to all other income and resources then readily available to the surviving spouse for use for these purposes and that are then known to the trustee. All decisions of the trustee regarding payments under this subparagraph, if any, are within the trustee's discretion and shall be final and incontestable by anyone. Any net income not expended under the foregoing provisions of this subparagraph shall be accumulated and added to the principal of the trust.

(b) Right of Surviving Spouse to Withdraw Principal. The surviving spouse shall have the power to withdraw from the principal of the trust each calendar year those amounts as shall not exceed the greater of five thousand dollars ($5,000) or five (5) percent of the assets, valued as of the end of the calendar year. The surviving spouse shall exercise this power by a written instrument signed by him or her and delivered to the trustee. This power is noncumulative and to the extent it is not exercised by the end of the calendar year, it shall lapse. This power shall exist each year until the death of the surviving spouse.

6.3. Disposition of Credit Shelter Trust Upon Death of Surviving Spouse. Upon the death of the surviving spouse, the property in the Credit Shelter Trust shall be disposed of as follows:

(a) To KENNETH MICHAEL GOODALL, by right of representation, those issue to take that share in the manner provided in California Probate Code section 240.

(b) If the property is not completely disposed of by the preceding provisions, twenty thousand dollars ($20,000.00) to each of the living brothers and sisters of the trustors and the remainder to GUIDE DOGS FOR THE BLIND OF MARIN, INC., of San Rafael, California.

(c) If the property is not completely disposed of by the preceding provisions, the trustee shall pay over and deliver the undisposed portion outright as follows: one-half (1/2) to the heirs of the deceased spouse and one-half (1/2) to the heirs of the surviving spouse.

6.4. Disclaimer Trust. The property allocated to the Disclaimer Trust shall be held, administered, and distributed

Exhibit C

Death Certificate of Kenneth Goodall

STATE OF CALIFORNIA

CERTIFICATION OF VITAL RECORD

COUNTY OF MARIN

SAN RAFAEL, CALIFORNIA

0695

CERTIFICATE OF DEATH

STATE OF CALIFORNIA

STATE FILE NUMBER — LOCAL REGISTRATION NUMBER: 394 21-001303

DECEDENT PERSONAL DATA

- 1. Name of decedent—first (given): Kenneth
- 2. Middle: Filmore
- 3. Last (family): Goodall
- 4. Date of birth (MM/DD/CCYY): 03/01/1916
- 5. Age yrs: 78
- 6. Sex: Male
- 7. Date of death (MM/DD/CCYY): 09/10/1994
- 8. Hour: 0930
- 9. State of birth: KS
- 10. Social security no.: 444-40-8884
- 11. Military service: 1935 to 1962
- 12. Marital status: Married
- 13. Education—years completed: 12
- 14. Race: Caucasian
- 15. Hispanic—specify: [X] No
- 16. Usual employer: US Goverment
- 17. Occupation: Retired Military
- 18. Kind of business: Military
- 19. Years in occupation: 27

USUAL RESIDENCE

- 20. Residence—street and number or location: 461 Peachstone Terrace
- 21. City: San Rafael
- 22. County: Marin
- 23. Zip code: 94903
- 24. Yrs in county: 35
- 25. State or foreign country: CA

INFORMANT

- 26. Name, relationship: Rachel A. Goodall, Wife
- 27. Mailing address: 461 Peachstone Terrace, San Rafael, CA 94903

SPOUSE AND PARENT INFORMATION

- 28. Name of surviving spouse—first: Rachel
- 29. Middle: Antionette
- 30. Last (maiden name): Bentley
- 31. Name of father—first: Fred
- 32. Middle: Armitage
- 33. Last: Goodall
- 34. Birth state: KS
- 35. Name of mother—first: Pearl
- 36. Middle: Odelia
- 37. Last (maiden): Baird
- 38. Birth state: KS

DISPOSITION(S)

- 39. Date (MM/DD/CCYY): 09/15/1994
- 40. Place of final disposition: Valley Memorial Park, Novato, CA

FUNERAL DIRECTOR AND LOCAL REGISTRAR

- 41. Type of disposition(s): BU
- 42. Signature of embalmer: ▶ Adrian Rodriguez
- 43. License no.: 7547
- 44. Name of funeral director: Keaton's Redwood Chapel
- 45. License no.: FD-1137
- 46. Signature of local registrar: ▶ Fred S. Schwartz, M.D. X
- 47. Date MM/DD/CCYY: 09/14/94

PLACE OF DEATH

- 101. Place of death: Residence
- 102. If hospital, specify one: [ ] IP [ ] ER/OP [ ] DOA
- 103. Facility other than hospital: [ ] Conv hosp. [ ] Res. [ ] Other
- 104. County: Marin
- 105. Street address—street and number or location: 461 Peachstone Terrace
- 106. City: San Rafael

CAUSE OF DEATH

- 107. Death was caused by (enter only one cause per line for A, B, C, and D):
  - Immediate cause (A): Metastatic Carcinoma of Esophagus — Time interval between onset and death: 17mos.
  - Due to (B):
  - Due to (C):
  - Due to (D):
- 108. Death reported to coroner: [ ] Yes [X] No — Referral number:
- 109. Biopsy performed: [X] Yes [ ] No
- 110. Autopsy performed: [ ] Yes [X] No
- 111. Used in determining cause: [ ] Yes [ ] No
- 112. Other significant conditions contributing to death but not related to cause given in 107:
- 113. Was operation performed for any condition in item 107 or 112? If yes, list type of operation and date: Feeding Jejunostomy 07/25/1994

PHYSICIAN'S CERTIFICATION

- 114. I certify that to the best of my knowledge death occurred at the hour, date and place stated from the causes stated.
  - Decedent attended since (MM/DD/CCYY): 04/27/1993
  - Decedent last seen alive (MM/DD/CCYY): 08/30/1994
- 115. Signature and title of certifier: ▶ Timothy J Crowley
- 116. License no.: G50995
- 117. Date MM/DD/CCYY: 09/13/1994
- 118. Type attending physician's name, mailing address, zip: Timothy Crowley, MD 1350 S.Eliseo Dr. Greenbrae, CA 94904

CORONER'S USE ONLY

- 119. I certify that in my opinion death occurred at the hour, date and place stated from the causes stated.
- Manner of death: [ ] Natural [ ] Suicide [ ] Homicide [ ] Accident [ ] Pending investigation [ ] Could not be determined
- 120. Injury at work: [ ] Yes [ ] No
- 121. Injury date MM/DD/CCYY:
- 122. Hour:
- 123. Place of injury:
- 124. Describe how injury occurred (events which resulted in injury):
- 125. Location (street and number or location and city and zip code):
- 126. Signature of coroner or deputy coroner: ▶
- 127. Date MM/DD/CCYY:
- 128. Typed name, title of coroner or deputy coroner:

STATE REGISTRAR

A	B	C	D	E	F	G	H	FAX AUTH. #	CENSUS TRACT

CERTIFIED COPY OF VITAL RECORDS

STATE OF CALIFORNIA, COUNTY OF MARIN

000232845

RICHARD N. BENSON

MARIN COUNTY ASSESSOR-RECORDER-COUNTY CLERK

DATE ISSUED AUG 12 2011 BY ________ , Deputy

This copy is not valid unless prepared on an engraved border displaying the seal, date of issuance and the original signature of the Deputy.

ANY ALTERATION OR ERASURE VOIDS THIS CERTIFICATE

Exhibit D

Declaration by Nancy Rodgers

SAM WARE (State Bar No. 105005)
700 Larkspur Landing Circle, #199
Larkspur, CA 94939

Telephone 415-464-4872

E-mail sam@samware.us

Attorney for Sam Sloan, administrator of Estate of K. Michael Goodall

SUPERIOR COURT OF THE STATE OF CALIFORNIA

FOR THE COUNTY OF SAN FRANCISCO

In the Matter of the Goodall Family Trust dated September 12, 1990	Case No. PTR-99-273030 Declaration of Nancy Rodgers Hearing Date: February 8, 2012 Time: Department: 204

Nancy Rodgers declares:

1. I make this declaration based upon my own personal knowledge unless otherwise stated.

2. I reside at 470 Peachstone Terrace, San Rafael, CA 94903 and have resided there since before 1970.

3. I have examined the signature page of the purported Will of Kenneth F. Goodall, attached hereto in Exhibit A, and the signature page of the purported Last Will of Rachel A Goodall, attached hereto in Exhibit B.

4. At page 7 of each of these Exhibits, I see what purports to be my signature as a witness to those wills, along with James R Hastings as the other witness, purportedly executed on August 24, 1994 in San Rafael California.

5. Although the signatures there looks like mine, I do not recall ever acting as a witness to any will for either Kenneth Goodall or Rachel Goodall at any time, and I am sure that I would remember having done so, so these are not my signatures.

6. I do recall that at some time after Kenneth Goodall died that Rachel Goodall asked me and Barbara Dagitz, another of our neighbors, to be the two witnesses to a legal document pertaining to Rachel Goodall, which I recall being a health care directive or similar document, but never any will at any time.

7. I do not recall ever witnessing any signing of any document by Kenneth Goodall at any time, though I do remember quite clearly my husband and I visiting him in his home shortly before his death.

I declare under penalty of perjury under the laws of the state of California that the foregoing is true and correct.

Date: February 3, 2012 Nancy Rodgers

Exhibit E

Transcript of the Deposition of James R. Hastings

0700

In re: Goodall Trust

PTR 99-273030

James Hastings

November 14, 2011

WEST COAST REPORTERS INC

117 Paul Drive, Suite A
San Rafael, CA 94903
(800) 979-2361

EXHIBIT D

SUPERIOR COURT OF THE STATE OF CALIFORNIA
FOR THE COUNTY OF SAN FRANCISCO

In the Matter of the — NO. PTR-99-272030

Trust for Michael created under the Goodall Trust dated January 19, 1999

Deposition of
JAMES R. HASTINGS

NOVEMBER 14, 2011

DEPOSING ATTORNEY: SAM WARE, ESQ.

REPORTED BY: CINDY J. KAISER, CSR #7647

I N D E X

EXAMINATION BY	PAGE
MR. WARE	4

EXHIBITS

RESPONDENT'S FOR IDENTIFICATION	DESCRIPTION	
1	Deposition Subpoena for James R. Hastings	4
2	Objections to Attachment 3 Demand For Production	7
3	Declaration of James R. Hastings	15

--oOo--

Pursuant to Notice of Deposition, and on Monday, November 14, 2011, commencing at the hour of 2:03 p.m., at the Law Offices of Sam Ware, 700 Larkspur Landing Circle, #199, Larkspur, California, before me, CINDY J. KAISER, a Certified Shorthand Reporter and Deposition Officer of the State of California, there personally appeared

JAMES R. HASTINGS,

called as a witness by the Respondent, who having been duly sworn, was examined and testified as hereinafter set forth.

--oOo--

APPEARANCES

SAM WARE, Attorney at Law, LAW OFFICES OF SAM WARE, 700 Larkspur Landing Circle, #199, Larkspur, California 94939, appeared as counsel on behalf of the Respondent. (415) 464-4872.

DON A. LESSER, Attorney at Law, LESSER LAW GROUP, 101 B Street, Suite 350, San Rafael, California 94901, appeared as counsel on behalf of the Subpoenaed Witness, James R. Hastings. (415) 453-7600.

ALSO PRESENT: Sam Sloan.

--oOo--

EXAMINATION

(Respondent's Exhibit 1 was were marked for identification.)

BY MR. WARE:
Q. Mr. Hastings, would you state your name for the record, please.
A. James Hastings.
Q. My name is Sam Ware. I represent Sam Sloan, who is the administrator of the estate of Michael Goodall. Do you understand that?
A. I understand it, yes.
Q. Have you had your deposition taken before on any occasion?
A. Yes.
Q. How many times?
A. Once.
Q. How long ago was that?
A. Approximately nine years ago.
Q. Have you ever taken a deposition as an attorney?
A. Yes.
Q. How many times, would you say?
A. I don't know.
Q. More than 100?
A. I don't believe so.

Q. Are you generally familiar with the law with regard to depositions?
A. I don't think so.
Q. Okay. I'll give you my understanding of what a deposition is and we'll take it from there.
A deposition is an opportunity, it's a discovery device, it gives me an opportunity, representing Mr. Sloan, to ask you as a witness to the matters involving the Goodall trust, questions on that subject. If my question isn't clear, I'll ask you to tell me you don't understand, I'll try and clarify it. Your attorney has the right on your behalf and is duty bound to make objections as he sees fit. We'll take those objections as we go.
With regard to answering a question that I have posed and an objection has been made by your attorney, or another attorney in the room, if you understand the question, notwithstanding the objection, I'll expect you to answer it, unless your attorney instructs you not to answer the question, then that's a different matter to be taken up by the court.
Do you understand that?
A. Do I understand which?
Q. Do you understand that you're under oath?
A. Yes.

Q. Do you understand that this process is a process for me to gather information from you?
A. Yes.
Q. You're here pursuant to a subpoena, correct?
A. Yes.
Q. Let me show you what's been marked as Exhibit 1, and ask you to look at that document, please. Once you've had an opportunity to review that document, I have questions for you.
A. I've reviewed the document.
Q. Have you seen that document before?
A. This particular document? No.
Q. Have you seen a copy of that document before?
A. I believe so.
Q. When did you see that for the first time?
A. I don't know.
Q. Do you recall being served with a subpoena in this matter?
A. Yes.
Q. Do you recall that the subpoena that you were served with asks that you bring certain documents today?
A. Yes.
Q. Do you have any documents --
A. No.
Q. -- that you brought today? Why not?

MR. LESSER: Mr. Ware, as you know, we served some objections with respect to the documents on your office sometime ago. I won't take the time now to reiterate the objections, but I will tell you that Mr. Hastings, at my instruction, searched for documents that he understood to reflect the intentions of the settlors with respect to the trust that's at issue in this matter. He has done a search for those documents. You can certainly ask him about the search that he did, but that is the limit to which we believe Mr. Hastings is required to respond to the subpoena, pursuant to the court's order.
MR. WARE: Okay. That's fine.
This is next marked Number 2, and I'll ask you to take a look at that.
(Respondent's Exhibit 2 was marked for identification.)
MR. WARE: Those are the objections that I received.
Q. Mr. Hastings, have you ever seen a copy of Exhibit 2 before?
A. No.
Q. I'll represent to you, Mr. Hastings, that those are the objections to which your counsel has referred.
MR. WARE: Mr. Lesser, would you just confirm

that that's --
MR. LESSER: They are.
BY MR. WARE:
Q. Let me ask you something.
When you looked for documents which reflected the intentions of Kenneth Goodall, where did you look?
A. In all of the locations in my office where documents would be and in the particular files that would be related.
Q. That is related to the Goodall matter?
A. Yes.
Q. And how voluminous are those documents? Bankers box? Two bankers boxes? A couple files? What's the universe of documents with regard to the Goodalls that you looked at?
A. Less than a bankers box.
Q. Are they categorized by file, that is, Goodall trust 1990? Goodall trust 1994? How are those kept in your office?
A. Which is the question? You asked two questions.
Q. Can you give me a description of how those documents related to the Goodalls are kept in your office.
A. Some were in manila folders, some were in

Page 9

expandable folders, some were marked with file numbers and some aren't.
Q. How recently did you review those documents?
A. This weekend.
Q. Are they all kept in one place in your office?
A. Yes.
Q. In one box?
A. Well, apparently not.
Q. What does that mean to you?
A. There were some documents I could not locate.
Q. Documents which you thought existed, which you just couldn't find, is that what you're saying to me?
A. Yes.
Q. What documents did you expect to find that you did not find?
A. A file marked G 080-01.
Q. What does that number mean to you, in your record keeping practices?
A. It means it's the initial estate planning file for Mr. and Mrs. Goodall.
Q. G 080-01?
A. That's right.
Q. What files did you find there, in your office, when you were reviewing your files to see whether you had documents which reflected the intentions of the

Page 10

Goodalls?
A. G 080-05 and G 080-86 and G 181-01.
Q. Now, what sorts of documents are included within the dash 05 file?
A. Mr. Goodall's trust administration.
Q. The 06 number.
A. Mrs. Goodall's trust administration.
Q. And the G 181-01 file.
A. That's Michael Goodall's will.
Q. Then I'll focus, if I may, on the G 080-01. Does the G stand for Goodall?
A. Yes.
Q. I notice that the numbers jump from dash 01 to dash 05. Would you expect to find a 02. 3, 4 someplace?
A. No.
Q. The reason for that gap is what?
A. That's not the way I identify files.
Q. Now, the G 080-01 file, what would you expect that file to contain?
A. The initial paperwork concerning the estate plan of Mr. and Mrs. Goodall.
Q. Initial paperwork would include your notes regarding your discussions with them?
A. It may.
Q. And in your record keeping practices, would you

Page 11

expect that file to contain such notes?
A. Yes.
Q. Typically during the estate planning process, do you keep notes --
A. Yes.
Q. -- with regard to the client?
MR. LESSER: Let him finish the question before you answer.
MR. WARE: I paused, and I should have nodded. So there you have it. Thank you.
Q. Do you recall when it was you last saw that file?
A. No.
Q. Let's turn to the dash 05 file, which is Mr. Goodall's trust administration file.
A. Yes.
Q. What sorts of things would be contained within such a file, the trust administration file?
MR. LESSER: Well, you're asking him generally as a matter of custom and practice, or this particular client?
BY MR. WARE:
Q. Fine. This particular file, let's go for that. What sorts of documents did you find in there when you looked at it?

Page 12

A. The trust, the will.
Q. Anything else?
A. Any other estate planning documents which had become obsolete.
Q. Such as? Would you give me an example.
A. Power of attorney is obsolete at the death, any paperwork relating to the trust administration.
Q. And when you say "trust administration" in this instance, what did the trust administration of Kenneth Goodall's trust administration include?
A. That pieces of the process that are necessary to make the distributions required by the trust.
Q. Okay. With regard to the dash 06 file, that's Mrs. Goodall's trust administration file, what sorts of documents are in there?
A. The same sorts of documents as in Mr. Goodall's file.
Q. That is a copy of the trust, right?
A. Yes.
Q. Would there be a copy of the 1990 trust in there? Was there a copy of the 1990 trust in there?
A. I don't know.
Q. You don't recall?
A. I don't recall.
Q. Do you recall seeing a copy of the 1994 trust

in there? That's in the 06 file.
A. At this point you're making some sort of assumption as to when I looked at those files and I'm supposed to remember something about the files and I don't know what that assumption is, so I can't answer that question.
Q. Fine. My assumption is you looked at them over the weekend.
A. That's -- that's not a valid assumption.
Q. When was the last time you looked at the 05 file?
A. I don't know.
Q. Do you recall when it was you last looked in the 06 file?
A. I don't know.
Q. How about the 01 file, the G 181-01 file, Michael Goodall's file?
A. I don't know.
Q. When did you begin looking for the G 080-01 file in preparation for this deposition?
A. Several weeks before I hired Mr. Lesser, and I don't know when that is.
Q. So you began looking for it several weeks before hiring Mr. Lesser, you discovered that it wasn't where it was supposed to be?

A. That's not a valid statement.
Q. When did you first start looking for the G 080-01 file?
A. Several weeks before I hired Mr. Lesser. I don't know when that was. Someplace within the last three months.
Q. Within the last three months you discovered that it did not exist, when you looked for it at that time?
A. I can't answer that question, because it has a predicate in it that's not true.
Q. What's untrue about that question? What's the predicate that's not true there?
A. You're saying something does not exist.
Q. Where is it? Where's the file?
A. I do not know.
Q. Why not?
A. Because I can't find it.
Q. When was the last time you saw it?
A. I don't know.
Q. Was it that several weeks ago when you first started looking for the file, before you hired Mr. Lesser?
A. No.
Q. You couldn't find it then either?

A. Not that I recall.
MR. WARE: We'll mark this next.
(Respondent's Exhibit 3 was marked for identification.)
THE WITNESS: I looked at Exhibit 3.
BY MR. WARE:
Q. Have you ever seen that document before?
A. I've seen a similar document before, yes.
Q. You've seen a copy of that document before?
A. Yes.
Q. You've probably seen the original of that document before, right, because you prepared it?
A. Yes.
Q. Is that a complete copy of your declaration?
A. It appears.
Q. I beg your pardon, please.
A. It appears to be there.
Q. There's an attachment to it, an Exhibit A, that's referred to in the body of the document, correct?
A. That's true.
Q. You prepared Exhibit A, as well, correct?
A. Yes.
Q. When you prepared that Exhibit 3, did you have the G 080-01 file in front of you?
A. The question was too broad.

Q. What you're saying is the G 080-01 file is unavailable to us today, right?
A. Okay, you're talking about the 1 file?
Q. The 1 file, right. That's unavailable to you right? It's unavailable to us, right?
A. Yes.
Q. It's unavailable to you, right?
A. Yes.
Q. Have you ever given the file to Mr. Lesser, for example?
A. No.
Q. You looked for that file, the dash 01 file, and you can't find it, over the weekend?
A. That's true.
Q. What I'm trying to figure out is the last time you saw that file. You don't remember when you last saw that file, right?
A. I do not remember the last time I saw the file.
Q. Does it refresh your recollection that you saw the file when you were composing Exhibit 3?
A. No, it does not refresh my recollection.
Q. So you may have had the file available to you when you drafted 3, you may not have, you don't remember. Is that what you're saying?
A. I do not know.

Q. So you don't recall whether when you were drafting Exhibit 3 you had that file, the dash 01 file, to look at, do you?
A. No, I do not.
Q. How about when you were looking, drafting attachment A, or Exhibit A, to Exhibit 3, which is the declaration that you signed apparently in January of 2011, do you recall whether you had the dash 01 file available to you when you drafted that declaration?
A. I don't recall.
Q. Just so I'm clear, you don't recall whether you referred to the dash 01 file when you drafted either of the declarations which compose Exhibit 3?
A. I may have, but I do not recall.
Q. You don't recall, okay.
Do you recall, when you were drafting Exhibit 3, that you referred to the dash 05 file?
A. I referred to documents in the file.
Q. The 06 file, did you refer to that when you were drafting Exhibit 3?
A. I referred to documents in the file.
Q. And the G 181-01 file, did you refer to that when you were drafting Exhibit 3?
A. I would refer to documents in the file.
Q. Over the weekend you took a look for the dash

01 file and you couldn't find it, right?
A. That's true.
Q. Where did you look? In your office, or storage, or where?
A. I looked in my office and in storage.
Q. Is your storage offsite from your office?
A. Yes.
Q. Did you personally look in your office to find that file?
A. Yes.
Q. Did you ask anybody in your office to help you find that file?
A. Prior to that point, yes.
Q. When did you ask somebody to help you find that file, prior to that point?
A. Sometime within the last two months.
Q. Do you remember who it was that you asked to help you find that file?
A. I asked René Moore.
Q. Did you ask anybody else to help you find that file?
A. No.
Q. Would René Moore know as much as anybody on the planet as to where that file might be?
A. No.

Q. Okay. Who would know more?
A. No one.
Q. Now, did you ask René Moore this weekend to help you find that file again?
A. No.
Q. Several months ago when you asked René Moore to help you find the 01 file, she couldn't find it either. Is that what she reported to you?
A. When we last looked for it, she could not find it.
Q. And have you asked her recently to help you find that file?
A. Yes.
Q. When was the last time you asked her to help you find that file?
A. Within the last two months.
Q. How about over the weekend?
A. She doesn't work on the weekend. I did not ask her on the weekend.
Q. Did you ask her this morning to help you find that file, the 01 file?
A. No.
Q. Does she work today?
A. Yes.
Q. Is there a reason you didn't ask her to try and

help you find that file this morning, knowing you had a deposition this afternoon?
MR. LESSER: What's the point of this?
MR. WARE: I want to know how thoroughly he's looked for that file.
MR. LESSER: Well, I think he's told you what he did.
BY MR. WARE:
Q. Okay, the question stands.
A. I can't answer that question, because it has some predicates in it that are emotional and not factual.
Q. Let me ask you again.
Did you ask René Moore any time today to help you find the 01 file?
A. No.
Q. Why not?
MR. LESSER: Objection. Relevance.
THE WITNESS: It was not necessary that I ask her.
BY MR. WARE:
Q. Why not?
A. I had made a thorough search of three offsite locations. I had made a thorough search at the office in all possible locations. I have not found the file at

this moment.
Q. That's fine. Okay, I understand.
At some point back in, I think it was 2000, the year 2000, you represented the Bank of America as trustee in the San Francisco proceedings, BPR 99273030, correct?
A. I don't know anything about the numbers, but I did represent the Bank of America in a motion hearing.
Q. Right, the motion was brought by Michael Goodall to replace the Bank of America as the trustee. Do you remember that?
A. I remember the motion was brought by Michael Goodall, that's all I remember.
Q. Do you remember that you represented Bank of America in that proceeding?
A. Yes.
Q. Is there a file that you have with regard to your representation of the Bank of America in that proceeding?
A. Yes.
Q. Is it one of those four files that we talked about earlier?
A. Yes.
Q. In which file would records of that proceeding be contained?

A. I presume it was after the death of his mother, so it would be the 06 file.
Q. Thank you.
MR. WARE: Just, Mr. Lesser, for the record, you're objecting to producing the 05, 06, and that is the files G 080-05, correct?
MR. LESSER: Well, we've objected to the form of the requests, on the grounds that we've stated in the objections. I told you before that we have, in the interest of avoiding disputes, made an investigation for the existence of documents that would reflect the intentions of the settlors, so that's what Mr. Hastings has looked for. I think he's told you where he looked and what he found.
BY MR. WARE:
Q. My question is this. Earlier in this proceeding we identified that G 080-05 has to do with Kenneth Goodall, correct?
MR. LESSER: Objection. Vague and ambiguous.
BY MR. WARE:
Q. Does G 080-05 have to do with Kenneth Goodall?
MR. LESSER: Same objection.
BY MR. WARE:
Q. The question stands.
A. I don't remember the father's name at this

moment.
Q. You don't remember Michael Goodall's father's name?
A. Right at this moment, I don't, no.
Q. Would you refer to the declaration that I marked as Exhibit 3, and I ask whether that refreshes your recollection.
A. The dash 05 file concerns Kenneth Goodall.
Q. Then referring you to the deposition note, the deposition subpoena, Exhibit 1, you see attachment 3 asks for, "Any and all writings as defined by Evidence Code section 250, which include e-mails which is in any way related to the following: 1, Kenneth F. Goodall."
Do you see that?
A. Yes, I see that.
Q. Would you agree with me that G 080-05 relates to Kenneth Goodall?
MR. LESSER: Mr. Ware, one of our objections, as you know, is that a request for documents that relate to a particular individual is not just vague and ambiguous, but unintelligible, and so to ask him whether the file somehow relates to Mr. Goodall has the same problem and warrants the same objections.
MR. WARE: Okay.
(Record read as requested.)

MR. LESSER: Same objections.
BY MR. WARE:
Q. The question stands.
A. I don't understand the question.
Q. Why not? What's unintelligible about the question?
A. To me it's unintelligible.
Q. Why?
A. Because that's my understanding. It is unintelligible, in my understanding.
Q. So what you're saying is that you can't tell me as you sit here today whether G 080-05, which you've described as the trust administration file for Kenneth Goodall, relates to Kenneth Goodall, you can't tell me that?
MR. LESSER: Same objections.
THE WITNESS: Same response.
BY MR. WARE:
Q. Which is? You can't answer that question?
A. I can't answer that question.
Q. It's too vague and unintelligible?
A. Among the answers, yes.
Q. Let me ask you this. Can you tell me whether in your understanding G 080-06, which you've described as the trust administration file for Mrs. Goodall,

relates to Rachel Goodall, which is number 2 on attachment 3 to the subpoena that I served upon you.

MR. LESSER: Same objections.

THE WITNESS: Same answer.

BY MR. WARE:

Q. You can't tell me whether in your mind the trust administration file, the 06 file, relates to Rachel Goodall?

MR. LESSER: Well, look, Mr. Ware. I don't see the point of asking Mr. Hastings to give you his personal understanding of what the word relates to. The problem with the subpoena is that you have propounded one that does not comply with the Code of Civil Procedures requirement that the categories be specifically and reasonably specified, so whatever Mr. Hastings may or may not think is the relationship between the Goodalls and these files is really irrelevant. The problem is that the subpoena is procedurally invalid, and so I think we're just wasting everybody's time here to argue with Mr. Hastings about whether these relate or don't relate to the Goodalls.

MR. WARE: Okay. I'm not arguing with Mr. Hastings, I don't intend to argue with Mr. Hastings to obtain information from Mr. Hastings, one of which is his understanding as to the meaning of certain words and

certain names and files, and if he doesn't understand whether or not his dash 06 file, which he's described as Mrs. Goodall's trust administration file, relates to Mrs. Goodall, so be it, but I can ask the question to find out whether or not he is able to answer questions such as that. That's all.

MR. LESSER: If that's the way you want to use your time, that's your choice.

MR. WARE: Okay.

Q. So just back, do you understand that the G 080-06 file relates to the administration of the trust of Mrs. Rachel Goodall?

MR. LESSER: Objection. Vague, ambiguous, unintelligible, not likely to lead to discovery of relevant evidence.

(Record read as requested.)

MR. LESSER: Same objections.

Go ahead.

THE WITNESS: I don't know what to say, because I'm being harassed and harangued by a word that you want to put in something, and you want to argue about that as opposed to get on with the case. I'm here to help you find out that the Goodalls intended the Guide Dogs for the Blind to get the assets of their trust. And if you want to find that out, then ask me the questions that

relate to my affidavit. Don't play games with me.

No, I do not understand what you say when you say those things in this document.

MR. WARE: Okay. I'll move to strike as nonresponsive.

Can you just ask the question one more time, then we'll move on.

(Record read as requested.)

MR. LESSER: Same objections. Also asked and answered.

MR. WARE: The question stands.

MR. LESSER: You can answer one more.

THE WITNESS: No, I don't understand your question.

BY MR. WARE:

Q. Okay.

With regard to the G 181-01 file, which you described as Michael Goodall's file, do you understand that that file relates to Michael Goodall?

MR. LESSER: Objection. Same objections.

THE WITNESS: No, I do not understand.

BY MR. WARE:

Q. Well, is that the reason that you did not bring these files, the 05, 06, and 01 files, is that you didn't understand that the subpoena asked you to bring

such documents?

MR. LESSER: Mr. Hastings didn't bring the documents for the reasons that we have set forth in the objections.

MR. WARE: So it was you who decided not to bring the files, Mr. Lesser. I want to know who is going to pay the sanctions here.

MR. LESSER: I'm not testifying, Mr. Ware.

BY MR. WARE:

Q. I'll ask any one of you to answer the questions. Is the reason you didn't bring the 05, 06, and G 181-01 file is because you didn't understand that those files were requested in the subpoena?

MR. LESSER: The reasons that Mr. Hastings has or has not brought things to the deposition is set forth in the objections.

MR. WARE: Okay.

Let me just state here for the record. As the representative of the estate of Michael Goodall, we request that you provide to us, at the very least, a copy of the G 181-01 file, which is Michael Goodall's file, without further ado, and that request is made pursuant to Rules of Professional Conduct, Rule 3-00 D, open paren D, which says that subject to any protective order or non-disclosure agreement, a lawyer is to

0708

promptly release to the client, at the request of the client, all the client's papers and property, and that of course is Mr. Sloan. Mr. Goodall is dead now, so that's Mr. Sloan who is making that request. That's in addition to the subpoena. That's just another reason why we're entitled to at least documents. We'll table that request, just so you know it's out there.

MR. LESSER: All I'll say to that is this is the first time that we've heard that request. So we'll take that under advisement.

MR. WARE: Other than in the subpoena, that of course --

MR. LESSER: Well, the subpoena didn't ask anything to be produced pursuant to the rules of professional responsibility or --

MR. WARE: Professional Conduct, yeah.

MR. LESSER: Well, I'm adding that as a further request.

BY MR. WARE:

Q. Now, I guess I'd better get clear what we're going to be doing here.

G 080-01 is not being produced because it doesn't exist and because based upon the objections which are raised in Exhibit 2, right?

A. That's wrong.

MR. LESSER: Say that again.

BY MR. WARE:

Q. G 080-01, what would you call that, best description of that file? The estate planning file?

A. Yes.

Q. That the estate planning file is not being produced today because it doesn't exist. That's one reason?

MR. LESSER: That misstates his testimony. He didn't say it didn't exist. He said he can't find it, after a reasonable and diligent search.

BY MR. WARE:

Q. It doesn't exist in your possession, correct?

A. I don't believe that's correct.

Q. It does exist in your possession?

A. I don't believe that's a correct statement.

Q. Because the file is lost? How are we going to talk about this file?

MR. LESSER: You can talk about it in the way he testified, which is that he looked for it and he can't find it. We're just wasting everybody's time. You keep trying to put words in his mouth. He said he's looked for it, he told you how he looked for it, he told you where he looked for it, he told you who he asked to help, and he can't find it. That's what the witness has

testified to.

MR. WARE: Okay. Can we agree, Mr. Lesser, that a motion to compel production of these documents and to answer -- to compel production of these documents, can be served on you so that I don't have to personally serve Mr. Hastings with that motion?

MR. LESSER: Yeah. I mean, without conceding that you have done anything necessary to, as a predicate to bringing such a motion, including meeting and conferring, yeah, you can serve me rather than Mr. Hastings.

MR. WARE: Great. Thanks. Okay.

Q. Now, turning to Exhibit 3, I've got some questions about some statements that were made in that. Exhibit 3 is your declaration.

At page 1, at line 28, you say that "I was the family estate planning counsel for the son of Kenneth F. Goodall and Michael A. Goodall, K. Michael Goodall, from on or about 1999 until his death on October 5, 2010."

Do you see that?

A. Yes.

Q. What is the source of your recollection when you were drafting this declaration that you represented him from about July 1, 1999? Do you recall looking at any notes or anything then?

A. Well, I see in that statement, the word "for the son" should not be there. I was trying to say I was the family estate planning counsel for Kenneth and Rachel and Michael.

Q. Then you see on page -- sorry?

A. Let me look and understand what is the sentence taken out of the paragraph. I have to make sure what I'm looking at here.

Okay, "for the son" does belong there.

Q. When you refer to "from on or about July of 1999," do you recall what you were looking at when you drafted that statement?

MR. LESSER: If anything.

BY MR. WARE:

Q. If anything, correct.

A. The 1999 is incorrect. I was trying to build that I was with the parents -- well, I don't know if July of 1999 is correct, because I don't know when Michael first came to me to assist him. So I presume that's what the file would show.

Q. That's Michael Goodall's file?

A. Yes.

Q. Then the paragraph goes on and says, I'm paraphrasing, that you were the estate attorney for the Executors Ray Hoppe and Frank Thornally from October of

Page 33

2010, until about January of 2011. Do you see that?
A. Yes.
Q. Do you have a file with regard to that representation?
A. Yes. It's within the Michael Goodall file.
Q. So that would be within the G 181-01 file?
A. Yes.
Q. Did they retain you to represent them?
A. Yes.
Q. Was it a written retention?
A. I don't recall.
Q. Would you expect that you got those dates from looking at Michael Goodall's file?
A. Yes.
Q. Do you recall what it was in your mind, if you do recall, why it was that it was October of 2010? Is there something that happened on that date that would make you write that date?
A. The previous sentence says -- one of the previous sentence says Michael died on October 5th of 2010.
Q. Do you recall that Ray Hoppe and Frank Thornally came to you after Michael died and asked you to represent them?
A. I don't recall that. But generally yes, that

Page 34

would be true.
Q. Do you recall what it was that terminated that relationship in January of 2011?
A. Essentially all the work was done and they were not responsive any more.
Q. Moving down a little bit here on your declaration, if I can refer you to page 2.
MR. WARE: Do you have a copy of these things?
MS. ADORNATO: I don't.
MR. WARE: Do you want me to shoot you a copy so you can follow along here?
MS. ADORNATO: Yes.
MR. WARE: Off the record.
(Off the record.)
BY MR. WARE:
Q. Page 2, I'm still on page 2, about line 9, it says, "On their own volition, Kenneth Goodall and Rachel Goodall chose Guide Dogs for the Blind in San Rafael as the residual beneficiary of their estate."
Do you have any records which reflect that assertion?
A. I don't know.
Q. If you did, it would be in the misplaced file?
A. I presume so.
Q. Do you have a recollection as to why they chose

Page 35

Guide Dogs for the Blind?
A. No, I do not.
Q. Did you ever discuss that with them?
A. Yes.
Q. Do you recall what they said to you with regard to choosing Guide Dogs for the Blind as the residual beneficiary?
A. I recall that we had a discussion. I don't recall the details of the discussion.
Q. Do you recall that they said anything to you about having a blind family member, or anything like that, which is of particular interest in -- strike that.
Do you recall any significant fact, such as having a family member who was blind, as part of their explanation, if any, as to why they chose Guide Dogs for the Blind?
A. No.
Q. It's my overall understanding of this declaration that you had nothing to do with suggesting to the Goodalls that Guide Dogs for the Blind be a beneficiary of their estate in any fashion, is that true?
A. That's my recollection.
Q. The next statement with regard to Michael Goodall's understanding. Your statement there with

Page 36

regard to Michael Goodall's understanding is based upon what he told you?
MR. LESSER: Excuse me. Are we talking about the statement that starts on line 11, page 2?
MR. WARE: Yes.
THE WITNESS: The statement comes from the discussion I had with Michael Goodall.
BY MR. WARE:
Q. So that conclusion as to Michael Goodall's understanding is based upon your recollection of what he told you, is that true?
A. It's based upon the discussion that he and I had, yes.
Q. That was a communication that you had when you were representing him in the construction of his estate plan?
A. Yes.
Q. That was a conversation that he had with you in confidence, correct?
A. Yes.
Q. The cat is sort of out of the bag here throughout as to what Mr. Michael Goodall's understanding was with regard to his rights and whatnot. But I'm going to say that with regard to lawyer-client communications with Mr. Goodall, Michael Goodall,

0710

Mr. Sloan intends to assert the privilege, the lawyer-client privilege, as to statements that Mr. Goodall, Michael Goodall, made to you. So just for the record, we want to assert that privilege, what's been said has been said, and I'll deal with that in the papers.

To be polite about this, but still clear, as Michael Goodall's attorney, it's Michael Goodall's privilege -- and we don't want you talking about it, okay? That's just for the record. We don't want you saying anything more to anybody. Counsel is another matter, but he'll be bound by the same. Those are privileged communications between you and Michael and we want to maintain that privilege until further notice. That's just a statement for the record.

MR. LESSER: In that case, do you anticipate asking Mr. Hastings anything further about his discussions with Mr. Michael Goodall, because if that's true, I'm wondering what you want to do with the transcript of this deposition.

MR. WARE: That's why I'm cutting it off right now, because we haven't talked about that so far. If we're going to talk about that, I just want it to be Mr. Sloan and Mr. Hastings and you and me. I don't want anybody else being privy to those things. That's

exactly where we're going here. I mean, with regard to communications from Mr. Goodall as to his understanding of things, those are privileged and we want to keep them between ourselves until further notice.

Q. So I'm going to skip over that part.

Now, just as a general proposition, there are statements which follow on page 2 with regard to agreements with Guide Dogs for the Blind for any remuneration. You just flatly deny that, right? Guide Dogs for the Blind didn't pay anything to get Guide Dogs for the Blind on this trust, right?

A. That is true.

Q. They didn't pay anybody on your staff?

A. That is true.

Q. They've never done that sort of thing, right, that is pay you to encourage clients to put them as beneficiaries, is that correct?

A. That's true.

Q. That's something you wouldn't do, right?

A. No, I would not do that.

Q. All right. Thanks.

Moving to page 3, please, at paragraph 5. I'm going to focus at about line 11 here, Mr. Hastings. It says, "Unfortunately, his parents found him subject to the undue influence of others, resulting in caution in

their ultimate estate plan."

Are there any notes that you recall looking at to remind you that that was his parents' finding with regard to their son at the time you drafted this declaration?

A. No, that is my clear memory.

Q. Is that memorialized anywhere, such as notes or letters or anything that might be in the file that has been misplaced?

A. I have no idea.

Q. But you have a clear understanding, you have a clear recollection of that?

A. Yes.

Q. Do you recall that that was expressed to you by the Goodalls?

A. Yes.

Q. And do you recall when that was expressed to you by the Goodalls?

A. Prior to amending their trust.

Q. Do you remember what they said in that regard?

A. No.

Q. What you're saying is as you sit here today, you just recall that impression from the words they said, you don't recall the exact words they used. Is that basically true?

A. I do not recall exact words they used.

Q. That's the impression, based upon what you recall them communicating to you. Is that true?

A. It's more than an impression. It was their communication.

Q. Again, with regard to asking you to recall for us here today what words they used to express that feeling or intention, can you tell us anything specifically that they said?

A. No.

Q. Do you recall whether or not they gave you any examples of instances where they had begun to mistrust his management of money?

A. I believe they always mistrusted that. Michael is concerned regarding the original will, where they talked about their concerns for him and decided to do what they did at that time and later changed their mind after watching his conduct.

Q. Do you recall what they later watched to make them change their mind?

A. No.

Q. Did they tell you what they had seen?

A. I do not recall what they told me.

Q. Do you recall whether or not you have notes in your file, the missing file, that might relate to that

subject?
A. I do not know.
Q. In 1990, the Goodalls engaged you to advise them and draw up an estate plan, correct?
A. Yes.
Q. And at that time you drew up a trust for them. That's the September 12, 1990 trust, correct?
A. Yes.
Q. And at that time did you sit down with them and review their assets, to know the universe of their estate?
A. Yes.
Q. And do you recall that at that point the Peach Stone house was part of their estate, correct?
A. Yes.
Q. What else was part of their estate at that time?
A. I don't recall.
Q. Do you recall that they had investments with USAA?
A. At some point in time that came to my attention.
Q. Do you recall that that was brought to your attention at the time that you were employed by them in 1990, to draw up the original trust?

A. Whatever their investments were was brought to my attention at that time.
Q. Okay. The 1990 trust includes, as in the list of the corpus of the trust, it includes the house, which is stated. Do you recall that?
A. Yes.
Q. And plus $1, right?
A. No.
Q. What else is there?
MR. SLOAN: $10.
THE WITNESS: $10.
BY MR. WARE:
Q. Thanks. There's nothing else listed there, right?
A. That's true.
Q. Now, at some point later the house was transferred or quitclaimed to the house, correct?
A. Probably the same day, yes.
Q. That's something you were instrumental in, as I recall the county records. Do you recall that?
A. Yes.
Q. Now, at that point did you assist them in moving any other property into the trust?
A. Yes.
Q. What else?

A. All of the other assets.
Q. Do you recall how that was accomplished in 1990?
A. I would make the exception all of the other aspects, as discussed with them. We made decisions about all the assets, and then the major assets we definitely transferred to the trust. It's possible that the bank accounts were not, because that was not the practice at the time. But any major asset was transferred to the trust, accomplished through paperwork, initiated and monitored by my office.
Q. That's your practice and procedure, correct?
A. Yes.
Q. Do you recall that that happened in this case, with regard to the Goodalls?
A. To my best of recollection, yes.
Q. Mr. Hastings, the distinction I'm trying to draw is this. Clearly that is your practice and procedure, and I respect that, but my question is very specific, and that is, do you recall transferring anything but the house to the Goodalls' trust in 1990? As you sit here today, do you recall specifically transferring anything else to the trust other than the house?
A. I can't answer the question the way it's posed.

Q. What's ambiguous about it? If it's unclear, let me fix it, but I don't know how to fix it.
A. I know those things were transferred. Whether I recall it right now is a different question.
Q. You know those things were transferred because that's the way you always do things. Is that basically it?
A. No.
Q. How do you know that they were done?
A. Because I know they were done.
Q. Okay. So why wasn't it listed on the schedule of assets?
A. It's not my practice. It's a waste of time.
Q. Because?
A. It's more important to change the title to the assets.
Q. Like the real property title was changed, right?
A. Yes.
Q. So the idea is that you don't include in the schedule of assets anything but real property in your practice?
A. That's true. In almost every case.
Q. Would the file, the missing file, contain a record of your office's activity in transferring assets

to the trust?
A. Yes.
Q. That's the sort of thing that file would contain, is that true?
A. Yes. The record may be elsewhere, as well.
Q. Such as in the coffers of the asset management company that had the assets, for example?
A. Yes.
Q. So, for example, in if the assets, if it did turn out that USAA had investment portfolios or annuities, that sort of thing, in the names of the Goodalls, USAA might have those records, correct?
A. That's true.
Q. But as far as your universe of records is concerned, the only place that those records would exist would be in the missing file, correct?
A. No.
Q. Where else would they be in your office?
A. There may be some reference to them in the other trust administration files.
Q. I see. That would be in the 05 or 06 files?
A. Yes.
Q. Just to close the loop on that, though. If your office participated in the transferring of assets to the trust in 1990, a record of that activity would

have been retained or made, kept, by your office in one of the files, correct?
MR. LESSER: You're asking as a matter of --
MR. WARE: Procedure.
MR. LESSER: Matter of procedure?
MR. WARE: Right.
THE WITNESS: There should be some record of what we did, yes.
BY MR. WARE:
Q. Okay, great. Thanks.
MR. LESSER: Going for an hour. Could we take a short break?
MR. WARE: You betcha.
(Short break taken.)
THE COURT REPORTER: Are you going to want a copy of this deposition?
MR. LESSER: Yes, please. Thank you.
(Off the record.)
(Record read as requested.)
BY MR. WARE:
Q. Continuing. Do you recall instructing or advising the Goodalls that they should execute, transfer, title documents with regard to assets that they wanted to put into the trust?
A. Yes.

Q. It's the practice and procedures to advise clients generally that if they want something in the trust, transfer the title into the trust, correct?
A. Yes.
Q. Just to ask. You've had a chance, a little break here. Is there anything you would like to add or change to anything you've said here today so far?
A. I want the opportunity to review the deposition after the fact.
Q. Just as you sit here today, you wouldn't change any answers to any answers you recall making so far?
MR. LESSER: He just wants to know as a result of our conversation on the break if you want to change your testimony.
BY MR. WARE:
Q. Right, that, or your own musings.
A. I'd have to review the whole deposition to know if there's anything. I would doubt it.
Q. That's fine. Thank you.
Then if I can direct your attention to 1994, you recall that there's another document that purports to be a restatement of the trust, and some changes were made to the 1990 trust or estate plan in 1994, correct?
A. Yes.
Q. And if I can direct your attention to page 4,

I'm beginning at paragraph 7, at page 3. It describes that in late July or early August of '94, you met again with the Goodalls.
Do you see that, generally speaking, there?
A. Where are you talking about?
Q. Page 4, paragraph 7.
A. Okay.
Q. Beginning at line 3, "On or about late July, early August 1994." Do you see that?
A. Yes.
Q. "Kenneth Goodall and Rachel Goodall again visited me for advice."
Do you recall what date specifically that was that they visited you?
A. No.
Q. Do you recall whether they visited you on more than one occasion, or one occasion when they were in the process of doing that activity?
A. They visited me at least once. I don't recall how many times.
Q. That was in 1994, correct?
A. Yes.
Q. And would the missing file contain notes with regard to what they wanted to change in their estate plan at that meeting?

A. Probably.
Q. Would the missing file also contain notes with regard to what their assets were at that time?
A. Probably.
Q. When it says they came to visit you, did they visit you at your office, is that your recollection?
A. That is my recollection.
Q. Do you recall your observations with regard to Mr. Goodall's health at that time?
A. No, I don't.
Q. Do you recall anything with regard to Mrs. Goodall's health?
A. No.
Q. Do you recall that Mrs. Goodall was in a wheelchair?
A. I don't recall on that date whether she was or was not.
Q. Do you recall ever seeing Mrs. Goodall in a wheelchair?
A. As you speak of it, it sounds familiar, but I don't have a visual of that in my mind.
Q. Do you recall ever seeing Mr. Goodall in a wheelchair?
A. I don't have a recollection, no.
Q. If I can direct your attention to page 5,

paragraph 10, which begins at line 3, you state there, "Kenneth F. Goodall died on September 10, 1994."
Does that refresh your recollection as to any observations you made about Kenneth Goodall's health when he met with you and Mrs. Goodall in July or early August 1994?
A. No.
Q. This page 4, paragraph 7, it goes on, "During the discussions," this is picking up at line 5, "During the discussion they told me of the changes they wished to make to their estate plan."
Do you recall what changes they described they wanted to make to their estate plan, as you sit here today?
A. The primary one is to revise the direct gift to their son, to a trust for their son.
Q. Anything else come to mind of any changes they had in mind?
A. No.
Q. Do you recall whether they made any provisions or expressed to you what they wanted to happen to their assets, should their son die after they were gone?
A. Yes.
Q. What did they say?
A. If they're both gone and when their son dies,

things are supposed to go to Guide Dogs for the Blind.
Q. Unless he had gotten married and had kids or something like that, is that right?
A. I'd have to read back. I presume that's in there, yes.
Q. Okay. At the time that they made that change in 1994, do you recall the size of their estate that they were going to be leaving to Guide Dogs for the Blind, when their son died?
A. I recall in general terms they had their house and investments equal, at least to the value of their house.
Q. Value of the house being in the neighborhood of 5 or $6,000, something like that, do you recall?
A. I don't recall the value of the house.
Q. Less than a million?
A. Less than a million.
Q. So you recall that their assets, other than their home, were in the neighborhood of about the same value of their house, correct?
A. That's generally what I recall, yes.
Q. When they, in the 1994 trust, appointed Bank of America as the trustee, did you have any influence on that appointment?
A. No.

Q. Do you know why they chose Bank of America as opposed to any other bank?
A. No.
Q. In 1994, was it necessary to obtain some input from Bank of America as to what size an estate they would be interested in administering, as a trustee?
A. Not that I recall.
Q. When you're going to describe an institution as a trustee, do you typically check with that institution to see whether or not they're willing to act as trustee?
A. No.
Q. That's something for your clients to figure out, is that basically right?
A. No.
Q. How do you figure that out, who to designate as the trustee in trusts that you draw up in, say, 1994?
A. The clients and I have a discussion and the clients select a trustee.
Q. Do you have any recollection, again, did any of that discussion refresh your recollection as to why Bank of America was described as the trustee in this 1994 trust?
A. No.
Q. Do you recall who the trustee was in the 1990 trust?

A. I don't recall the trust. I couldn't tell you.
Q. At the bottom of paragraph 7 there on page 4, it refers to Exhibit A, to your declaration. Oh, but before we get to that.
As a general proposition, when you were drafting this declaration, that is August 18, 2011, do you recall discussing the contents of that declaration when drafting it with any person, such as a secretary, did you have any discussions with Bank of America or anybody else, trying to put together this chronology?
A. Not that I recall.
Q. Have you ever had any discussions with the attorney in this proceeding, Mr. Rothstein?
A. Yes.
Q. Did you ever discuss with him the matters of the Goodall family's matters at any time prior to drafting this declaration?
A. I don't understand the question.
Q. Before you drafted this declaration, Exhibit 3, on August 18, 2011, had you had any discussions with Mr. Rothstein?
A. Yes.
Q. About what?
A. I don't recall.
Q. Do you recall making any notes of your

discussions with Mr. Rothstein, at any time, any discussions?
A. No.
Q. Now, digress, now we're on Exhibit A to Exhibit 3, it's Declaration in Support of Petition for Determination of the Beneficiaries, et cetera. Second page is of interest to me, paragraph 4, begins on line 2. I'm sorry, I think we've covered that.
Let me ask it, anyway. At page 4, line 4, it begins, "It was my understanding, based on that discussion," that is with Kenneth and Rachel Goodall, "that Rachel and Kenneth intend the balance of the trust established for the benefit of Michael remaining at Michael's death to be distributed," et cetera.
Do you see that?
A. Yes.
Q. Again, we don't have any notes of that discussion, correct?
A. I don't know.
Q. Would you expect to have notes of that discussion in the missing file, knowing what you know about your practice of discussing matters with clients, that sort of thing?
A. I would probably have a statement as to the direction as to what they wanted me to do.

Q. That's all for Exhibit A. Let me just review my notes here, please.
If you recall, Mr. Hastings, at the time of the 1994 amendment and restatement, did you have a discussion with the Goodalls as to what assets were in the trust at that time, in the 1990 trust at that time?
A. You asked that question already.
Q. I beg your pardon. If I did, I forgot the answer.
A. Probably.
Q. It would be your practice and procedure to find out what's in the 1990 trust, if we're going to amend that trust and restate it, let's find out what's in there, right?
A. Probably.
Q. Probably, as we discussed, you would have made notes of that, correct?
A. If it was discussed, I would have made notes.
Q. I'd like to ask you about the execution of those documents in 1994.
You recall that two documents were prepared. One was a trust -- three, actually. A trust and two pour-over wills, correct?
A. Yes.
Q. Those documents were signed by the Goodalls in

your presence?
A. Yes.
Q. The trust is not witnessed, correct?
A. That's true.
Q. But it is notarized, correct?
A. Yes.
Q. At that point you were a notary public, correct?
A. Correct, yes.
Q. And you notarized the trust, correct?
A. Yes.
Q. With regard to the pour-over wills, they were witnessed, as I recall?
A. Yes.
Q. They were witnessed by you and your secretary, was that it?
A. I believe so.
Q. That's the usual practice, as you recall your activities in 1994?
A. Yes.
Q. Was your secretary then still your secretary?
A. No.
Q. Your secretary then who witnessed that will, is she still around, as far as you know? She hasn't died or anything, I hope.

A. I don't recall who it was.
Q. Let me just pull that up, so I can ask that. Let me ask you this. I have asked the clerk's office to pull those two wills for me. They're able to find Mrs. Goodall's will, they can't find Kenneth's will. Do you know why that might be?
A. Of course not.
Q. Other than just the clerk, yeah, who knows. Unless I ask the question, I can't be sure. There's nothing that happened that you know of that would explain why the clerk seems to have misplaced Mr. Goodall's will?
A. I know of nothing.
Q. Thank you. That's what I need to know. At page 5, paragraph 12, at line 24, it says, "During the administration of the estate of Rachel Goodall, all assets of the bypass trust and the survivor's trust were passed to Bank of America as trustee and placed into the trust for Michael, as directed by the declaration of trust dated August 24, 1994."
Do you see that statement?
A. Yes.
Q. Do you recall what assets were transferred to Bank of America at that time?

A. The house, USAA assets and all investment assets. I don't recall the specific assets beyond that.
Q. The house and the USAA assets and what else?
A. All other investment assets.
Q. Do you recall what those included?
A. I just said I do not.
Q. Thank you. In the files that you maintain, would there be a list of those assets which were transferred to Bank of America, as described in that paragraph?
A. Probably.
Q. Do you know probably what file they would be in?
A. In Mrs. Goodall's file.
Q. Mrs. Goodall's file that we still have. That's the 06 file, right?
A. Yes.
Q. Do you recall how long it took to get those assets transferred?
A. No.
Q. Do you recall whether there was any resistance by USAA to transferring those assets to Bank of America?
A. I don't recall that there was any resistance.
Q. Neither of the pour-over wills are probated, right?

A. That's true.
Q. What role did you have in transferring the assets to Bank of America, if you recall?
A. We ran the trust administration, and it was our job to get all the assets to Bank of America once it was determined that the trust administration was complete.
Q. Once the trust administration was complete, will you tell me what you mean by that.
A. The trust administration is a process.
Q. The trust administration process to which you refer is the process of transferring the assets to the new trustee, which was then Bank of America, correct?
A. That's the end result of the process, yes.
Q. At that point the trust administration process is concluded, correct?
A. Yes.
Q. Thank you. Was the trust administration process, the trust administration process of the estate of Rachel Goodall, complete before you met with Michael to draw up his will?
A. Yes.
MR. WARE: I would just like to take a brief recess, talk to Mr. Sloan and we'll come back. We're nearly done.
(Short break taken.)

BY MR. WARE:
Q. Mr. Hastings, I'm almost through. When you met were the Goodalls to change the plan in 1994, it's your recollection that they came to your office to do that?
A. I don't believe they did. I thought about that since you asked the question.
Q. Thank you. Tell me what you recall about that meeting, or meetings.
A. I don't really recall anything about the meeting, but I refreshed my recollection as to where it might have been.
Q. Thank you.
A. And it apparently was at their house.
Q. Do you recall what it is that refreshed your recollection?
A. Looking at the trust document.
Q. The trust document. You looked at it here? Do you have a copy of the trust document?
A. This one right here.
Q. This one. What is it about the trust document that --
A. It says was executed in San Rafael, California.
Q. Your office at the time was not in San Rafael?
A. That's true.

Q. Where was your office at the time?
A. San Anselmo.
Q. Fair enough. Does that further refresh your recollection as to the physical condition of Mr. Goodall at the time?
A. At the moment it does not.
Q. But at this point, so we're clear, you recall probably you went to their office in San Rafael rather than met at your office in San Anselmo at the time?
A. I would say I went to their house in San Rafael, yes.
Q. That is a fine point, but let me just ask you this.
The document that you're looking at, the trust, the amendment and restatement of the trust, says what it says. It says San Rafael, fair enough. But what you're saying is that seeing that San Rafael refreshes your recollection, as you sit here today. So you're beginning to recall it was at their house that you met them?
A. Yes.
Q. I hate to belabor it. Thank you very much.
Do you recall that you met them together, that you were all together at the same time, you did not meet them separately?

A. The only time I met separately was with Mrs. Goodall, after his death.
Q. Thank you. Do you recall that your secretary came with you to their house to witness the signing of the will, as well?
A. I don't specifically recall that she did, but she would have, yes.
Q. It's something in your practices and procedures in 1994, at times you would need a witness, you would bring your secretary with you when you were calling on clients, doing house calls, so to speak?
A. Yes.
Q. It was not unheard of?
A. No.
Q. Now, with regard to your representation of Mr. Thornally and Hoppe, if there is a signed retention agreement between you and them, it would be in the Michael Goodall file, correct?
A. Yes.
Q. The dispositive provisions which make Guide Dogs for the Blind the beneficiary of this trust, now that Michael has died, is where in the trust? I put the trust here. I don't intend to defoliate the planet by attaching it, but if you would help me find those provisions.

MR. SLOAN: Page 18.
MR. LESSER: I'll object to the question on the grounds it calls for a legal conclusion.
MR. WARE: Yeah, I understand.
Q. If you would answer the question, I would be appreciative.
A. I have not reviewed all of this. I have not read the trust completely today.
Q. Yes.
A. But the gist of the whole thing is that after the Goodalls, everything goes to the trust for Michael. The trust for Michael then says what happens on the termination of the trust, which doesn't take into effect, doesn't take into account that Michael may die. Or it takes into account that he died, but it wasn't the intention of the clients that it go just by B.
What the intention was, was that instead, at that point in time, it would revert back to 6.3, as if Michael had predeceased them and will go through, without issue, and you would go through the line and then it gets to 6.3-D, which gives the $20,000 gifts to family members and then to Guide Dogs for the Blind.
Q. Okay. You were just pointing to page 19 and then back to 18?
A. That's true.

Q. I understand.
MR. SLOAN: My question, since he's an attorney, why doesn't the document that he drafted say what he says it says? Because it doesn't say that.
BY MR. WARE:
Q. Well, you have referred us to pages 18 and 19 of the trust, correct?
A. Yes.
MR. WARE: That's enough. The document says what the document says.
That's all I have.
MR. SLOAN: You're not going to ask him why he didn't do a better job of drafting the document?
MR. WARE: No, I'm not.
MR. SLOAN: To say what he claims it should have said?
MR. WARE: No, I'm not.
BY MR. WARE:
Q. The only thing I'd like to say, is that I don't know, you know -- not quite yet, not quite yet.
Because if that file turns up, I'd sure like to find out what it says. So is there any place that you might look for it, that file, that you haven't looked for it, Mr. Hastings?
A. I'll answer that question off record, so you

have an understanding.
Q. That's okay, for now at least. I don't want to embarrass anybody here, but you can understand how it's pretty important to me.
MR. WARE: We'll go off the record for a moment.
(Off the record.)
MR. WARE: So just for the record, we had a discussion off the record, and Mr. Hastings was describing what sounded like a diligent search of the file, and we've also been discussing that he will continue to look for the file and if it shows up, I will be notified promptly by Mr. Lesser that the file has been discovered and then we can figure out where to go from there with regard to reconvening the deposition.
Q. I'm not just throwing this twist at the end. I'm not asking you to come back when you find the file, but I'll do what I have to do to accomplish that. All I'm asking for is your continued good efforts to find the file, please.
A. Yes.
Q. And notification if it turns up.
MR. LESSER: The problem is I don't want some ambiguous commitment to continue to look for this forever. I think his testimony reflects what's already

been a diligent search. If Mr. Hastings wants to commit to looking in a few places that he hasn't already looked, that's fine with me, but I want the record to be clear that he has already made a diligent search and that we are not committing to anything that will support some additional motion or legal proceeding to try to force Mr. Hastings to do anything more than he's already done.
MR. WARE: Right. Now, with regard to getting other files, though, you, Mr. Lesser, will accept service of any motions with regard to compelling the production of those other files that I would file, so I need not trouble Mr. Hastings with serving him with that document, correct? We've covered this before, but I just want to cover it again.
MR. LESSER: Yes, I think you have some meeting and conferring to do before you do that, but as a matter of service, yes, I will self-service of whatever you choose is fine.
MR. SLOAN: May I ask you a question? I'll ask him.
Our understanding is that the original signed 1994 trust is in the missing file and he does not know where that trust is.
MR. WARE: That's a question, if we could, this

last one.
Q. Where is the original 1994 restatement of trust?
A. I don't know. I would presume I have it.
Q. You would think it would be in one of the files that you do have?
A. Yes.
Q. Not the missing file?
A. Yes.
MR. WARE: Okay.
MR. SLOAN: We want to see the signed original 1994 trust to see if he really signed it, because we don't believe he did sign it, we think it's a forgery. I'll go on record right now. We think it's a forgery. We do not think that Colonel Goodall signed the 1994 documents. We don't think he was capable of signing that 1994 document because he had a feeding tube inserted in his abdomen, he was hospitalized, in the hospital, he wasn't walking anywhere, he never saw Mr. Hastings. The whole thing is a fraud. I'm right on the record telling you exactly what's going on in this case.
BY MR. WARE:
Q. Where would you expect to find the original 1994 trust, among the files that we were discussing

earlier, in the Kenneth Goodall trust administration file?
A. I don't know which one.
Q. It would be in one of the two, either the Kenneth or the Rachel Goodall trust administration files?
A. Yes.
MR. WARE: Thanks. I'll take that up.
(Whereupon, the proceedings were concluded at 4:06 p.m.)
-oOo-

____
JAMES R. HASTINGS

STATE OF CALIFORNIA
SONOMA COUNTY

I, CINDY J. KAISER, duly authorized to administer oaths pursuant to Section 2093(b) of the California Code of Civil Procedure, do hereby certify that

JAMES R. HASTINGS,

the witness in the foregoing deposition, was duly sworn by me to testify to the truth in the within entitled cause, that said deposition was taken at the time and place set forth; that the testimony of said witness was reported by me, a Certified Shorthand Reporter and a disinterested person, and was thereafter transcribed by computer under my direction into booklet form; that the witness was given an opportunity to read and correct said deposition and to subscribe to the same.

I further certify that I am not of counsel or attorney for either or any of the parties in the foregoing deposition and caption named, nor in any way interested in the outcome of the cause named in said caption.

Executed November 28, 2011, at Rohnert Park California.

Deposition Officer

WEST COAST REPORTERS, INC
117 Paul Drive, Suite A
San Rafael, CA 94903
(415) 472-2361 * 1-800-979-2361
FAX (415) 472-2371

November 28, 2011

To: JAMES R. HASTINGS
1003 Third Street
San Rafael, CA 94901

Re: In the Matter of the Goodall Trust

Dear Mr. Hastings:

Please be advised that the transcript of your deposition, taken on November 14, 2011 in the above-entitled matter, has been transcribed and is now ready for your review by calling for an appointment in our San Rafael Office

In the alternative, you may choose to discuss this matter with your attorney to determine if counsel requires that you do read, make any corrections that you think are appropriate, and sign the transcript of your deposition before it is sealed.

Your rights regarding signature of this deposition are contained in the Code of Civil Procedure, and the original deposition transcript will be sealed after 30 days plus 5 days for mailing, from the date of this letter, and thereafter sent to the noticing attorney

Yours very truly,
WEST COAST REPORTERS, INC

CINDY J. KAISER, CSR 7647

cc: Original transcript
All Counsel

Exhibit F

Purported Last Will of Kenneth F. Goodall

LAST WILL OF
KENNETH F. GOODALL

I, KENNETH F. GOODALL, a resident of Marin County, California, declare that this is my will. I hereby revoke all my previous wills and codicils.

ARTICLE ONE
INTRODUCTORY PROVISIONS

1.1. Marital Status. I am married to RACHEL A. GOODALL, and all references in this will to "my wife" are to her.

1.2. Identification of Living Child. I have one living child, KENNETH MICHAEL GOODALL.

1.3. No Deceased Children. I have no deceased children.

ARTICLE TWO
RESIDUARY PROVISIONS

2.1. Disposition of Residue. I give the residue of my estate to the trustee of the GOODALL TRUST, created under the declaration of trust executed on September 12, 1990, by KENNETH F. GOODALL and RACHEL A. GOODALL, as Settlors and Trustees. The trustee of that trust shall add the residue of my estate to the trust principal and hold, administer, and distribute the property in accordance with the provisions of that declaration of trust, including any amendments of that declaration of trust that have been made before or after execution of this will.

2.2. Alternate Disposition of Residue. If the GOODALL TRUST has been revoked, terminated, or declared invalid for any reason, I give the portion of the residue of my estate not taken to the executor of this will, as trustee, who shall hold, administer, and distribute the property under a testamentary trust, the terms of which shall be identical to the terms of the GOODALL TRUST that are in effect on the date of execution of this will.

ARTICLE THREE

EXECUTOR

3.1. Nomination of Executors. I nominate my wife as executor of this will. If, for any reason, my wife fails to qualify or ceases to act as executor, I nominate BANK OF AMERICA, NT & SA, San Francisco, California, or any corporation that is a successor thereto by merger, consolidation, transfer of assets, or other manner provided by law, as executor of this will.

3.2. Waiver of Bond. No bond or undertaking shall be required of any executor nominated in this will.

3.3. General Powers of Executor. The executor shall have full authority to administer my estate under the California Independent Administration of Estates Act. The executor shall have all powers now or hereafter conferred on executors by law, except as otherwise specifically provided in this will, including any powers enumerated in this will.

3.4. Power to Invest. The executor shall have the power to

invest estate funds in any kind of real or personal property, as the executor deems advisable.

3.5. Division or Distribution in Cash or in Kind. In order to satisfy a pecuniary gift or to distribute or divide estate assets into shares or partial shares, the executor may distribute or divide those assets in kind, or divide undivided interests in those assets, or sell all or any part of those assets and distribute or divide the property in cash, in kind, or partly in cash and partly in kind. Property distributed to satisfy a pecuniary gift under this will shall be valued at its fair market value at the time of distribution.

3.6. Power to Sell, Lease, and Grant Options to Purchase Property. The executor shall have the power to sell, at either public or private sale and with or without notice, lease, and grant options to purchase any real or personal property belonging to my estate, on such terms and conditions as the executor determines to be in the best interest of my estate.

3.7. Power to Purchase Estate Property. The executor shall have the power to sell any property of my estate to, or exchange any property of my estate with the property of, my wife, even though she is also an executor at the time of the sale or exchange, provided that any such sale or exchange shall be for adequate consideration.

3.8. Payments to Legally Incapacitated Persons. If at any time any beneficiary under this will is a minor or it appears to the executor that any beneficiary is incapacitated, incompetent,

or for any other reason not able to receive payments or make intelligent or responsible use of the payments, then the executor, in lieu of making direct payments to the beneficiary, may make payments to the beneficiary's conservator or guardian; to the beneficiary's custodian under the Uniform Gifts to Minors Act or Uniform Transfers to Minors Act of any state; to one or more suitable persons, as the executor deems proper, such as a relative or a person residing with the beneficiary, to be used for the benefit of the beneficiary; to any other person, firm, or agency for services rendered or to be rendered for the beneficiary's assistance or benefit; or to accounts in the beneficiary's name with financial institutions. The receipt of payments by any of the foregoing shall constitute a sufficient acquittance of the executor for all purposes.

ARTICLE FOUR

CONCLUDING PROVISIONS

4.1. Nonprobate Transfers of Community Property. If I predecease my wife, I revoke any consent I have given during my lifetime to any nonprobate transfer on the death of any person, to anyone other than my wife, of all or part of my community property interest in any asset described in California Probate Code Section 5000 (or any successor section), and instead I give to my wife my community property interest in any assets affected by this revocation of consent. Notwithstanding the preceding sentence, this revocation of consent shall be inapplicable to any community property included in any express trust of which I am the settlor or a cosettlor, which shall continue to be governed by the terms of the applicable trust instrument. It is my intention that my wife shall have full power to dispose of all community property assets to which this section of the will applies. If my wife and I die simultaneously or if it cannot be established by clear and convincing evidence whether my wife or I died first, this section shall not apply.

4.2. Definition of Death Taxes. The term "death taxes," as used in this will, shall mean all inheritance, estate, succession, and other similar taxes that are payable by any person on account of that person's interest in my estate or by reason of my death, including penalties and interest, but excluding the following:

(a) Any addition to the federal estate tax for any "excess retirement accumulation" under Internal Revenue Code Section 4980A.

(b) Any additional tax that may be assessed under Internal Revenue Code Section 2032A.

(c) Any federal or state tax imposed on a "generation-skipping transfer," as that term is defined in the federal tax laws, unless the applicable tax statutes provide that the generation-skipping transfer tax on that transfer is payable directly out of the assets of my gross estate.

4.3. Payment of Death Taxes. Pursuant to the declaration of trust executed on September 12, 1990, by KENNETH F. GOODALL and RACHEL A. GOODALL, as Settlors and Trustees, all death taxes, whether or not attributable to property inventoried in my probate estate, shall be paid by the trustee from that trust. However, if that trust does not exist at the time of my death, or if the assets of that trust are insufficient to pay the death taxes in full, I direct the executor to pay any death taxes that cannot be paid by the trustee from the assets of my probate estate by prorating and apportioning those taxes among the beneficiaries of this will, as provided in the California Probate Code.

4.4. Period of Survivorship. For the purposes of this will, a beneficiary shall not be deemed to have survived me if that beneficiary dies within forty (40) days after my death.

4.5. No-Contest Clause. If any person, directly or indirectly, contests the validity of this will in whole or in part, or opposes, objects to, or seeks to invalidate any of its provisions, or seeks to succeed to any part of my estate otherwise than in the manner specified in this will, any gift or other interest given to that person under this will shall be revoked and shall be disposed of as if he or she had predeceased me without issue.

4.6. Captions. The captions appearing in this will are for convenience of reference only, and shall be disregarded in determining the meaning and effect of the provisions of this will.

4.7. Severability Clause. If any provision of this will is invalid, that provision shall be disregarded, and the remainder of this will shall be construed as if the invalid provision had not been included.

4.8. California Law to Apply. All questions concerning the

validity and interpretation of this will, including any trusts created by this will, shall be governed by the laws of the State of California in effect at the time this will is executed.

Executed on 8/24/94, at San Rafael, California.

Kenneth F Goodall
KENNETH F. GOODALL

On the date written above, we, the undersigned, each being present at the same time, witnessed the signing of this instrument by KENNETH F. GOODALL. At that time, KENNETH F. GOODALL appeared to us to be of sound mind and memory and, to the best of our knowledge, was not acting under fraud, duress, menace, or undue influence. Understanding this instrument, which consists of seven (7) pages, including the pages on which the signature of KENNETH F. GOODALL and our signatures appear, to be the will of KENNETH F. GOODALL, we subscribe our names as witnesses thereto.

We declare under penalty of perjury under the laws of the State of California that the foregoing is true and correct. Executed on 8/24/94, at San Rafael, California.

James R. Hastings residing at 18 San Rafael Avenue
San Anselmo, California

Nancy Rodgers residing at 470 Peachstone Terrace
San Rafael, California 94903

0727

Will

RECEIVED FOR
SAFE KEEPING

NOV 17 1994

FROM J.R. Hastings

HOWARD HANSON
MARIN COUNTY CLERK

BY

D. ROSS

LAW OFFICE OF
J. R. HASTINGS
18 SAN RAFAEL AVENUE
SAN ANSELMO, CALIFORNIA 94960
(415) 459-6635

Exhibit G

Purported Last Will of Rachel Goodall

LAST WILL OF

RACHEL A. GOODALL

I, RACHEL A. GOODALL, a resident of Marin County, California, declare that this is my will. I hereby revoke all my previous wills and codicils.

ARTICLE ONE

INTRODUCTORY PROVISIONS

1.1. Marital Status. I am married to KENNETH F. GOODALL, and all references in this will to "my husband" are to him.

1.2. Identification of Living Child. I have one living child, KENNETH MICHAEL GOODALL.

1.3. No Deceased Children. I have no deceased children.

ARTICLE TWO

RESIDUARY PROVISIONS

2.1. Disposition of Residue. I give the residue of my estate to the trustee of the GOODALL TRUST, created under the declaration of trust executed on September 12, 1990, by KENNETH F. GOODALL and RACHEL A. GOODALL, as Settlors and Trustees. The trustee of that trust shall add the residue of my estate to the trust principal and hold, administer, and distribute the property in accordance with the provisions of that declaration of trust, including any amendments of that declaration of trust that have been made before or after execution of this will.

2.2. Alternate Disposition of Residue. If the GOODALL TRUST has been revoked, terminated, or declared invalid for any reason, I give the portion of the residue of my estate not taken to the executor of this will, as trustee, who shall hold, administer, and distribute the property under a testamentary trust, the terms of which shall be identical to the terms of the GOODALL TRUST that are in effect on the date of execution of this will.

ARTICLE THREE

EXECUTOR

3.1. Nomination of Executors. I nominate my husband as executor of this will. If, for any reason, my husband fails to qualify or ceases to act as executor, I nominate BANK OF AMERICA, NT & SA, San Francisco, California, or any corporation that is a successor thereto by merger, consolidation, transfer of assets, or other manner provided by law, as executor of this will.

3.2. Waiver of Bond. No bond or undertaking shall be required of any executor nominated in this will.

3.3. General Powers of Executor. The executor shall have full authority to administer my estate under the California Independent Administration of Estates Act. The executor shall have all powers now or hereafter conferred on executors by law, except as otherwise specifically provided in this will, including any powers enumerated in this will.

3.4. Power to Invest. The executor shall have the power to

invest estate funds in any kind of real or personal property, as the executor deems advisable.

3.5. Division or Distribution in Cash or in Kind. In order to satisfy a pecuniary gift or to distribute or divide estate assets into shares or partial shares, the executor may distribute or divide those assets in kind, or divide undivided interests in those assets, or sell all or any part of those assets and distribute or divide the property in cash, in kind, or partly in cash and partly in kind. Property distributed to satisfy a pecuniary gift under this will shall be valued at its fair market value at the time of distribution.

3.6. Power to Sell, Lease, and Grant Options to Purchase Property. The executor shall have the power to sell, at either public or private sale and with or without notice, lease, and grant options to purchase any real or personal property belonging to my estate, on such terms and conditions as the executor determines to be in the best interest of my estate.

3.7. Power to Purchase Estate Property. The executor shall have the power to sell any property of my estate to, or exchange any property of my estate with the property of, my husband, even though he is also an executor at the time of the sale or exchange, provided that any such sale or exchange shall be for adequate consideration.

3.8. Payments to Legally Incapacitated Persons. If at any time any beneficiary under this will is a minor or it appears to the executor that any beneficiary is incapacitated, incompetent,

or for any other reason not able to receive payments or make intelligent or responsible use of the payments, then the executor, in lieu of making direct payments to the beneficiary, may make payments to the beneficiary's conservator or guardian; to the beneficiary's custodian under the Uniform Gifts to Minors Act or Uniform Transfers to Minors Act of any state; to one or more suitable persons, as the executor deems proper, such as a relative or a person residing with the beneficiary, to be used for the benefit of the beneficiary; to any other person, firm, or agency for services rendered or to be rendered for the beneficiary's assistance or benefit; or to accounts in the beneficiary's name with financial institutions. The receipt of payments by any of the foregoing shall constitute a sufficient acquittance of the executor for all purposes.

ARTICLE FOUR

CONCLUDING PROVISIONS

4.1. Nonprobate Transfers of Community Property. If I predecease my husband, I revoke any consent I have given during my lifetime to any nonprobate transfer on the death of any person, to anyone other than my husband, of all or part of my community property interest in any asset described in California Probate Code Section 5000 (or any successor section), and instead I give to my husband my community property interest in any assets affected by this revocation of consent. Notwithstanding the preceding sentence, this revocation of consent shall be

inapplicable to any community property included in any express trust of which I am the settlor or a cosettlor, which shall continue to be governed by the terms of the applicable trust instrument. It is my intention that my husband shall have full power to dispose of all community property assets to which this section of the will applies. If my husband and I die simultaneously or if it cannot be established by clear and convincing evidence whether my husband or I died first, this section shall not apply.

4.2. Definition of Death Taxes. The term "death taxes," as used in this will, shall mean all inheritance, estate, succession, and other similar taxes that are payable by any person on account of that person's interest in my estate or by reason of my death, including penalties and interest, but excluding the following:

(a) Any addition to the federal estate tax for any "excess retirement accumulation" under Internal Revenue Code Section 4980A.

(b) Any additional tax that may be assessed under Internal Revenue Code Section 2032A.

(c) Any federal or state tax imposed on a "generation-skipping transfer," as that term is defined in the federal tax laws, unless the applicable tax statutes provide that the generation-skipping transfer tax on that transfer is payable directly out of the assets of my gross estate.

4.3. Payment of Death Taxes. Pursuant to the declaration of trust executed on September 12, 1990, by KENNETH F. GOODALL and RACHEL A. GOODALL, as Settlors and Trustees, all death taxes, whether or not attributable to property inventoried in my probate

estate, shall be paid by the trustee from that trust. However, if that trust does not exist at the time of my death, or if the assets of that trust are insufficient to pay the death taxes in full, I direct the executor to pay any death taxes that cannot be paid by the trustee from the assets of my probate estate by prorating and apportioning those taxes among the beneficiaries of this will, as provided in the California Probate Code.

4.4. Period of Survivorship. For the purposes of this will, a beneficiary shall not be deemed to have survived me if that beneficiary dies within forty (40) days after my death.

4.5. No-Contest Clause. If any person, directly or indirectly, contests the validity of this will in whole or in part, or opposes, objects to, or seeks to invalidate any of its provisions, or seeks to succeed to any part of my estate otherwise than in the manner specified in this will, any gift or other interest given to that person under this will shall be revoked and shall be disposed of as if he or she had predeceased me without issue.

4.6. Captions. The captions appearing in this will are for convenience of reference only, and shall be disregarded in determining the meaning and effect of the provisions of this will.

4.7. Severability Clause. If any provision of this will is invalid, that provision shall be disregarded, and the remainder of this will shall be construed as if the invalid provision had not been included.

4.8. California Law to Apply. All questions concerning the validity and interpretation of this will, including any trusts created by this will, shall be governed by the laws of the State of California in effect at the time this will is executed.

Executed on 8/24/94, at San Rafael, California.

Rachel A. Goodall
RACHEL A. GOODALL

On the date written above, we, the undersigned, each being present at the same time, witnessed the signing of this instrument by RACHEL A. GOODALL. At that time, RACHEL A. GOODALL appeared to us to be of sound mind and memory and, to the best of our knowledge, was not acting under fraud, duress, menace, or undue influence. Understanding this instrument, which consists of seven (7) pages, including the pages on which the signature of RACHEL A. GOODALL and our signatures appear, to be the will of RACHEL A. GOODALL, we subscribe our names as witnesses thereto.

We declare under penalty of perjury under the laws of the State of California that the foregoing is true and correct. Executed on 8/24/94, at San Rafael, California.

James R. Hastings — residing at 18 San Rafael Avenue, San Anselmo, California

Nancy Rodgers — residing at 470 Peachstone Terrace, San Rafael, California 94903

Exhibit H

Declaration filed by James R. Hastings in San Francisco Probate Court

Don A. Lesser (SBN #112887)
THE LESSER LAW GROUP
1010 B Street, Suite 300
San Rafael, California 94901
Telephone: (415) 453-7600
Facsimile: (415) 295-4122
E-mail: DLesser@LesserGroup.com

Attorney for Subpoenaed Witness
JAMES R. HASTINGS

CALIFORNIA SUPERIOR COURT

SAN FRANCISCO COUNTY

In the Matter of the Trust for Michael created under the Goodall Trust dated January 19, 1999	Case No. PTR-99-273030 **DECLARATION OF JAMES R. HASTINGS PURSUANT TO COURT ORDER ON RESPONDENT'S MOTION TO COMPEL PRODUCTION OF DOCUMENTS AND FURTHER DEPOSITION** Hearing: January 12, 2012 Time: 2:15 p.m. Department: 204

I, James R. Hastings, declare as follows:

1. I am an attorney at law licensed to practice in the State of California. I provide this declaration in response to this Court's order on Respondent's Motion to Compel Production of Documents and Further Deposition. The following facts are personally known to me. If called upon to do so, I could and would testify competently to them.

2. This declaration describes my further search for my Estate Planning file relating to Kenneth and Rachel Goodall, following my November 14, 2011 deposition in this matter. Since then, I have re-examined the two groups of files I have at my home. As the number of the file I

am looking for begins with the letter "G," I looked at every "G" file in those files at my home and did not find the Goodalls' file. I also looked in both storage areas at my office, active and inactive, again looking at every "G" file, and again found nothing. I also looked at all of the Goodall files retained in an armoire near my assistant's work area, which contains "active" files. I then looked at *all* of the files in that armoire, and still found nothing. I have searched my entire office, where I prepared the declarations I have submitted in this matter. Previously I inquired of all the staff people who work in my office when and where they last saw the file, and no one could recall.

3. I have not knowingly discarded or destroyed the file, or instructed anyone else to do so, nor have I knowingly given it to anyone else. At this point, I have searched everywhere I can think of where the file might be found.

I declare under penalty of perjury under the laws of the State of California that the foregoing is true and correct and that this declaration was executed this 1 day of February, 2012 at San Rafael, California.

James R. Hastings

PROOF OF SERVICE

I, the undersigned, declare: I am over the age of 18 years at the time of service, and am not a party to the within action. I am employed in the County of Marin. My business address is 1010 B Street, Suite 350, San Rafael, California 94901.

On this date, February 2, 2012, the following document(s) were served:

DECLARATION OF JAMES R. HASTINGS PURSUANT TO COURT ORDER ON RESPONDENT'S MOTION TO COMPEL PRODUCTION OF DOCUMENTS AND FURTHER DEPOSITION

on the parties, through their attorneys of record, by means of service designated below:

Samuel G. Ware 700 Larkspur Landing Circle Suite 199 Larkspur, CA 94939	**(By First Class Mail)** I caused each such envelope, with first-class postage thereon fully prepaid, to be deposited in the United States mail at San Rafael, California.
John L. McDonnell, Jr. Reed Smith LLP 1999 Harrison Street, 24th Floor Oakland, CA 94612	**(By First Class Mail)** I caused each such envelope, with first-class postage thereon fully prepaid, to be deposited in the United States mail at San Rafael, California.
Gary D. Rothstein Manat Phelps Phillips One Embarcadero Center, 30th Fl. San Francisco, CA 94111	**(By First Class Mail)** I caused each such envelope, with first-class postage thereon fully prepaid, to be deposited in the United States mail at San Rafael, California.

I declare under penalty of perjury that the foregoing is true and correct and that this Declaration was executed on February 2, 2012, at San Rafael, California.

Gina Anthony

GINA ANTHONY

Exhibit I

Power of Attorney by Rachel Goodall given to Michael Goodall

COPY

DURABLE POWER OF ATTORNEY

FOR MANAGEMENT OF PROPERTY AND PERSONAL AFFAIRS

I, RACHEL A. GOODALL, a resident of Marin County, California, appoint KENNETH MICHAEL GOODALL of 461 Peachstone Terrace, San Rafael, California 94903, whose telephone number is (415) 479-3599, as my attorney in fact. All references herein to "my attorney in fact" refer to the attorney in fact acting at the pertinent time.

I intend to create a Durable Power of Attorney (herein referred to as "this Power") pursuant to California Probate Code Section 4000 and following, specifically including the Uniform Durable Power of Attorney Act but specifically not including Section 4600 and following relating to health care. This Power is effective immediately upon its execution and shall not be affected by my subsequent disability or incapacity.

I give my attorney in fact the powers specified in this Power with the understanding that they will be used for my benefit and on my behalf and will be exercised only in a fiduciary capacity.

ARTICLE ONE

POWERS

1.1. Real and Personal Property. I give my attorney in fact the power to take any actions he believes necessary or desirable for the management or maintenance of any real or personal property in which I own an interest when this Power is executed, or in which I later acquire an interest, specifically including the real property listed on Exhibit A, including the power to acquire, sell, and convey ownership of property; control the manner in which property is managed, maintained, and used; change the form of title in which property is held; satisfy and grant security interests and other encumbrances on property; obtain and make claims on insurance policies covering risks of loss or damage to property; accept or remove tenants; collect proceeds generated by property; ensure that any needed repairs are made to property; exercise rights of participation in real estate syndicates or other real estate ventures; make improvements to property; and perform any other acts described in California Probate Code Sections 4451 and 4452, except those acts that conflict with or are limited by a more specific provision in this Power.

1.2. Securities. I give my attorney in fact the power to take any actions he believes necessary or desirable with respect to any securities that I own when this Power becomes effective, or that are acquired thereafter, including the power to purchase and sell securities; exercise voting rights with respect to securities; collect dividends, interest, and any other proceeds generated by securities; transfer title to securities; and perform any other acts described in California Probate Code Section 4453, except those acts that conflict with or are limited by a more specific provision in this Power. For the purposes of this paragraph, the term "securities" includes stocks, bonds, mutual funds, and all other types of securities and financial instruments, except commodity futures contracts and call and put options on stocks and stock indexes.

1.3. Financial Institutions. I give my attorney in fact the

power to take any actions he believes necessary or desirable in connection with any financial institution in which I have an account or an interest in an account when this Power is executed, or in which I later acquire an account or an interest in an account, including the power to continue, modify, or terminate existing accounts; open new accounts; draw, endorse, and deposit checks, drafts, and other negotiable instruments; prepare, receive, and deliver financial statements; establish, maintain, or close safe deposit boxes; borrow money; apply for and receive travelers checks and letters of credit; extend payment periods with respect to commercial paper; and perform any other acts described in California Probate Code Section 4455, except those acts that conflict with or are limited by a more specific provision in this Power. For the purposes of this paragraph, the term "financial institution" includes, but is not limited to, banks, trust companies, savings banks, commercial banks, building and loan associations, savings and loan companies or associations, credit unions, industrial loan companies, thrift companies, and brokerage firms.

1.4. Business Operations. I give my attorney in fact the power to take any actions he believes necessary or desirable in connection with any business venture in which I have an interest when this Power is executed, or in which I later acquire an interest, including the power to execute and enforce my obligations and rights as a partner in any general or limited partnership to the extent permitted by law and any applicable partnership agreement; enforce my rights as the holder of a bond or similar instrument issued by any business in which I have an interest; discharge my duties and enforce my rights in any sole proprietorship; expand, recapitalize, or reorganize any business to the extent my interest in that business allows; collect proceeds generated by any business in which I have an interest and to which I am entitled; sell or liquidate my interest in a business; and perform any other acts described in California Probate Code Section 4456, except those acts that conflict with or are limited by a more specific provision in this Power.

1.5. <u>Insurance and Annuities</u>. I give my attorney in fact the power to take any actions he believes necessary or desirable with respect to any insurance or annuity contracts in which I have an interest when this Power is executed, or in which I later acquire an interest, including the power to acquire additional insurance coverage of any type or additional annuities; continue existing insurance or annuity contracts; agree to modifications in the terms of insurance or annuity contracts in which I have an interest; borrow against insurance or annuity contracts in which I have an interest, to the extent allowed under the contract terms; change beneficiaries under existing contracts and name beneficiaries under new contracts, including the power to designate himself as the beneficiary; receive dividends, proceeds, and other benefits generated by the contracts; transfer interests in insurance or annuity contracts to the extent permitted under the terms of those contracts; and perform any other acts described in California

Probate Code Section 4457, except those acts that conflict with or are limited by a more specific provision in this Power.

1.6. Retirement Plans. I give my attorney in fact the power to take any actions he believes necessary or desirable in order to maintain or participate in any retirement plan in which I have an interest when this Power is executed, or in which I later acquire an interest, including the power to select the manner in which benefits under the plan are to be paid; designate beneficiaries under the plan, including the power to designate himself as the beneficiary; make voluntary contributions to the plan; make rollovers from one plan into another; to the extent authorized by the plan, borrow from the plan and sell the assets of the plan; and perform any other acts described in California Probate Code Section 4462, except those acts that conflict with or are limited by a more specific provision in this Power.

1.7. Estate, Trust, and Other Beneficiary Transactions. I give my attorney in fact the power to take any actions he believes necessary or desirable in order to act, to the extent an agent is permitted to do so by law and by any controlling instrument, with respect to any estate or trust in which I have an interest when this Power is executed, or in which I later acquire an interest, including the power to receive payments to which I am entitled from any estate or trust; participate in all proceedings concerning any estate or trust in which I have an interest; execute disclaimers of any interests I may have in any estate or trust; convey or release any contingent interests I may have in any estate or trust; make any election available to a surviving spouse under California Probate Code Section 13502 or 13503; and perform any other acts described in California Probate Code Section 4458, except those acts that conflict with or are limited by a more specific provision in this Power. For the purposes of this paragraph, the term "estate or trust" means all matters that affect a trust, probate estate, guardianship, conservatorship, escrow, custodianship, or other fund from which I am, may become, or claim to be entitled, as a beneficiary, to a share or payment. The powers described in this paragraph do not include the power to create, modify, or revoke trusts.

1.8. Power to Create, Modify, and Revoke Trusts. I give my attorney in fact the power to take any action he believes necessary or desirable with respect to trusts that exist when this Power is executed or that are established thereafter (other than powers that I hold in a fiduciary capacity or solely by virtue of being a beneficiary of any trust), including the power to establish trusts for my benefit or the benefit of my husband, my issue, and any other of my dependents; contribute or transfer assets to any trust in which I have an interest; and exercise any power I may have as an individual (not as a fiduciary), other than as a trust beneficiary, such as borrowing trust assets, amending or revoking a trust agreement, and voting shares of stock, but subject to the limitation that any trust I have created may be modified or revoked by my attorney in fact only if expressly permitted by the trust instrument. This paragraph shall not be construed as limiting the authority of my attorney in fact to exercise any power, with respect to trusts, that I may hold in a fiduciary capacity or as a trust beneficiary, to the extent that such authority is specifically given elsewhere in this Power.

1.9. Claims and Litigation. I give my attorney in fact the power to take any actions he believes necessary or desirable with respect to any claim that I may have or that has been asserted against me and with respect to any legal proceeding in which I have an interest when this Power is executed, or in which I later acquire an interest, including the power to institute, prosecute, and defend legal proceedings and claims on my behalf; file actions to determine adverse claims, intervene in litigation, and act as amicus curiae in any proceedings affecting my interests; seek preliminary, provisional, or intermediate relief on my behalf; apply for the enforcement or satisfaction of judgments that have been rendered in my favor; participate fully in the development of claims and proceedings; submit any dispute in which I have an interest to arbitration; submit and accept settlement offers and participate in settlement negotiations; handle all procedural aspects, such as service of process, filing of appeals, stipulations, verifications, waivers, and all other matters in any way affecting the process of any claim or litigation; fully participate in any voluntary or involuntary bankruptcy proceeding involving me or in which I am a claimant; satisfy judgments that have been rendered against me; and perform any other acts described in California Probate Code Section 4459, except those acts that conflict with or are limited by a more specific provision in this Power.

1.10. Tax Matters. For any tax year for which the statute of limitations has not run and to the tax year in which this durable power of attorney was executed and any subsequent tax year, I give my attorney in fact the power to prepare and file any and all documents and take all actions that are necessary or that he believes to be desirable with respect to my local, state, or federal tax liability, including the power to participate in audits; exercise my rights to protest and appeal assessments; pay amounts due to the appropriate taxing authority; execute waivers, consents, closing agreements, and similar documents related to my tax liability; participate in all procedural matters connected with my tax liability; exercise any elections that may be available to me under applicable state or federal tax laws or regulations; and perform any other acts described in California Probate Code Section 4463, except those acts that conflict with or are limited by a more specific provision in this Power. My Social Security number is 440-07-8489.

1.11. Personal and Family Maintenance. I give my attorney in fact the power to take any actions he believes necessary or desirable in order to effectively conduct my personal affairs and to discharge any and all obligations I may owe to myself and to family members and other third persons who are customarily or legally entitled to my support when this Power is executed, or that are undertaken thereafter, including the power to take steps to ensure that our customary standard of living is maintained; arrange for medical and dental care; continue existing charge accounts, open new charge accounts, and make payments thereon; provide for transportation; maintain correspondence; prepare, maintain, and preserve personal records and documents; maintain membership in any social, religious, or professional organization and make contributions thereto; and perform any other acts described in California Probate Code Section 4460, except those acts that conflict with or are limited by a more specific provision in this Power.

1.12. Funeral and Burial. I give my attorney in fact the power to arrange for my funeral or other memorial service and for burial or cremation of my remains, including the purchase of a burial plot or other place for interment of my remains or ashes.

1.13. Gifts. I give my attorney in fact the power to make gifts, grants, or other transfers without consideration, of cash or other property, either outright or in trust, including the power to forgive indebtedness and consent to gift splitting under Internal Revenue Code Section 2513 or successor sections. The powers granted under this paragraph shall be exercised, if at all, in favor of my husband, my issue, and any other of my dependents. Any gifts made pursuant to this paragraph shall not be future interests within the meaning of Internal Revenue Code Section 2503, and the aggregate amount of any gifts made in any one calendar year to any one individual shall not exceed the amount that may be made free of federal gift tax to a person. The limitations in the preceding sentence shall not apply to any gifts that incur no federal gift tax, such as, for example, gifts that qualify for the unlimited federal gift tax marital deduction or charitable deduction.

1.14. Gifts to Attorney in Fact Limited to Ascertainable Standard. Notwithstanding any other provision in this Power, my attorney in fact may make gifts in amounts not to exceed the annual federal gift tax exclusion to himself, but only if he is in need of funds to meet the reasonable expenses of the following: (1) support in accordance with his accustomed manner of living; (2) medical, dental, hospital, and nursing services, and other costs relating to the health care of my attorney in fact; and (3) education of my attorney in fact.

1.15. Government Benefits. With respect to any government benefits either existing when this Power is executed or accruing thereafter, whether in this state or elsewhere, I give my attorney in fact the power to take all actions he believes necessary or desirable, including the power to execute and deliver vouchers related to government benefits; take possession of and store property as allowed under any government benefit program in which I have an interest; prepare and submit claims for government benefits to which I may be entitled; collect proceeds due to me under any government benefit plan; and perform any other acts described in California Probate Code Section 4461, except those acts that conflict with or are limited by a more specific provision in this Power. For the purposes of this paragraph, the term "government benefits" means benefits from social security, medicare, medicaid, or other governmental programs, or from civil or military service.

1.16. Nomination of Conservator. If proceedings are initiated for the appointment of a conservator of my person or my estate or both, I hereby nominate the attorney in fact then serving as conservator of my person, estate, or person and estate. I hereby waive the requirement of a bond if this person is appointed as conservator. I request that, if the person named above is appointed conservator of my estate, the court make an order granting to that person all or as many of those independent powers listed in California Probate Code Section 2591 as the court deems appropriate.

1.17. All Other Matters. Except for those actions that conflict with or are limited by another provision in this Power, I give my attorney in fact the power to act as my alter ego with respect to all matters and affairs that are not included in the other provisions in this Power, to the extent that a principal can act through an agent. This paragraph does not authorize my attorney in fact to make health care decisions, as defined in California Probate Code Section 4612.

1.18. Incidental Powers. In connection with the exercise of any of the powers described in the preceding paragraphs, I give my attorney in fact full authority, to the extent that a principal can act through an agent, to take all actions that he believes necessary, proper, or convenient, to the extent that I could take such actions myself, including the power to prepare, execute, and file all documents and maintain records; enter into contracts; hire, discharge, and pay reasonable compensation to attorneys, accountants, expert witnesses, or other assistants; engage in litigation regarding a claim in favor of or against me; execute, acknowledge, seal, and deliver any instrument; and perform any other acts described in California Probate Code Section 4450, except those acts that conflict with or are limited by a more specific provision in this Power.

ARTICLE TWO

AMPLIFYING PROVISIONS

2.1. Reimbursement for Costs and Expenses. My attorney in fact shall be entitled to reimbursement from my property for expenditures properly made in the execution of the powers conferred by me in this Power. My attorney in fact shall keep records of any such expenditures and reimbursement.

2.2. Reasonable Compensation. My attorney in fact shall be entitled to reasonable compensation for the services rendered in the execution of any of the powers conferred in this Power. In determining the reasonableness of compensation, all relevant factors shall be taken into consideration, including, but not limited to, the time expended by my attorney in fact, the value of the property over which my attorney in fact exercises control and management, and the complexity of the transactions entered into by my attorney in fact. My attorney in fact may make the payment of such amount from my assets every month. My attorney in fact shall keep records that include the amount of time spent in performing the services, a description of the services performed, and the amount of compensation paid to himself for each such time period.

2.3. Reliance by Third Parties. To induce third parties to rely upon the provisions of this Power, I, for myself and on behalf of my heirs, successors, and assigns, hereby waive any privilege that may attach to information requested by my attorney in fact in the exercise of any of the powers described herein. Moreover, on behalf of my heirs, successors, and assigns, I hereby agree to hold harmless any third party who acts in reliance upon this Power for damages or liability incurred as a result of that reliance.

2.4. Release of Medical Information. I authorize in advance all providers of health care, including hospitals, to release to my attorney in fact all information or photocopies of any records that my attorney in fact requests. If I am able to confirm this authorization at the time of the request, third parties may seek such confirmation from me, but this authorization shall not be conditional on my confirmation. All providers of health care shall treat the request of my attorney in fact as that of a legal representative of an incompetent patient, as contemplated by California Civil Code Section 56.11(c)(2), or any successor section, and shall honor that request on such a basis. I hereby waive any privilege applicable to such information and records, and to any communication pertaining to me and made in the course of a physician-patient or psychiatrist-patient relationship, and I hold the provider of health care harmless for any liability for the release of such information.

2.5. Ratification. I ratify and confirm all that my attorney in fact does or causes to be done under the authority granted in this Power. All instruments of any sort entered into in any manner by my attorney in fact shall bind me, my estate, my heirs, successors, and assigns.

2.6. Exculpation of My Attorney in Fact. My attorney in fact shall not be liable to me or any of my successors in interest for any action taken or not taken in good faith, but shall be liable for any willful misconduct or gross negligence.

2.7. Revocation and Amendment. I revoke all prior General Powers of Attorney that I may have executed and I retain the right to revoke or amend this document and to substitute other attorneys in fact in place of my attorney in fact. Amendments to this document shall be made in writing by me personally (not by my attorney in fact) and they shall be attached to the original of this document and recorded in the same county or counties as the original if the original is recorded.

2.8. Power to Petition Court. I expressly eliminate, pursuant to California Probate Code Section 4903, the authority of all persons except the attorney in fact then serving and me to file a petition for the following purposes:

(a) To determine whether this power is in effect or has terminated.

(b) To request that the court pass on the acts or the proposed acts of my attorney in fact.

(c) To compel my attorney in fact to submit accounts.

(d) To request that the court declare this power terminated.

ARTICLE THREE

GENERAL PROVISIONS

3.1. Signature of Attorney in Fact. My attorney in fact shall use the following form when signing on my behalf pursuant to this Power: "RACHEL A. GOODALL by KENNETH MICHAEL GOODALL, her attorney in fact."

3.2. Photostatic Copies. Persons dealing with my attorney in fact may rely fully on a photostatic copy of this Power.

3.3. Severability. If any of the provisions of this Power are found to be invalid for any reason, such invalidity shall not affect any of the other provisions of this Power, and all invalid provisions shall be wholly disregarded.

3.4. Governing Law. All questions pertaining to validity, interpretation, and administration of this Power shall be determined in accordance with the laws of California.

3.5. Explanation of Durable Power for Property Management. I understand that this Power is an important legal document. Before executing this document, my lawyer explained to me the following: (1) this document provides my attorney in fact with broad powers to dispose of, sell, convey, and encumber my real and personal property; (2) the powers granted in this Power will exist for an indefinite period of time unless I limit their duration by the terms of this Power or revoke this Power, and they will continue to exist notwithstanding my subsequent disability or incapacity; and (3) I have the right to revoke or terminate this

Power at any time.

This Durable Power of Attorney is executed by me on ____________________, at Novato, California.

____
RACHEL A. GOODALL

Acceptance by Attorney in Fact

______________________________ Dated: ______________________
KENNETH MICHAEL GOODALL

ACKNOWLEDGMENT

State of California)
) ss
County of Marin)

On ______________________________ before me, James R. Hastings, a notary public in and for the State of California, personally appeared RACHEL A. GOODALL, personally known to me (or proved to me on the basis of satisfactory evidence) to be the person whose name is subscribed to the within instrument and acknowledged to me that she executed the same in her authorized capacity, and that by her signature on the instrument, the person, or the entity upon behalf of which the person acted, executed the instrument.

WITNESS my hand and official seal.

Signature ______________________________ (SEAL)

LAWYER'S CERTIFICATE

I am a lawyer authorized to practice law in the state where this power of attorney was executed, and the principal was my client at the time this power of attorney was executed. I have advised my client concerning her rights in connection with this power of attorney and the applicable law and the consequences of signing or not signing this power of attorney, and my client, after being so advised, has executed this power of attorney.

Dated:____________________ ______________________________
James R. Hastings

Law Firm: Law Office of James R. Hastings

Address: 18 San Rafael Avenue, San Anselmo, California 94960

Telephone Number: (415) 459-6635

STATEMENT OF RACHEL A. GOODALL

I, RACHEL A. GOODALL, am the principal under a Durable Power of Attorney for Property Management and Personal Affairs, which was prepared for me by James R. Hastings and which I am executing at the same time that I am executing this statement. I hereby acknowledge that James R. Hastings advised me fully concerning my rights in connection with this Durable Power of Attorney for Property Management and Personal Affairs and explained the applicable law and the consequences of signing or not signing this Durable Power of Attorney for Property Management and Personal Affairs. I have been shown and have read the warnings contained in subdivision (a) of California Probate Code Section 4128, a copy of which is attached hereto and which I have initialed.

Executed on ______________, at Novato, California.

____
RACHEL A. GOODALL

California Probate Code Section 4128(a)

NOTICE TO PERSON EXECUTING DURABLE POWER OF ATTORNEY

A DURABLE POWER OF ATTORNEY IS AN IMPORTANT LEGAL DOCUMENT. BY SIGNING THE DURABLE POWER OF ATTORNEY, YOU ARE AUTHORIZING ANOTHER PERSON TO ACT FOR YOU, THE PRINCIPAL. BEFORE YOU SIGN THIS DURABLE POWER OF ATTORNEY, YOU SHOULD KNOW THESE IMPORTANT FACTS:

YOUR AGENT (ATTORNEY IN FACT) HAS NO DUTY TO ACT UNLESS YOU AND YOUR AGENT AGREE OTHERWISE IN WRITING.

THIS DOCUMENT GIVES YOUR AGENT THE POWERS TO MANAGE, DISPOSE OF, SELL, AND CONVEY YOUR REAL AND PERSONAL PROPERTY, AND TO USE YOUR PROPERTY AS SECURITY IF YOUR AGENT BORROWS MONEY ON YOUR BEHALF.

YOUR AGENT WILL HAVE THE RIGHT TO RECEIVE REASONABLE PAYMENT FOR SERVICES PROVIDED UNDER THIS DURABLE POWER OF ATTORNEY UNLESS YOU PROVIDE OTHERWISE IN THIS POWER OF ATTORNEY.

THE POWERS YOU GIVE YOUR AGENT WILL CONTINUE TO EXIST FOR YOUR ENTIRE LIFETIME, UNLESS YOU STATE THAT THE DURABLE POWER OF ATTORNEY WILL LAST FOR A SHORTER PERIOD OF TIME OR UNLESS YOU OTHERWISE TERMINATE THE DURABLE POWER OF ATTORNEY. THE POWERS YOU GIVE YOUR AGENT IN THIS DURABLE POWER OF ATTORNEY WILL CONTINUE TO EXIST EVEN IF YOU CAN NO LONGER MAKE YOUR OWN DECISIONS RESPECTING THE MANAGEMENT OF YOUR PROPERTY.

YOU CAN AMEND OR CHANGE THIS DURABLE POWER OF ATTORNEY ONLY BY EXECUTING A NEW DURABLE POWER OF ATTORNEY OR BY EXECUTING AN

AMENDMENT THROUGH THE SAME FORMALITIES AS AN ORIGINAL. YOU HAVE THE RIGHT TO REVOKE OR TERMINATE THIS DURABLE POWER OF ATTORNEY AT ANY TIME, SO LONG AS YOU ARE COMPETENT.

THIS DURABLE POWER OF ATTORNEY MUST BE DATED AND MUST BE ACKNOWLEDGED BEFORE A NOTARY PUBLIC OR SIGNED BY TWO WITNESSES. IF IT IS SIGNED BY TWO WITNESSES, THEY MUST WITNESS EITHER (1) THE SIGNING OF THE POWER OF ATTORNEY OR (2) THE PRINCIPAL'S SIGNING OR ACKNOWLEDGMENT OF HIS OR HER SIGNATURE. A DURABLE POWER OF ATTORNEY THAT MAY AFFECT REAL PROPERTY SHOULD BE ACKNOWLEDGED BEFORE A NOTARY PUBLIC SO THAT IT MAY EASILY BE RECORDED.

YOU SHOULD READ THIS DURABLE POWER OF ATTORNEY CAREFULLY. WHEN EFFECTIVE, THIS DURABLE POWER OF ATTORNEY WILL GIVE YOUR AGENT THE RIGHT TO DEAL WITH PROPERTY THAT YOU NOW HAVE OR MIGHT ACQUIRE IN THE FUTURE. THE DURABLE POWER OF ATTORNEY IS IMPORTANT TO YOU. IF YOU DO NOT UNDERSTAND THE DURABLE POWER OF ATTORNEY, OR ANY PROVISION OF IT, THEN YOU SHOULD OBTAIN THE ASSISTANCE OF AN ATTORNEY OR OTHER QUALIFIED PERSON.

____

Initials

EXHIBIT A

The following described real property in the City of San Rafael, County of Marin, State of California:

Lot No. 1068, "Map of Marinwood Unit 7", County of Marin, Initially recorded 19 Oct. 1959 in Map Book #10, Page 42, Marin County Records.

MIKE GOODALL
461 PEACKSTONE TERRACE
SAN RAFAEL, CA 94903-1327
(415) 491-1269

U.S. POSTAGE
PAID
SAN RAFAEL, CA
JAN 28 '99
AMOUNT
$1.21
00083722-13
UNITED STATES POSTAL SERVICE
0000
78288

USAA INVESTMENT MANAGEMENT COMPANY
9800 FREDERICKSBURG ROAD
SAN ANTONIO, TEXAS 78288

0763

Exhibit J

Hand written notes regarding Kenneth's plans for his estate

Hastings, 305 San Anselmo Ave

WILLS

Both Kenneth and Rachel have wills, [being re-made in Apr 89] made in ~~May 1974~~, by attorney ~~[illegible]~~, ~~[illegible]~~, ~~San [illegible]~~. Copies are in home strong box. Originals are in Safety Deposit Box at First ~~Federal~~ Western Savings and Loan, ~~[illegible]~~, San Rafael.

General terms of the wills leave all property to the survivor of Ken or Rachel, and then to Mike, our son.

Rachel or Kenneth is designated as executor. No trust fund is established.

Rachel has Ken's Power of Attorney, located in home strong box. It expires upon Ken's death. Being revised.

It is probable that legal assistance will be required. Try to get this from the Post Legal Officer, at the Presidio. If he cannot handle it, then hire a lawyer. Do not hire Mr. Pendergrass as he is not to be trusted. Be extremely cautious in dealing with any lawyer and proceed on the assumption that he will do all he can to enlarge his fees. When in doubt, get a 2d opinion, from another lawyer. At your first visit with the lawyer, have him spell out completely just what his total fee will be. If he's reluctant or circumspect in this regard, get another lawyer. You have an absolute right to know exactly what his services will cost you.

It is best that you have some time to think about the subjects discussed at the first meeting, so try to defer any commitments until the next meeting. I have never encountered a lawyer who did not leave me feeling poluted afterwards. I despise them as a class and as individuals.

Exhibit K

Letters by Hastings written after the death of Rachel Goodall demanding that funds be transferred to Bank of America

RTAS
12504767 695

A PROFESSIONAL CORPORATION
MEMBER OF CALIFORNIA, NEVADA, COLORADO and DISTRICT OF COLUMBIA BARS

LAW OFFICES OF
J. R. HASTINGS
18 SAN RAFAEL AVENUE
SAN ANSELMO, CALIFORNIA 94960

AREA CODE 415
TELEPHONE 459-6635
FACSIMILE 459-6756

October 18, 1999

USAA Investment Management Company
9800 Fredricksburg Road
San Antonio, TX 78288

Re: Deceased: Rachel A. Goodall
Date of Death: June 7, 1999
Social Security Number: 440-07-89489
Trust Name: Goodall Trust Dated September 12, 19090
Successor Trustee: Ms. Susan Scribner, Trust Officer
Employer Identification Number: 68-6185978

Account Number: 61900213768
Member Number: 012504767

Dear Sir or Madam:

Your firm responded to my request for valuation, but did not forward the appropriate forms to transfer ownership of this Account. Please see my request No. 2 in the attached letter. I look forward to hearing from you soon.

Cordially,

JAMES R. HASTINGS

JRH:ccw
cc: Susan D. Scribner
Enclosure

A PROFESSIONAL CORPORATION
MEMBER OF CALIFORNIA, NEVADA, COLORADO and DISTRICT OF COLUMBIA BARS

LAW OFFICES OF
J.R. HASTINGS
18 SAN RAFAEL AVENUE
SAN ANSELMO, CALIFORNIA 94960

AREA CODE 415
TELEPHONE 459-8635
FACSIMILE 459-6755

October 14, 1999

USAA Life and Health Insurance Division
9800 Fredricksburg Road
San Antonio, Texas 78288

5251070

Re: Deceased: Rachel A. Goodall
Date of Death: June 7, 1999
Social Security Number: 440-07-8489
Trust Name: Goodall Trust dated September 12, 1990
Successor Trustee: Ms. Susan Scribner, Trust Officer
Employer Identification Number: 68-6185978

Account Number(s): Annuity 00048135TA

Dear Sir of Madam:

I am the attorney assisting Ms. Susan Scribner, Trust Officer, the successor trustee to the Goodall Trust. I enclose for your review an "Affidavit of Death of Trustee and Acceptance of Office of Trustee," showing the succession of Trustee to the office of trustee, and a letter "To Whom it May Concern," authorizing you to follow the requests and directions of this letter:

1. I ask you to forward to me at your earliest convenience the following information (please copy as necessary and use the attached information sheet):

   a. The type of account of any Account(s) held by Rachel A. Goodall as of June 7, 1999;

   b. The owner of any Account(s) held by Rachel A. Goodall as of June 7, 1999;

4720644

c. The value of each such Account as of June 7, 1999; and,

d. The value of any accrued value (interest or dividends) not included in (b) as of June 7, 1999.

2. I ask you forward to me appropriate forms to claim the benefits of this Account. As you do so, please send a copy of your written communication to the successor trustee, Ms. Susan Scribner, Trust Officer, at Bank of America Investment Management and Trust Services P.O. Box 3700, Unit 6753, San Francisco, California, 94137-0001.

Should you have any questions, please do not hesitate to telephone me. I thank you for your prompt and accurate assistance.

Cordially,

JAMES R. HASTINGS

G080ann1.doc

Made in United States
Orlando, FL
04 November 2026

90202364R00234